The Story of

Ernest Gilliat-Smith

Alpha Editions

This edition published in 2024

ISBN : 9789362920256

Design and Setting By
Alpha Editions
www.alphaedis.com
Email - info@alphaedis.com

Contents

PREFACE ....- 1 -

CHAPTER I The First Flemings...............................- 2 -

CHAPTER II Earliest Bruges ....- 7 -

CHAPTER III Arnulph the Great ....- 14 -

CHAPTER IV Progress of the City ....- 17 -

CHAPTER V The Murder of Charles the
Good..- 26 -

CHAPTER VI *Vengeance*.......................................- 37 -

CHAPTER VII Bruges in the Days of
Charles the Good, etc..- 48 -

CHAPTER VIII *William Cliton*............................- 52 -

CHAPTER IX Dierick of Alsace and the
Precious Blood ....- 58 -

CHAPTER X Philip of Alsace and the
Charter of the Franc ....- 66 -

CHAPTER XI Baldwin of Constantinople ....- 70 -

CHAPTER XII The Love Story of
Bourchard d'Avesnes..- 77 -

CHAPTER XIII The French Annexation ....- 86 -

CHAPTER XIV Peter de Coninck.........................- 91 -

CHAPTER XV The Battle of the Golden
Spurs ....- 97 -

CHAPTER XVI The Great Charter—The
Belfry and the Tower of Notre Dame ....- 104 -

CHAPTER XVII Louis of Nevers......................- 109 -

CHAPTER XVIII *Louis of Maele*......................- 124 -

CHAPTER XIX Bruges under the Princes
of the House of Burgundy—Philip le Hardi
and John Sans Peur—1385-1419 ....- 134 -

CHAPTER XX The Great Humiliation ....- 147 -

CHAPTER XXI The Terrible Duke and
his Gentle Daughter ....- 159 -

CHAPTER XXII The Final Catastrophe ....- 171 -

CHAPTER XXIII The Architects and
Architecture of Bruges in the Fifteenth
Century...- 194 -

CHAPTER XXIV The Painters and the
Pictures of Bruges in the Fifteenth Century........- 210 -

CHAPTER XXV *Modern Bruges*.......................- 241 -

PREFACE

FEW great mediæval towns possess so many memorials of the past, alike in masonry and on parchment, as does 'the ancient town of Bruges.'

They have been indited by the patience of the scribe in breviary and in charter-roll; they have been perpetuated by the art of the painter, in gold and glowing tones, in portrait and in altar-piece; they have been graven with an iron pen in wood and metal and stone; they have been handed down by word of mouth through countless generations.

The municipal rolls go back to the year 1280, and included amongst them are the annual accounts of the city from 1281 to 1789, almost complete; those of the Collegiate Church of *Notre Dame* to early in the eleven hundreds; and there are, too, the rolls of *St. Sauveur*, of the old Cathedral of St. Donatian, of the great Abbey of Dunes, and of many other time-honoured corporations; whilst the Municipal Library and the Library of the Diocesan Seminary contain together, no less than seven hundred and thirty-four manuscripts, not a few of which were written in the city itself or in its immediate neighbourhood.

There are buildings in Bruges which carry us back to the days of Baldwin Bras de Fer, perhaps to a still more remote period; four of the seven parish churches date from the twelve hundreds; the oldest of the civic monuments to at latest 1280, and from this epoch until the close of the Middle Age almost every year is marked by the erection of stately edifices, of which very many have come down to us.

Lack of material will not hamper the future historian of Bruges, for the history of Bruges has yet to be written. The present work lays no claim to such title. It is but a bare outline, a mere sketch, and in this it resembles, in some degree, the beautiful map at the end of the volume, and many of the illustrations by which the book is adorned.

The artists who designed these fascinating pictures have succeeded by means of a few skilful touches in laying before us a faithful reflection of the beauty of Bruges, and, following in their footsteps, I, too, have essayed to render my story of the men who created it alike faithful and picturesque.

If my efforts have not been crowned with the same measure of success, the fault lies not in the material, but rather in the manner in which it has been handled; for the life's story of the builders of Bruges is no less marvellous and no less alluring than are the monuments which they reared.

E. G.-S.

BRUGES, *June 1901.*

CHAPTER I

The First Flemings

IT is not to the stalwart Celtic tribes which Cæsar found scattered about the low-lying sandy plain which stretches along the coast from the mouth of the Rhine to the Canche that this part of Europe owes either its name or its greatness.

The Menapii and the Morini, the bravest of them all and the last to withstand the Roman legions, were at length compelled to bend their necks beneath the yoke of Rome's enervating and effete civilization, and when, four centuries later, a whirlwind of Northern barbarism had swept the land, only a handful of them, sparsely scattered, abject, cringing, hidden away in forest and marsh, were left to tell the tale.

The civilization of Rome had been clean wiped out in that quarter of Europe. Silence unbroken settled down on the land, and for two hundred years the Latin-Celts of the Netherlands slipped out of the world's memory.

It was not until the middle of the six hundreds that men began once more to think of them.

The cause of their reappearance upon the stage of European history is chronicled for us in a contemporary life of St. Amand, Bishop of Bourges.[1] It happened in this wise.

Towards the close of the year 630, Amand, who had journeyed to Rome, was one day praying before the tomb of the Apostles, when suddenly he heard the voice of St. Peter bidding him be up and return to Gaul, where he must preach the Gospel.

So impressed was he with the reality of the warning, that he at once set out for the northern province, and presently reached Sens.

Here he was told that there was a country beyond the Scheldt called Gand, where dwelt a wild people who had forgotten God, and who worshipped trees, and that so rude was this land, and so fierce were its inhabitants, that no missionary had hitherto ventured there. This must be the field, said Amand, which St. Peter would have me till, and with a small band of companions he landed on the further bank of the Scheldt.

The reception the new comers met with was not one calculated to inspire confidence. The natives, men and women alike, showed unmistakable signs of hostility, and at length, in a wild outburst, seized upon Amand himself and plunged him into the stream. This so terrified his companions that they, all of them, drew back in fear of their lives. But Amand, nothing daunted, went on with the work he had undertaken, and in course of time won the confidence of the natives, many of whom he baptized.

For thirty years he wandered up and down this forlorn district, enduring all manner of hardships, preaching and teaching wherever he went. Presently he was joined by other missionaries. Here and there churches and monasteries were built. The land around soon began once more to be brought under cultivation, and, beneath the shelter of their walls, villages and little towns gradually sprung up. Bruges, St. Omer, Thorhout, Tronchienne, each of them claims as its founder one or other of the missionaries who at this time were evangelizing the country; and at Bruges they still show the rude chapel on the banks of the Roya in which St. Amand baptized his first neophytes.

It was not, however, to this remnant of resuscitated Celts that the Netherlands owed the important part they played later on in the civilization of Europe. A race ignorant alike of the refinement and the corruption of Roman civilization, and which, because it was barbarous itself, had never had its spirit crushed beneath the heel of barbarism, a race which hailed from the same fatherland from whence came our own ancestors, akin to them in habit of thought and speech and blood, animated by the same intense passion for liberty and hatred of servitude, by the same reverence for woman and love of home, by the same keen admiration for the brave and the true, was destined to build up that marvellous stronghold of mediæval freedom, culture and commercial enterprise called Fleanderland, the land that is of the Fleming, of the exile, the land whose hospitable shore had given to the victorious Viking a haven for his ships and a foot or two of solid earth on which to pitch his tent.

How or when the first Flemings came here are subjects wrapt in mystery. Perhaps the same upheaval which, in the middle of the four hundreds, drove our own Saxon forefathers from their old homes in Jutland and Friesland and Sleswicke-Holstein to seek new homes in Britain, impelled also the Saxon Flemings to the northern shore of Gaul. Be this as it may, all along the coast line of the Netherlands were scattered, at a very early date, settlements of men of Saxon origin, of this there can be no doubt, who possessed in a very marked degree the qualities and characteristics of their race. They were chaste, proud, daring, avaricious, given to plunder. Mutual responsibility was the basis of their social system; the Karl, or free land-holder, the pivot on which hinged their entire political organization. Like all Saxons, they had a horror of slavery. Courage for them was the queen of virtues; freedom dearer than life; vengeance but the cultus of filial piety, and family ties the most sacred of all.

These were the dominant tones which coloured all their institutions. At the uproarious banquets at which in Fleanderland, as elsewhere, the Karls assembled to deliberate on public affairs, to choose their leaders, and deposit in a common hoard the *gulden* destined for an insurance fund in case of shipwreck, fire or storm, the first goblet drained was in honour of Woden, for victory, and the last to the memory of those heroes who had fallen on the battlefield.

When, after the carnage of *Fontanet* (A.D. 841) all Europe was overrun by robber bands, who killed, burnt and harried at will, in those rude days when 'not to be slain,' as Stendhal says, 'and to have in winter a good leathern jerkin, and,' in the case of a woman, not to be violated by a whole squadron, was, for very many, the supreme sum of human happiness, and all the world were seeking in feudalism a refuge from anarchy such as this, and patiently accepting even the right of *marquette* as something less horrible than the horrors which they would otherwise have to endure,[2] these hardy sons of the North, almost alone among the peoples of Europe, retained their independence. Again and again the feudal lords endeavoured to reduce them to serfdom, and again and again their endeavour proved abortive.

In Fleanderland at least they preserved their liberty, living under their own laws and their own elected chiefs; a nation of free men, practically independent of the sovereigns who nominally ruled over them, until, at all events, the advent of the House of Burgundy.

Of this stock was the real founder of Bruges—Baldwin of the Iron Hand—first Count of Flanders.

His coming was in this wise.

It was the time of the break up of Charlemagne's artificial empire—A.D. 850—and strong men on all sides were gathering up the fragments and laying the foundations of great houses, sometimes of kingdoms. The Danes were everywhere harrying Neustria, and the old Frank king, Charles the Bald, unable to purchase peace by the strength of his own arm, was buying it at the best markets he could, with gold and concessions. Guntfried and Gosfried, two Northern chieftains, had lately sworn him fealty, and for the moment were exercising paramount influence over the feeble will of their lord, whilst Rotbert, surnamed *le fort*, an adventurer of obscure origin whom people had lately begun to talk about, was at this time the strongest man along Loire, a freebooter, as some said, from the forests of Germany, in whose veins ran the blood of Charlemagne himself, according to others, the son of a butcher from the shambles of Paris, matter of little moment. In days when a mighty hand and an outstretched arm alone could lead to fortune, his reputation for strength of will and thew was of far greater importance. This man, then, it were politic to bind to the crumbling fortunes of the royal house, so thought Guntfried and Gosfried, in all singleness of heart, and at their instigation King Charles the Bald consented to receive his homage, little thinking that he was thereby laying the foundations of a house which would one day wreck his dynasty.

But the new vassal was something more than a strong man, he was a man, too, of tact and address, and his influence soon became so great, and the favours showered on him so large, that Guntfried and Gosfried, jealous of the rival whom they themselves had set up, determined to compass his overthrow.

To this end, supported by Louis, son of Charles the Bald, and by Judith, his beautiful and accomplished daughter, they called to their assistance the Flemish chief, Baldwin, son of Odoaker, a man of whose antecedents we know nothing. Judith was at this time one of the most remarkable women in Europe. Her career had been a strange and a stormy one. First married, in his old age and as his second wife, to our own King Ethelwolf of Wessex, it was to Judith, his step-mother, that Alfred the Great was indebted for his earliest training.

When Ethelwolf died she had contracted an alliance with Ethelbald, a son of the old king by a former marriage, and upon his death in 860 she retired to Senlis, where she was living in queenly state under the sovereign protection of its bishops when Baldwin saw her, became enamoured of her beauty, and it would seem, with her own connivance, carried her off for his bride.

King Charles was holding his Court at Soissons when the news of the abduction and of his son's confederacy with Guntfried and Gosfried reached his ears, and furious at the disregard shown to his parental authority, he acted, for once, with energy and decision. Summoning the nobles of his Court to his presence forthwith, he pronounced judgment against the culprits in accordance with civil law, next obtained from his complaisant bishops their excommunication, and marching in person against the two conspiring vassals, surprised them at Meaux, and forced them to lay down their arms. The plot then had for the moment failed. Baldwin and Judith fled to the Court of Lothaire, and from thence to Rome, where they sought the aid of that sturdy old Pontiff, Nicholas II. Nor did they seek in vain.

'Your liegeman Baldwin,' he wrote to the King of France, 'has taken refuge at the sacred threshold of the blessed Apostles Peter and Paul, and with earnest prayers has approached our pontifical throne.

'We therefore, from the summit of our Apostolic power, beseech you for the love of our Lord Jesus Christ and of His Apostles Peter and Paul, whose support Baldwin has preferred to that of earthly princes, vouchsafe to grant him your pardon and to completely overlook his offence, in order that, supported by your goodness, he may live in peace along with your other faithful subjects; moreover, when we ask your sublimity to forgive him, we are not only moved thereto by reason of the charity we owe to all those who implore the pity and protection of the Apostolic See, but we are impelled likewise by fear lest your anger should drive Baldwin to ally himself with the Danes, the enemies of Holy Church, and thus prepare new evils for the people of God.' This effusion, however, does not seem to have made much impression on Charles, and the following year Pope Nicholas wrote again, and with vigour. ' "Consider the times," says the Apostle, "for evil days are at hand," and I say unto you that the danger which he announces is already at your door. See to it, then, that you do not bring down upon your head disasters yet more terrible. Have sufficient good sense to master your spleen, and be not for ever deaf to Baldwin.' At length, not without reluctance, and less from love of his daughter than from fear of his redoubtable son-in-law and the Danes, Charles yielded to the Pope's request. On the 25th of October 863, he received Judith at his palace at Verberie, and shortly afterwards her union with Baldwin was celebrated with great splendour at Auxerre. But though Charles had consented to acknowledge the marriage, no argument could induce him to be present at the ceremony by which it was made legal. 'I could not persuade the king,' runs the letter in which Archbishop Hincmar of Rheims recounts to Pope Nicholas the whole affair, and Hincmar had probably at this time more influence with Charles than anyone else, 'I could not persuade the king to go in person to the wedding, but he sent his ministers and officers of state, and in compliance with your request has conferred the highest honours on Baldwin.'

Thanks, then, to the intervention of the Pope, the main object which Guntfried and Gosfried had in view was at length obtained. Whilst Rotbert, who had been successively created Count of Anjou and Abbot of Tours, was consolidating his power on the banks of the Loire, Baldwin was being invested with still greater authority over the Northern 'Marches,' in the vicinity of the Lys and the Scheldt.

The first was the founder of the royal house of France, the second the ancestor to whom all the Counts of Flanders traced their descent.

CHAPTER II

Earliest Bruges

FROM a very early date, perhaps since the time of the Romans, there had stood some nine leagues west of Ghent, on a small, oblong-shaped island, formed by the confluence of the Boterbeke with an elbow of the Roya, and a deep, broad moat which united the two streams, a fortified camp or castle surrounded by a handful of cottages. Hard-by on the mainland, near the spot where the rivers met, stood a small, ancient sanctuary, which tradition said St. Amand had built, and further up stream, on the banks of the Boterbeke, a larger church dedicated to the Saviour, and said to be the handiwork of St. Eloi.

This place, perhaps from the *brugge* or heather which surrounded it, perhaps from the *brigge* or bridge by which it was approached, was called Brugge or Bruggestock or Bruggeswelle—a lonely, desolate place hemmed in by forest and marsh, and, from the nature of its site, well calculated to form a stronghold against the Danes.

Moved by this consideration, hither came Baldwin and Judith when they had made their peace with the irascible King Charles, determined to make Brugge the headquarters of their government and their principal abode. A felicitous choice of residence destined to be fruitful in results. Thanks to it, we shall see the tumbled-down ruins of Bruggestock develop later on into that wondrous conglomeration of picturesque civic splendour—rival, in its heyday, of Venice, alike in commerce and in treasures of art, and in glory of piled-up brick, which later generations called Bruges, the Queen of the North.

Before going further, let us linger awhile over the Brugge of Baldwin's day. The old fortress which he found there was built on an oblong-shaped island. The river Roya, which enclosed it on two sides (those facing S.E. and N.E.), still runs in its ancient bed; it flows alongside of that pleasant lime grove, which some old Burgomaster of a hundred years ago planted in front of that unlovely terrace of substantial, comfortable-looking eighteenth-century *bourgeois* homes which goes by the name of the Dyver.

Soon, however, after the bend of the stream, the Roya now burrows underground, vaulted over in the seventeenth century, and wends its subterranean course along the south-west side of the *Place du Bourg*, under Government House, and at the back of the houses which line the east side of the *rue Flamande*, and comes once more into daylight just opposite the old Academy in the *Place des Biscayens.*

As to the Boterbeke—the stream which formed the north-west boundary of the old Bourg, its course has long since been diverted, and it now only skirts the city. It formerly entered Bruges beyond the station, near the spot where the old Bouverie gate stood forty years ago, crept along near the cathedral, down the *rue du Vieux Bourg*, beneath the Belfry, built on piles thrust into its bed, and finally mingled its waters with those of the Roya at the corner of the *rue Breidal.* The moat which formed the south-western boundary of the old Bourg has also been filled in, and the present *rue Neuve* is built over its ancient bed.

Of the actual buildings which Baldwin found at Brugge, it is doubtful whether any remain. Possibly the Baptistry Chapel, in the rear of the Chapel of St. Basil, is of the date which tradition claims for it, and, if so, it may perhaps be identified with St. Amand's Chapel on the banks of the Roya, but recent expert investigation makes it almost certain that this portion of the Chapel of St. Basil dates from the same epoch as the rest of the building, and that Baldwin, Bras de Fer, was himself its founder. St. Eloi's Church of Our Lady occupied the site of the present cathedral, but of the original structure no vestige remains, save perhaps the lower portion of the tower, and even this is doubtful. The old Bourg itself had fallen into such a state of decay when Baldwin first came to Bruges, that he did not dare deposit there the relics of St. Donatian which had been given to him by Archbishop Ebber of Rheims, but sent them for safe keeping to his castle at Thorhout, about three leagues south of Bruges, until the new bourg which he was building should be ready to receive them. The old fortress was never restored, but its stones were used later on during the reign of Baldwin II. for the construction of a wall round the city, and of this wall no vestige remains.

Baldwin's new Bourg was built on an island formed by a backwater of the Roya—an irregular-shaped strip of land of considerably smaller dimensions than the island of the old Bourg. The backwater in question branched off at right angles to the main stream, and running for a short distance straight on, presently turned sharp round to the left, at a little beyond the site of the present fish market; and then gradually curved round till it again met the river at the corner of the *Grand' Place*, and of the *rue Philipstock.*

VIEW OF THE QUAI VERT

The course of this backwater has long since been entirely changed. Running on in a straight line past the fish market, it now empties itself into the *grand coupure*, and is one of the most picturesque waterways in Bruges.

Along the right bank of this beautiful stream, going towards the great canal, runs a towing-path, well shaded with poplar trees and limes, and fringed on the side with some delightful old gabled houses, and by

others less interesting and of more recent date. But it is the left bank which gives the stream its greatest charm, for here, at the angle where the backwater turns off from the main stream, stand certain phlegmatic municipal offices of the last century, laving their feet in the water—comfortable-looking, old-fashioned red-brick buildings which, somehow or other, 'the golden stain of time' has managed to make beautiful. Behind them soar the high-pitched roofs and dormer windows of an old city hall, whose pinnacles and turrets and spires give play to light and shade, and break up the sky line. Hard-by, at the end of a narrow street which runs back from the water, behold a rival of the Bridge of Sighs, and in a gilded gatehouse without gates, the marriage of the Middle Age and the Renaissance, and to the right, quaint, venerable and picturesque in weather-beaten brick, the Palace of the Liberty of Bruges, and further still, a vista of old homes, and shady lawns, and overhanging trees and bridges, hunch-backed and of ancient date.

But to return to Baldwin's bourg, the Castle itself—a spacious and strongly-fortified building, which stood on ground now occupied by the Palais de Justice, the Hotel de Ville, and the unsightly modern erections on the east side of the square—included within its precincts not only Baldwin's own residence, but the residence of the Châtelains or Viscounts of Bruges, the *Ghistelhaus* where hostages were lodged, the Court chapel and the Court prison; opposite this group of buildings on the north side, that is, of the Bourg, stood a sanctuary dedicated to Our Lady, which Baldwin had founded to receive the relics of St. Donatian, and further on the cloisters of the priests who served it.

The whole island was encircled by a strong and lofty wall, pierced by four great gateways, each one protected by a portcullis and a drawbridge, which were the only means of communication with the outer world. Such was the citadel reared on the banks of the Roya by the father and founder of Bruges. Of his handiwork only a fragment has come down to us, but a fragment so perfect, that as one enters the gloomy crypt beneath the Chapel of the Precious Blood, the mind is involuntarily carried back to the time when Baldwin and his family worshipped there, a thousand years ago.

THE CRYPT OF ST. BASIL'S

Clustering around Baldwin's great fortress were the houses and huts and hovels of such members of the sovereign's household as were unable to find lodgings within the bourg, of the purveyors who catered for his daily needs, and of a handful of traders and country folk who sought and found safety beneath the shadow of its walls. Even at this early date Bruges must have been a place of some commercial note, for the coins which from time to time have been found in the neighbourhood show that a mint had been already established there in the days of the first Baldwin (865-879), and before the close of his son's reign, so greatly had the settlement increased, that it was deemed necessary to surround the whole with a moat and a great wall, built up of the *veltsteen* (field stone) and rubble, which had once been the old bourg (A.D. 912).

Baldwin, Bras de Fer, that redoubtable warrior whom no man had ever seen in the day-time without his coat-of-mail, and who in time of war was said to have not even doffed it at night, had received the County, or, as it was called in those days, Marquisate of Flanders, on terms of defending that quarter of Neustria from the ravages of the Danes, and though with a mighty hand and an outstretched arm, he managed to keep the sea-dogs at bay, his reign of fourteen years was one unbroken hurricane of effort and strife, until he saw the shadow of death on the horizon, and then at last the old soldier sheathed his sword and withdrew to the Abbey of St. Bertin, there in the quiet of its cloister to gather up his strength for the last great battle.

So, too, was it during the days of the second Baldwin, but the mantle of the old Marquis had not fallen on his son. The hard head and iron will and iron hand of Baldwin, Bras de Fer, was not the heritage of Baldwin the Bald, and the wild courage of the Karls of the seaboard, who had to bear the brunt of the battle whilst their panic-stricken chief was safely entrenched in his fortress at Bruges, could do little more than stem the tide. Why dwell on the woes of Neustria, laments Adroald, a monk of Fleury, why dwell on the woes of Neustria? From the shore of the ocean right away to Auvergne there is no country which has preserved its freedom, no city, no village but has been overwhelmed by the devastating fury of these Pagans, and this has been going on for thirty years. Such was the state of affairs at the close of the eight hundreds, and no land on the Continent of Europe had suffered more than Flanders, but though the rural population had been all but wiped out, though hamlet and abbey had gone up in flames, though cities like Courtrai and Arras and Ghent had been pillaged or razed to the ground, somehow or other Bruges had escaped, nay, in spite of the surrounding devastation, perhaps by reason of it, she had prospered, had increased her population, had enlarged her borders, had girded herself, as we have seen, with ramparts, and added to her crown of sanctuaries a new gem.

In the year 880, on the left bank of the Roya, a little higher up stream than the old bourg, the citizens of Bruges built for themselves a chapel, and dedicated it to St. Mary and St. Hilarius—a sufficiently humble structure, knit together like so many churches in the eight hundreds, of rudely-hewn beams and rough planks.

From this grain of mustard seed in after ages there sprang up a tree that is still the glory of Bruges—a stately shrine, adorned by a steeple, than which, in its grand simplicity, there is not one perhaps more lovely in the world.

Baldwin II., who died in the year 918, was buried in the Abbey Church at Blandinium.

The circumstances which led to his interment there are sufficiently curious. They had at first laid him alongside his father at St. Omer, but when his widow Alfrida, who wished to share her lord's grave, was informed by the abbot of that monastery that his rule forbade him to admit even a dead woman within the precincts of his cloister, she gave orders that Baldwin's remains should be translated to Blandinium, where they buried him with much solemnity *in ædicula Parentis Virginis*, and where she herself was laid to rest eleven years later.

THE CHURCH OF NOTRE DAME

CHAPTER III

Arnulph the Great

SOME six years before the death of Baldwin Calvus, his suzerain, Charles the Mild, had endeavoured to buy off Rolf the Ganger, a pirate chief who about this time had carved out for himself 'a sphere of influence' along Seine, with an offer of Baldwin's fief. But Baldwin meanwhile had got wind of the plot, had set his house in order, had strengthened his border towns. Rolf refused to exchange the land which his sword had won for a less advantageous holding, which perhaps he might never obtain, and the famous treaty of Claire-sur-Epte was the outcome of his common sense.

By it he became the French King's vassal for the province we now call Normandy, received the hand of his daughter in marriage, and embraced the Christian faith. And though to the cynical Norman chief his oath of fealty may have been little more than an empty form, and his change of religion but a move in the game, the signing of the treaty of Claire-sur-Epte was, for Neustria, the first streak of dawn. Then it was that the storm which had been so long whirling its fury on the land at last began to lull, and when, in 918, Baldwin Calvus was gathered to his fathers, and Arnulph his son reigned in his stead, the times were sufficiently tranquil to enable him to gather up the slackened reins of government, and to set about a work much needed after the long years of bloodshed and anarchy—a work of healing, and restoration, and reform.

It was chiefly in the reorganization of the Church in Flanders, and, in the first place, of the great religious houses, that Arnulph sought to accomplish the object he had in view. Matter of no little moment in days when the lay aristocracy knew no trade but war, and the peasant was still his lord's chattel, when the monastery was not only the last shelter of learning and the arts, but the only agricultural college and the only technical school, when the monk was the one physician, and the one intelligent artisan, and the clerk, alike legislator, notary, scribe, was almost the only man who knew how to sign his name.

Though the Church had suffered much at the hands of the Danes, monasticism was not, at this time, at such a low ebb in Flanders as it was in England in the days of Alfred. In England it was practically extinct, in Flanders it had only languished. Nevertheless, and strange as it may seem, it was chiefly owing to the efforts of Count Baldwin's English wife, Alfrida,[3] the daughter of our own King Alfred, that monasticism became once more in Flanders a burning and a shining light. She it was who first tended the dying flame. The good work was completed by her son Arnulph, who, in this matter, played much the same part in his own dominions as that played in England by King Edred, his first cousin. He was the builder or restorer of eighteen great monasteries. The famous Chapter of St. Donatian at Bruges was founded and munificently endowed by him. The Collegiate Church of St. Mary at Ardenburg, and the Collegiate Church of St. Peter at Thorhout, were each of them his handiwork, and a host of minor foundations bear witness to his untiring energy and zeal.

He himself acted as abbot, or chief officer, of the great Abbey of St. Bertin at St. Omer. He was the friend and patron of St. Gerard, the thaumaturgus of Brogne, and through him he reformed more than one religious house. He had received St. Dunstan with hospitality when he fled before the fury of Æthelgifu, and in after years, when the storm had passed and Dunstan had returned to his own land, we find the Margrave of Flanders among his correspondents. A letter still extant—*Epistola Arnulfi ad Dunstanum Archiepiscopum* (MS. Cotton, Tiberius A. 15, fo. 159b)—bears witness to their mutual esteem and affection.

Dunstan's own munificence to the monasteries of Flanders, which, after those of his own country, as Dr. Stubbs[4] points out, were, in a special manner, the object of his solicitude, was doubtless prompted by gratitude for the kindness which he had received from the Flemish monks and their great Count Abbot Arnulph, and it was probably owing to Dunstan's laudatory stories concerning the Flemish Count, that 'the fame of his charity and good works was spread abroad throughout all the land of Albion.' This last fact we learn from a curious letter addressed to Arnulph himself by an English ecclesiastic of high position, whose identity, as Dr. Stubbs observes, it is almost impossible to establish. He was certainly the head of a monastery, perhaps a bishop. Dr. Stubbs conjectures Ethelwold of Winchester, or may be Elfege, Ethelwold's predecessor in the same See, and Dunstan's near relative. Whoever its author may have been, the letter is an interesting one, and sufficiently characteristic of the age in which it was written.

After expressing his best wishes, and enlarging on Arnulph's fame and good works, the writer of the epistle in question goes on to say that he was sending a messenger who would explain to Arnulph by word of mouth that he had in his possession a book of the Gospels which had been purloined from his—the writer's—Church by 'two clerks waxen old in wickedness, and who, a fact much to be marvelled at in such men, had afterwards confessed what they had done, and acknowledged that, journeying to Flanders to recover a little girl who had been carried off by his—Count Arnulph's—Danes, they had visited the Count in one of his country houses, perhaps Winendaele or Maele, and there sold to him the volume in question for the sum of three marks.' The writer concludes by begging Arnulph to restore the book, 'for the love of God and all His Saints.'[5] It would seem, then, from the above letter, that a certain number of Danes were at this time settled in Flanders, and that they had not yet entirely relinquished their predatory habits.

'Ego Arnulphus dictus Magnus'—I, Arnulph, whom men call the Great. Thus did the Count of Flanders style himself in the year 961. In a grant of fresh privileges to the great Benedictine house at Blandinium, indited perhaps when the hand of death was upon him, Count Arnulph writes in lowlier strain, 'Ego cognosco,' he says, 'Ego cognosco me reum et peccatorem.'

He knew himself better perhaps than did his people, and yet the surname which they gave him was one which he justly deserved. If any man merited to be called great,, that man was Arnulph of Flanders. Consider what he did.

In spite of almost insurmountable difficulties, in spite of a body eaten up by disease, and often racked and torn by pain, whilst with one hand he kept his garden gate, no child's play, with the other he went on patiently sowing and dressing, and watering the tender seeds of that plant which we call civilization, and this continued for forty years.

There is another side to the picture. The age of Arnulph was an age of blood, and some said his hands too were stained with it. Perhaps they were, but if this were so, at least he never sinned for mean or sordid or selfish ends. If the guilt of murder encumbered his soul, it was burthened for the sake of his people.

Of the greatest crime with which his enemies charged him, he denied all knowledge, and even that black crime found its sanction in the approval of the nation.

Flanders had so long been a prey to cruel and treacherous foes, that she had at length come to believe that perjury, treason, cool-blooded murder were legitimate means of defence, and the death of Wilhelm the Norman, lured to destruction with fair speech and false promises, covered Baldwin Baldzo[6] with glory, for if Arnulph had inspired the deed, it was Baldwin who struck the blow. It gained for him more credit in Flanders than if he had taken ten cities, and when he returned to his native land, still reeking with his victim's blood, he was everywhere received with frenzied ovations, and proclaimed the saviour of his country.

Perhaps he merited the title. Wilhelm was the mightiest man of his day, and he had always shown himself an implacable enemy to Flanders.

CHAPTER IV

Progress of the City

THE story of the long chain of discords and disasters which make up the reign of the grandson and successor of Count Arnulph the Great is not graven in the stones of Bruges.

Arnulph II. was the founder of no monastery, the builder of no church. No city hall nor hospital owes its origin to him. So far as Bruges is concerned, his reign is a blank.

It could hardly have been otherwise. The days of Arnulph were very evil. On all sides brute force had usurped the place of justice. Wars and rumours of wars were making the whole world shudder. Flood, famine and pestilence had filled Europe with an exceeding bitter cry. The thousand years which were to elapse between Christ's first and second coming had well-nigh run out. Surely His sign would soon appear in the heavens. Surely the advent of the great King was drawing very near. So thought all the world, and in an agony of hope and apprehension the whole world was waiting with bated breath. Presently a streak of light appeared on the horizon, but it was not the light which the world expected. With the ten hundreds a new era had opened in Europe. Scourged by the hand of misfortune, afflicted humanity seems to have at last realized the need of drawing closer together, and a very general revival of commerce, of literature, of art and of religion was the outcome.

Not least among the great leaders under whose auspices these things were taking place, was Count Baldwin IV. of Flanders. Baldwin of the Long Beard, as men called him.

He took up the work of civilization where Arnulph the Great had left it, and his one ambition was to bring it to a successful issue. 'He was noble and brave,' we read in the Flemish Chronicle, 'a man of good report, and one who feared God. His riches were immense, he marched at the head of his armies and sowed terror among his foes, and his sword was no less keen than his mother wit. He honoured righteousness, was a zealous promoter of reform, protected the Fatherland and defended the Church. Stern to law breakers and men puffed up by pride, to the meek and gentle he ever showed himself gentle and meek.'

Perhaps the picture is too highly coloured, but Flanders certainly prospered under Baldwin's government. The outcome of his dispute with the Emperor Henry II. was the island of Walcheren and the city of Valenciennes. The marriage of his son with Ethel of France added Corbie to the paternal inheritance, whilst his own marriage with Norman Eleanor, if it brought him no increase of territory, at least healed the old feud between Flanders and her powerful neighbour.

But this was not all. Under the fostering care of this prince, and thanks to the very large charter of liberties which he granted, the trade of Flanders increased by leaps and bounds. 'In these days,' we read, 'the ports of Montreuil and Boulogne were full of shipping, and traders from all sides crowded to Bruges, already famous by reason of the rich merchandise they brought there.' Nor did the national prosperity diminish when, in 1036, the old Count was gathered to his fathers. So greatly had Bruges increased, that his son Baldwin of Lille found it necessary, during the third year of his reign, to rebuild and extend its walls.

It was about this time that Flanders first began to consider herself the common fatherland of all foreigners who chose to reside within her borders. Indeed, Baldwin of Lille seems to have kept open house at Bruges for all the political refugees of the period. Hither, in 1036, came Emma of England, widow of Canute the Great, driven into exile by the machinations of Godwin, and the accession of her step-son Harold I.

Here she was joined later on by her own son Harthacnut, and here that prince received the English envoys when, upon the death of Harold in 1040, they waited on him with an offer of the English throne.

Queen Emma was a daughter of Duke Richard the Fearless of Normandy, and consequently the first cousin of Baldwin of the Long Beard. She did not prolong her stay at Bruges after Harthacnut's acceptance of the throne of England, but four years later Count Baldwin had an opportunity of receiving another English connection, the Princess Gunhilda, a niece of Canute the Great. She was accused of having opposed the election of King Edward the Confessor, and forthwith fled to Bruges.

When, in 1047, Godwin's son Swegen was outlawed, he too found shelter at Bruges, and when, four years later, the great English Earl himself had to flee his native land, he directed his steps to the same retreat. It was, doubtless, at his palace in the Bourg that Baldwin entertained his guests, and most likely the Crypt of St. Basil—sole relic of Bruges as Godwin saw it—was the place where they went to pray. Here Earl Godwin remained all the winter, busy with many things, anon negotiating a marriage for Tostig with Baldwin's daughter Judith, anon constructing a great fleet with which he would presently conquer the right to live in peace on his native soil.

Shortly before Baldwin's death, another great Englishman came to Flanders, perhaps to Bruges.

Hereward, son of Leofric, the last man who defied the right of the Conqueror's sword. Here he found for himself a wife, and here he would have ended his days in peace had not the insults heaped on his mother called him back to England. With him there went a band of Karls, and with him they laid down their lives at Thorney. If there had been in England three men like him, runs an old rhymed chronicle, the French would have never landed, and if he had only lived, he would have driven them back to France.

About this time, too, there came to Bruges two other victims of the Conqueror's ambition. Githa, Earl Godwin's widow, and his daughter, Gunhilda. Of Githa's subsequent career we are ignorant, but Gunhilda made Bruges her principal residence for nearly twenty years. Here she died on the 24th August 1087, and by way of acknowledgment for the kindness she had received at the hands of the burghers, she bequeathed her jewels to their Collegiate Church—jewels so precious that, when they were sold a century later, a sufficient sum was realized to pay for its restoration. They laid her to rest in the cloister of St. Donatian, and when, in 1786, her tomb was opened, they found therein a leaden tablet, still preserved in the Cathedral of Bruges, on which was graved the story of her virtues and her sorrows.

Baldwin of Lille was succeeded by his second son, Baldwin the Good. The tumultuous days of his immediate successors and the harshness and violence of nearly all the sovereigns who followed them, have enhanced perhaps the glory of his good fame. Be this as it may, the old Flemish chroniclers delight to dwell on the story of this gentle youth, but his name is not linked with Bruges.

He was a prince, they tell us, of wondrous dignity, and yet of a disposition so sweet that all men were drawn to him. He alone of the Counts of Flanders never once unsheathed his sword, and so great was his love of peace that he would never suffer his subjects to do so. 'His officers carried white wands, long and straight, symbols of justice and mercy,' and they maintained such good order throughout his domains, that no man was fain at night to bar his doors against thieves, and when the husbandman went home in the evening, he did not fear to leave his ploughshare in the fields, and this is the reason, they add, why all men called him 'the good Count of Flanders.'

In order to accurately appreciate the causes of the almost perennial struggles between the sovereigns of Flanders and their subjects throughout the Middle Ages, it is important to know something of the men, and of their position in the body politic who formed the backbone of the people's resistance; of the men from whose primitive institutions were gradually evolved the complicated municipal machinery by which all the great cities of Flanders were eventually governed, and in defence of which almost all the struggles in question were originally undertaken. These men were the Flemings or Karls of the seaboard, Saxons of pure blood, distinct in race, though not in speech, from the inhabitants of the towns, for in the veins of the townsman there often flowed a strain of Celtic blood, and at Bruges especially, where, as we know, at an early date there was settled a colony of foreign merchants, the population must soon have become one of mixed race.

The Karls then formed a class apart, a vast middle class of free landholders, distinct alike from the Court nobility—the comrades of the Count, his bodyguard, the great feudal lords who knew no trade but war—from the *vilains* or serfs who were their retainers; and from the inhabitants of the towns. But the Karl was not only a farmer, he was sometimes also a fisherman, often a merchant, and always, and above all things, a soldier. If it had been otherwise, he could never have preserved either his own personal freedom or the freedom of the soil he tilled. To him toil was no disgrace. The greatest of their chiefs, even those among them in whose veins ran noble blood, were not ashamed to dig.

Herred Krangrok, who dwelt along with his wife Ethel, a niece of the Bishop of Térouane, in the impregnable Castle of Salvesse in the midst of the marshy forest land, which in those days stretched away beyond Furnes, was a typical Karl of high degree. This man seems to have been a brewer by trade, and they gave him the surname *Krangrok* from a habit he had of throwing his cloak back over his shoulder when he was driving his own plough.

The home of the Karls was a long strip of territory stretching along the coast from the great Abbey of Muenickereede to the marshes of Wasconingawala in the county of Guines—a strip of territory of unequal width, of which the northern boundary would now be difficult to trace, but which certainly included within its borders the townships of Ardres, of Alveringhem and Furnes—the vast forest of Thorout, and all that district which was later on submitted to the jurisdiction of the Liberty of Bruges.

This land was divided up into a number of districts called circles or guilds, which the inhabitants themselves administered by means of their own elected chiefs, who were at the same time their magistrates and their legislators.

The ties which bound them to the sovereign were of the loosest nature, amounting to little more than this—personal service for the protection of the Fatherland, and the payment of a voluntary tribute which they themselves assessed.

Certainly up to the end of the tenth century, and perhaps for a century later, the Karls were still a fierce, wild race, much given to hereditary feuds and private warfare, still infected with Pagan superstitions, and still occasionally practising Pagan rites.

The vast majority of them were poor, but a certain number, especially after the triumph of Robert the Frisian, succeeded in amassing wealth, and of these not a few filled high positions alike in Church and State.

Under the sovereignty of the early Flemish Counts the Karls had little to complain of, and though doubtless the feudal tendencies of their rulers were fostered by the *rapprochement* with Normandy under Baldwin le Barbu and Baldwin of Lille, the Karls were still so independent of their princes, that whilst Baldwin, for a consideration, was helping William in his projects against England, the Karls were straining every nerve in behalf of their Saxon kinsmen on the other side of the water, and it was not till the regency of Richilde of Hainault, the widow of Baldwin the Good, that any systematic attempt was made to bring them under subjection.

In the neighbouring States of Guines and Normandy, Northern freedom and Northern notions of liberty had long ago given place to a feudal *régime* of the sternest type, under which the freehold farmer of olden days had rapidly sunk into the *vilain*. The untimely death of Baldwin the Good, in 1070, afforded the Flemish barons, as they thought, a fitting opportunity for reducing the Karls of Flanders to a similar condition. Arnulph, the heir to the throne, was a youth of fifteen years, and Richilde of Hainault, the Countess Dowager, had assumed the reins of government and taken for her chief councillor Albéric de Coucy, a man who, on account of his tyrannical tendencies, had experienced the wrath of Baldwin of Lille. The first measure of her reign showed the spirit by which she was animated—the imposition of a tax, an *inaudita et indebita tributa*, as Lambert of Ardres describes it, the proceeds of which were intended to defray the cost of maintaining town ramparts. Since these had hitherto been kept in repair by means of forced labour, and the *Böelfart* was only to be levied on the Karls of the seaboard, they naturally regarded the measure in question as a direct attack on their liberty.

That the men now called on to pay for the work were henceforth to be considered as of like condition with the slaves who had formerly toiled at it, this for the Karls was the meaning of Richilde's decree—in the bitter words of Lambert of Ardres, it was the outcome of the hatred she bore them, 'and they murmured to one another and to God, and they bethought them of the valiant deeds of Robert, the good Count's brother.' Flanders was in a state of ferment, but the widow of Baldwin was in no way daunted at the tokens of the coming storm. She had inflamed the heart of a mighty champion, who had had experience in the taming of Karls—William FitzOsberne, Earl of Hereford, the Conqueror's right hand at Senlac, but lately his Viceroy in England, and the bravest and the craftiest of all his knights. She had conciliated the good will of Baldwin's kinsman, Eustace, Count of Boulogne, and for 4000 livres she had purchased the help of Philip I. of France.

Confident in this added pillar of strength, Richilde made light of her subjects' complaints, and answered their appeal to Robert the Frisian by cutting off three-score heads and by invading his county of Alost.

But Richilde had reckoned without her host. Robert was away in Holland at the time, but he was not a man to tamely suffer an insult, nor to despise the prayer of those who asked his help. He had inherited from his Saxon forebears the courage, the daring, the generosity and the violence of their race, and he no sooner learned what had happened, than he set out for Alost, drove out Richilde, and made haste to occupy Cassel, an old Roman camp on the top of a solitary hill a thousand feet high, some three leagues south of Dunkirk. Cassel was in the heart of the Karl country, and the Karls from all sides flocked to his standard. The towns, too, sent their contingents. From Bruges, from Thorhout, from Furnes, from Courtrai, from Oudenburg, from Ypres, burghers came in by the thousand, and soon Robert the Frisian was at the head of a mighty host.

But Richilde and her allies had not been idle. FitzOsberne had summoned his cohorts from Normandy. Eustace had set his fighting men in battle array, all the chivalry of France was enrolled under Philip's banner, and presently, from the height of his stronghold, Count Robert saw a huge, disorderly rabble, knee-deep in snow and sand, slowly wending its way through the plain stretched out before him. Men of a hundred races were there, and may be as many motives had armed them, but the task they had sworn to accomplish was one—to stamp out for ever the last torch of Northern freedom.

On the evening of the 21st of February, shrivelled with cold and worn out with bad roads and hard marching, these men at length reached Bavichove and there made camp. From the heights of Mount Cassel, Count Robert saw them. In the small hours of the morning he swooped down from his eyrie, and when the sun rose the great Confederate host had melted away; all that was left of it at Bavichove was a mire of red slush and a heap of mangled corpses.

Richilde herself had escaped, and the swiftness of his heels had saved Philip, her hired champion, by a hair's breadth, but William FitzOsberne, the husband who had fought for love, was among the slain, and—cruellest blow of all—young Arnulph, too, had fallen, cut down when he thought the bitterness of death had passed.

Thus much had Richilde gained by mixing herself up in the conspiracy against the Karls, but she had not yet reaped the full harvest of her arrogance. The hour of their final triumph had not yet come. Immediately after the death of Arnulph, Philip of France had received the homage of his younger brother Baldwin, and it took five long years of fighting and diplomacy to establish Robert on the throne of Flanders.

At length, in 1076, Richilde yielded to the inevitable, acknowledged the pretensions of the rival of her son, and accepted from him as dower the châtelaincy of Audenarde. Here she remained till the end of her days, occupying herself with prayer and good works in expiation for the bloody war which her disastrous policy had entailed. The life of the châtelaine of Audenarde was one long act of contrition for the sins of the Countess of Flanders. The conquest of Robert meant the conquest of the Karls, and the effect of their triumph was immediately observable in the changed policy of the government, not only at home but abroad. Their rights as free men were now acknowledged throughout the country, and their chiefs were received at Court on an equality with the feudal lords, henceforth we find them occupying high positions alike in Church and State. Erembald, a simple Karl of Furnes, was appointed Châtelain of Bruges—the highest civil appointment in Flanders. One of his sons received the provostship of the Collegiate Church of St. Donatian (Bruges), the first ecclesiastical preferment in the county—not a few of their daughters were wedded to the proudest of the feudal lords, and Robert's own son, Philip, Viscount of Ypres, did not think it beneath his dignity to take a Karline for his wife.

The same policy was pursued during the reign of the Frisian's successor. Amongst the knights who followed Count Robert II. to Jerusalem were not a few Saxon chiefs. The names of some of them have come down to us—Siger of Ghistelles, Walter of Oudenburg, Engelram of Lillers, Erembald of Bruges, the mightiest of them all, and Erembald's son Robert, Count Robert's intimate friend and his most trusted servant. The influence of the Karls is distinctly traceable in the changed attitude of Flanders with regard to England. Baldwin had done all he could to strengthen William, Robert strained every nerve to oppose him. He would have brought back the line of Alfred, or restored the English throne to the house of the great Canute, had not the Conqueror been wily enough to circumvent him. Raised to supreme authority by the aid of Saxon Karls, Robert the Frisian could hardly have done otherwise than show himself friendly to the cause of their compatriots.

Although, as we have seen, the victory of Bavichove, 1071, or rather the peace of Mayence five years later, had for the moment settled the question of Karlish freedom, there were still not wanting among the feudal lords men who envied the power and prosperity to which the Karls had attained, and who wished to reduce them to slavery. Their plans had been foiled by Robert I. and kept in check by Robert II., but when that prince fell at the siege of Meaux (thrown from his horse in a narrow lane and trampled

I.—Genealogical Table of the Counts of Flanders from Baldwin I. to Baldwin V[7]

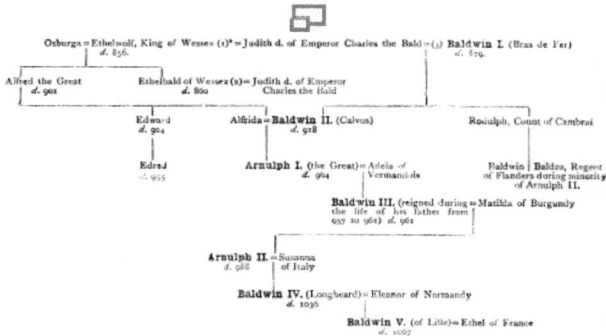

Osburga = Ethelwolf, King of Wessex (1)* = Judith d. of Emperor Charles the Bald = (1) Baldwin I. (Bras de Fer)
d. 856.   d. 879.

- Alfred the Great d. 901
- Ethelbald of Wessex (2) = Judith d. of Emperor d. 860 Charles the Bald
- Alftida = Baldwin II. (Calvus) d. 918
- Rodulph, Count of Cambrai

- Edward d. 924
- Arnulph I. (the Great) = Adela of d. 964 | Vermandois
- Baldwin | Baldzo, Regent of Flanders during minority of Arnulph II.

- Edred d. 955
- Baldwin III. (reigned during the life of his father from 957 to 961) d. 961 = Matilda of Burgundy

Arnulph II. = Susanna d. 988 | of Italy

Baldwin IV. (Longbeard) = Eleanor of Normandy d. 1036

Baldwin V. (of Lille) = Ethel of France d. 1067

to death by his own knights as they were pressing on to victory), the rights of the Karls of Flanders were once more called in question. His son and successor, Baldwin Hapkin, a youth of eighteen years, was entirely under the influence of the stern preceptor, whose iron will had trained him, his father's nephew, Charles of Denmark. In this man's veins flowed the blood of Canute the Great; the violence and the virtues of that redoubtable monarch were all his. Added to this, his whole being was tinged by the ghastly tragedy which had deprived him of a royal heritage and driven his trembling mother to flee with her infant boy to Bruges.

He had always before his eyes the murder, or, as he himself deemed it, the glorious martyrdom of his father, who was literally hacked to pieces as he was praying before the altar in the Church of St. Alban at Odensee (1086) by a band of rioters lashed to fury by his rigorous method of exacting tithe. Such being the man, and such his antecedents, it would have been surprising indeed if he had shown any sympathy for such bloodthirsty folk as the Karls. But if he hated the lawlessness of these men, he hated no less the lawlessness of the barons, and throughout the fifteen years during which he governed Flanders, first as Baldwin's minister and afterwards, when at that prince's death he himself succeeded to his inheritance, he never ceased to combat each of these elements of disorder, and in so doing he hurled himself with such violence against the rock of liberty, that at length he was dashed to pieces.

CHAPTER V

The Murder of Charles the Good

AMONG the tragedies enacted at Bruges—and their number is legion—not one is so weird, so mysterious, so repulsive, and at the same time so enthralling, as the blood-stained legend of Charles the Good.

It is the theme, as we all know, of Hendrick Conscience's *De Kerels van Vlaanderen*, a romance which approaches nearer to the original legend than almost any modern historical account that has come under our notice. For although for his details Conscience has drawn to a certain extent on imagination, the main outlines of his story coincide exactly with the main outlines of the legend handed down to us by writers contemporary with Charles himself.

Of these contemporary lives of the murdered Count we still possess at least three. The first is by Walbert, Court Notary, or, as we should say, Registrar of Bruges. He was a personal friend and staunch adherent of Count Charles, and, as he himself avers, an eye-witness of much that he relates. His evidence cannot, however, be regarded as altogether trustworthy. He was naturally animated with the bitterest feelings against the great house which compassed his patron's overthrow, and against Bertulph, one of the chiefs of that house, he seems to have nourished a personal grudge. On more than one occasion he contradicts himself flatly, and he is an inveterate backbiter and gossip. From his direst enemy to his dearest friend there is hardly a man in his crowded canvas whose character he does not directly or indirectly asperse. Indeed, in the case of his enemies, when he can find nothing to say against them, he not unfrequently hints that, in his opinion, their good actions were inspired by unworthy motives. For the rest, the story of this twelfth-century Saint-Simon is replete with the most interesting details, rich in local colour, and almost as thrilling to read as one of Wilkie Collins's novels. The second life is by Walter, Archdeacon of Tournai. It was written at the request of 'Blessed' John, who ruled the united churches of Noyon and Tournai from 1127 to 1130, and is dedicated to him. Walter, like Walbert, was personally acquainted with Charles. He was with him at Ypres three days before his death, but was not at Bruges when that event took place, and his narrative is based on information furnished by certain trustworthy clerks and citizens of Bruges who vouched for the truth of what they told him.

In some respects Walter's narrative is a work superior to Walbert's. The whole story hangs together, his language is often dignified, and generally temperate, nor are the judgments which he forms, on the face of them, inaccurate.

The third life is contained in the Acta of Louis the Fat, compiled by Suger, Abbot of St. Denis, who died in 1142. It must have been written, therefore, not later than this date, and not earlier than 1137, the year in which Louis died, from ten to fifteen years, that is to say, after the death of Charles. As for this account, there is only one thing to be said about it. Suger held a brief for Charles's avenger, Louis the Fat, and he did the best he could for his client.

In compiling the following narrative we have made use of these three lives, of the Danish life by Wegener, of the Bollandist's life, and of the notes and contemporary documents collected by Vredius in his *Flandrica Ethnica*. We have also consulted Gaillard, Gheldorf, Kervyn de Lettenhove, and various other modern Flemish historians.

When Count Charles assumed the government of Flanders the Erembalds were a power to be reckoned with. Their political influence was unrivalled, the number of their retainers was legion, their wealth was immense, by their marriages they had allied themselves with the first families in the county.

Desiderius Hacket, the head of this house, was Châtelain of Bruges, and, as such, second man in the realm; Bertulph, his brother, as Provost of St. Donatian's, was the greatest churchman in Flanders, and, as hereditary chancellor, chief of the Count's household, whilst other members of the family held honourable and lucrative appointments about their sovereign's person. Notwithstanding, however, their great position, the Erembalds were never included in the ranks of the feudal nobility. They were originally simple freeholders or Karls, perhaps hereditary chiefs of some circle or guild, who by commerce, and may be also by plunder, for the Karls were lawless folk, had amassed vast wealth, and thereby been enabled to climb to the high places they now held. That they could by the same means, if they had been so minded, have also been ennobled, there can be no doubt, but the Erembalds, like all Karls, despised feudalism and all its works and all its pomps; in their eyes the title of Freeman was a nobler one than any which princes could bestow.

Tancmar, the head of the great feudal house of Straten, was the owner of the lordship of Straten, in the neighbourhood of Bruges, where he had built himself an impregnable fortress, a wealthy devotee who had gained no little renown for piety and good works, the great Abbey of St. Andrew, hard-by his own domain, was the especial object of his munificence. He held high office in the Count's household, was a member of his Privy Council, and, what was worth more to him than anything else, his sovereign's confidential and devoted friend.

Tancmar himself had no children, but he had adopted two nephews, sons, perhaps, of his brother; Giselbert, or, as we should say Gilbert, and Walter, whom men called the Winged Lie.

Between the families of Erembald and Straten there had gradually grown up a deadly feud. As to the first cause of it both Walter and Walbert are silent, but the former writer tells us that, like many other great quarrels before and since, it arose out of a very small matter.

Wegener, indeed, comes to the conclusion that the primary quarrel was between Charles himself and Bertulph, that it sprang from the Count's hatred of the Erembalds, whose pride and lawlessness were marring his projects of reform, and that the Stratens on the one side, and Bertulph's kinsfolk on the other, were mere tools in the hands of these two wire-pullers, who themselves at first remained in the background.

Certainly all the facts of the case, taken together, go to show that if Charles himself was not its first instigator, he at all events exploited the quarrel for his own political ends.

In the early years of his reign, he had issued an edict by which he forbade all men save his own officers to go armed in time of peace—an edict particularly galling to the Karls, who regarded the bearing of arms as the inherent right of a freeman, and to deprive them of it was, in their estimation, and perhaps also in the estimation of the Count, to deprive them of their personal liberty. The Karls, it is true, were a cruel and a quarrelsome race. The territory in which they dwelt was often drenched with blood. Scenes of rapine and murder were with them matters of everyday occurrence; their hereditary feuds and petty wars were a constant menace to the State. Charles was determined to put an end to all this, and he knew of but one way of doing so—to submit the territory of the Karls to the tender mercies of feudalism, for, in his estimation, law and order were matters of far greater moment than mere personal freedom. This, however, was not the opinion of the Erembalds. Although they themselves, as officers of the Count, were in no way touched by the edict in question, they opposed it with all their might, and from that moment Charles determined to crush them.

To attack his old friends openly was an undertaking too hazardous. It was to the Erembalds, as Bertulph used to boast, that Charles owed his crown, and he had repaid the debt with gold and favours. Their power was now as great as his own, and their popularity perhaps greater. Moreover, to strike at them was to strike at the Church, for Bertulph, their chief, was chief also of the clergy of Flanders. It behoved Charles, then, to be very wary. He determined therefore for the moment to keep himself in the background, to bide his time, and when the plot was ripe to act through trusty agents. He had not long to wait, the crisis came early in 1126. It happened thus.

Richard of Raeske, one of the many barons allied by marriage to the house of Erembald, and a man of no little repute in Flanders, fell out about this time with Walter of Straten and defied him in the Count's presence to mortal combat. To the surprise of every one the challenge was refused, and the ground of the refusal was still more astounding. "I will never measure my sword," hissed 'the Winged Lie,' "with any but a free man, and the Lord of Raeske, by wedding a serf, has forfeited his right to that title." He was alluding to one of Charles's own edicts, perhaps made in anticipation of the quarrel, by which it was decreed that 'the freeman (*liber*) who married a slave (*ancillam*) should, after a year's wedlock, cease to be free, and sink to his wife's condition.'

The calumny, as Archdeacon Walter calls it, came like a bolt from the blue. The Erembalds had been châtelains of Bruges for well-nigh a hundred years, and no man heretofore had ever ventured even to hint at the possibility of a flaw in their escutcheon. Walter had aimed his shaft well, it had flown far and pierced deep. By it was threatened not only the honour and the liberty and the purse of every man in whose veins flowed the blood of an Erembald, but alike the honour and the liberty and the purse of each one of the score or more of proud barons allied by marriage to the dishonoured race. The Erembalds were cut to the quick, and the words of defiance which Bertulph himself hurled back, words which in the light of after events seem almost prophetic, voiced the indignation of the whole clan. 'I am a free man,' he thundered out; 'my forefathers were free men, and no one shall be found mighty enough to take away my freedom.' Strange as it may seem, the aristocracy, almost to a man, rallied round the attainted house, whilst almost alone at the side of his friend stood the Count.

He still hesitated, however, to show his true colours; he would himself, he said, in no way interfere, but leave the matter in the hands of his judges—a commission should be appointed to examine the affair, and he would abide by their decision. But Bertulph was not to be hoodwinked, and spread it abroad that the Count was plotting his ruin:—'This Charles of Denmark, whom I made, would fain through his judges reduce me to slavery. Let him try.' Nor did he hesitate to fling back in Charles's teeth the retort that he himself was illegitimate, aye and a bastard, too, base born. 'This Charles of Denmark!' he contemptuously cried—Bertulph, who was a true Fleming, could never forget or forgive his master's foreign extraction—'This Charles of Denmark, who boasts that he is a king's son! In good sooth, a scullion begat him! By what right doth he torment us?' Truly Provost Bertulph had a bitter tongue. But neither scorn nor threats nor bitter speech could turn the Count from his purpose. The promised commission was duly appointed, and after a lengthy inquiry made its award:—Let the Lady of Raeske swear that she is of free birth in the presence of twelve nobles who shall confirm her oath with their own; but with no little inconsistency a proviso was added that this decision concerned only the case of the Lady of Raeske personally, and in no way derogated from the Count's right, if he would, to proceed against any other member of the Erembald family. This compromise Charles accepted, and, partially laying aside the cloak of neutrality which hitherto prudence had bade him assume, lost no time in claiming the Erembalds for his serfs, nor until the day of his death, more than a year later, did he cease so to regard them.

They no less persistently repudiated the claim, and Charles either could not or would not enforce it, and for the moment was fain to content himself with slighting words and half-veiled threats. Meanwhile the Erembalds and the Stratens were flying at one another's throats. Cattle were being looted, boundaries were being razed, and blood was flowing in torrents. A hurricane of strife had been let loose on the land, and all the efforts of the sower of the wind, now thoroughly afraid at his own handiwork, and clumsily playing the double *rôle* of peacemaker and partisan, were powerless to quell it.

Suddenly, when the turmoil was at its height, Charles was called to France. An intermittent warfare had for years been carried on between the Count of Auvergne and the Bishop of Clermont, and things had at length come to a crisis. The former had made appeal to his liege lord, Duke William of Aquitaine, and the latter, by their united efforts, driven from his See, had now invoked, not vainly, the aid of Louis the Fat, who forthwith summoned his vassals (amongst whom of course was Charles) and set out for Clermont.

The Count of Flanders was undoubtedly placed in a very awkward predicament. To leave his realm at the present juncture was to risk revolution, and by staying at home he would certainly estrange his one reliable friend. The civil war at the beginning of his reign, and the famine and pestilence which followed, had sown broadcast misery and discontent, whilst the well-meant but arbitrary measures which Charles had taken for the relief of the poor, especially his edict as to the price of wheat, had alienated the rich, who openly accused him of showing favour to the people at their expense. 'If it be so,' he was wont to reply, 'it is because I know the misery of the poor and the pride of the upper classes,' but, unfortunately for Charles, in his day the classes alone counted, and the classes were in a high fever of suspicion and unrest. The great purveyors of bread-stuffs had been touched in their pockets, the free landholders of the sea-board thought themselves already slaves, the honour of the first family in Flanders had been trampled in the dust. No one was sure that it would not be his turn next. Others besides Bertulph were questioning Charles's right to torment them. The whole land was sick of foreign rule, and men were beginning to whisper in corners of William of Löo. It was probably this last consideration which prompted Charles to obey. If he had failed to do so, his powerful kinsman might have veered round to the side of the legitimate heir, and in that case he would in all probability have lost his county.

Charles must have taken a heavy heart with him to Clermont, but his biographers do not inform us that he was in any way disquieted.

Before starting, however, he seems to have summoned the Erembalds and the Stratens to his presence and to have made them swear to a truce, but to swear to a truce under existing circumstances was little better than a farce. Such was the hatred of the belligerents for one another, that even a temporary suspension of hostilities had become impossible, and during the whole period of Charles's absence the land was a prey to their mutual depredations.

It was not till the fall of the year that Charles came back to his domains. At Ypres he was met by a deputation of peasants, retainers seemingly of the Stratens, who made complaint that the Erembalds, headed by the provost's nephew Burchard, had plundered their dwellings, laid waste their land and driven off their cattle. Charles promised them justice, and having taken counsel with his barons, decreed that Burchard's house at Straten should be razed to the ground. The sentence was promptly carried out, and Walter adds that the Count in person superintended its execution. That this was only a prelude there can be no doubt. Charles had returned to Flanders crowned with the laurels of victory. His successes at Clermont had earned for him the gratitude of Louis the Fat, who had most likely promised him help. The time had come when he felt himself strong enough to carry out his plan against the Erembalds. Nor were these last ignorant of his intentions. At length, driven to bay, they were determined to make one desperate stand for liberty. They would save their honour, even if the price paid for it should be their sovereign's life.

Charles had arrived at Bruges late on the evening of 28th February, and towards the close of the next day a deputation waited on him on behalf of the threatened clan. There seems to have been little hope of bringing about a reconciliation, but Bertulph had most likely insisted that no effort should be left untried before having recourse to violence. The accounts which the contemporary lives give of this interview do not tally, but they are at one as to its issue—Charles was adamant. The die was cast. That night the Erembalds met in secret conclave. Early next morning Charles rose, feverish and ill at ease, from a couch overshadowed by the wraith of his coming doom. His servants would have had him remain indoors. Some rumour of the midnight meeting had leaked out, and they suspected foul play, but Charles refused to listen, and notwithstanding that the day had dawned so thick, 'that a man could see no further than a spear's length before him,' betook himself almost unattended to St. Donatian's, there to hear Mass.[8]

Hardly had the service begun than Burchard, accompanied by a crowd of retainers, entered the church by a side door, and sheltering himself behind the great columns of the northern aisle, stealthily crept up to the place where Charles was kneeling before the Lady altar, and touched him on the shoulder. The Count turned his head to see who was there, and for a moment their eyes met, and then, quick as thought, a blow from Burchard's sword felled him dead on the pavement.

'If this Dane should be cut down,' Burchard was reported to have said a few days before the murder—'If this Dane should be cut down, who will rise up to avenge him?' and now that the blow had been struck and Charles was dead, it at first seemed that Burchard had accurately gauged the situation.

Thémard, Châtelain of Brudburch, who was kneeling by Charles's side when the fatal blow was struck, indeed made some show at defending him, but he was quickly overpowered by numbers, and fell, mortally wounded, beside the body of his master. As to the other members of the Count's household, those of them who were not privy to the conspiracy were too terrified to think of anything but their own safety. The Stratens and their adherents had fled the county. William of Löo, the next heir to the throne, sent letters of salutation and promises of help. Even the clergy were silent, and the burghers, amongst whom the Erembalds had always been popular, so far from showing signs of disapproval of the crime, were working night and day at the fortifications of the town, in order to enable it to withstand a possible attack.

For the moment the Erembalds had triumphed. The death of their sovereign had brought them life.

After the long months of shame and suspense, during which wealth, honour, liberty, all that makes life dear, were trembling in the balance, it must have been no little consolation to these fierce, proud Karls to know that their enemy, the man who had persecuted them, had himself been brought low. But there was one thing which was a cause of anxiety and of reproach—that thing which to many another murderer before and after has been the source of no little embarrassment—the body.

There it lay, in the place where the deed had been done, set out in ghastly state amid flaming torches, a silent witness to their broken troth. What should they do with it?

Bertulph and Hacket had indeed from the first disclaimed all knowledge of the murder, and though perhaps their ignorance was wilful, in doing so they probably spoke the truth; but the guilt of Burchard and of several other members of the family was notorious and undenied, and so strong were ties of blood in the eyes of the Karl, that when one of them had sinned all his kindred deemed themselves not only responsible for, but, in a certain measure, also participators in the crime.

The ghastly trophy, then, in the choir of St. Donatian's, was as dire a reproach to Bertulph and his brother as to the blood-stained Burchard himself.

Time pressed. Every moment that the mutilated corpse remained above ground was increasing the risk that pity would goad men to rebellion. What should they do with it? This was the problem which the Erembalds assembled in Bertulph's house[9] had now to solve, and, if their new-born hope was not to be stifled, to solve quickly.

There were several weighty reasons why the interment should not take place at Bruges. To bury Charles in the capital, where the circumstances of his death were notorious, were to indelibly grave their own ignominy in the hearts of future generations. Perhaps, too, the presence of the body would entail also the presence of an avenging shade. Moreover, there was no precedent for a royal interment at Bruges, and the only church in the city where such a function could be fittingly celebrated had been defiled by blood, none but the Bishop of Tournai had the right to reconsecrate it, and even if there were time to communicate with him, it was in the highest degree improbable that old Simon of Tournai, Charles's own brother-in-law, would consent to smooth the path of his kinsman's murderers.

On the other hand, there was a strong feeling amongst the people in favour of Bruges, and Bertulph was sufficiently acquainted with the temper of his fellow-townsmen to know that any attempt to run counter to their wishes would be hazardous. After much confabulation, it was at length decided to request Arnulph, Abbot of Blandinium, a man whom Bertulph could trust, to secretly convey the body of Charles to his cloister and there give it Christian burial. Nor did Arnulph belie the confidence placed in him.

Although it was the hour of compline when Bertulph's messenger reached Ghent, on learning of his old friend's dilemma, he at once made ready to start, and pushing on through the darkness, in spite of bad roads and bad weather, made such expedition that he reached Bruges before cock-crow. All was in readiness, the body had been prepared for burial— the trusty abbot had secured a conveyance which was now drawn up in a secluded corner hard by the cathedral, before daybreak he would again be free of the town, and once in the open country there was little fear of hindrance or detection.

All that remained of Charles had been placed on the bearers' shoulders, and under the direction of Bertulph and the abbot, the weird *cortège* was slowly wending its way down the nave of St. Donatian's, had indeed almost reached the great western portal, when suddenly the stillness of the early morning became a whirl of angry voices and tramping feet. There could be no mistake as to its import. Somehow or other the project had become known, and all Bruges had turned out to oppose it.

In order to understand the cause of this seemingly sudden revulsion of feeling, a word of explanation is perhaps necessary.

The whole life of Charles of Denmark is wrapped and swathed from beginning to end in mystery and contradiction. Half soldier, half saint, with his Bible in one hand, and Charlemagne's sword 'Joyeuse' in the other, he flits across the stage of European history like some pale, crimson-robed phantom from another world.[10]

Was he a cunning schemer—a layer of deep plots which he never lived to carry out, or was he only a dreamer of dreams, tossed about by wayward impulses and passing fancies, this incomprehensible Dane, king's son or scullion's son, as the case may be, who almost accomplished so much and in reality achieved so little—this tissue of inconsistencies who usurped for himself a petty principality and despised an imperial diadem, who crushed his proud lords with a lion's fierceness, and went barefoot to kiss the hands of beggars, this most marvellous devotee who showed himself on occasions so generous and at times appears so mean, who deprived himself of meat and raiment that he might have the more to succour the needy, and spat on his best friends and trampled them in the dust? This friend and father of churches, who all his life long lavished on them wealth, honour, obedience, and whose end, by a strange irony of fate, was at length destined to be the outcome of an unjust quarrel which he himself had forced on his own ecclesiastical chief.

Questions difficult to answer these, with the evidence at present at our disposal. Dr. Wegener thinks (p. 6) there is ground for believing that the dream of Charles's life was to win his paternal heritage—the crown of

Denmark, and that if he had lived longer he might perhaps have realized it. May be his hopes flew higher still, and that the ultimate goal of his ambition was to carry out his father's darling project and establish once more, in all its glory, the kingdom of Canute the Great. But, however this may be, and whatever may have been Charles's failings and his foibles and his faults, one thing is certain: his good deeds alone followed him. The hospitals and asylums which he founded, the churches and monasteries which he built, his courtesy and sweetness to the poor and the simple, the sympathy and protection which he showed to the oppressed, the lordly feasts which he made in his palace at Bruges for the blind and the halt and the maimed— these are the things which lived after him, and friend and foe alike agreed to forget the rest.

Prayers and Masses were everywhere offered for the repose of his soul, perhaps even in his honour. Bertulph himself sang 'Requiem' for the foe who had once been his friend, and when all was over and the poor had returned to their houses enriched by his alms, his servants found him weeping over the grave. Even Burchard sought reconciliation. Despite the ban of the Church, Pagan practices died hard with the Flemish Karls of the seaboard, and Burchard, who was a true Karl, would make his peace with Charles after the manner of his forefathers. Accompanied by a band of wild retainers from the Forest of Thor, he entered at midnight the choir of St. Donatian's, where lay the body, and there, by the light of flaming torches, celebrated the weird *Dodsisas*, or banquet of the dead. Libations of wine and libations of ale were poured over the grave, and as the loving-cup passed from hand to hand each man muttered, 'We drink to thee, Count Charles,' and then Burchard alone knelt down on the pavement and with his lips touched the marble slab which covered his victim's remains, saying, as he did so, 'Accept, O shade, this kiss of peace and reconciliation, and, appeased by these our offerings, vouchsafe to lay aside all thought of enmity and vengeance.' In a word, owing to the tragic circumstances of his death, the memory of 'this Charles of Denmark' was clean wiped out. The citizens of Bruges were only mindful, and to this day they are only mindful, of 'Blessed Charles the Good.'

Such being the case, it is not to be wondered at that, in an age when relics were prized above rubies, the burghers should be loth to part with so precious a thing as the body of their martyred Count. At all hazards they would keep it, thus they averred, and with much clamour and a mighty rush they burst into the cathedral. In the midst of the uproar rumour passed from mouth to mouth that a hunchback had been actually healed, in the twinkling of an eye, there, in the midst of them all, by simply touching the holy thing they were fighting for—fresh confirmation, were any needed, of Charles's sanctity. Bertulph indeed only laughed at the tale; that poor

Charles should be able to work miracles after his death seemed to him so very improbable. But Bertulph was a sceptic, so it was said, and nobody minded him. Five hundred unimpeachable burghers could vouch for the truth of the story, and the tumult increased tenfold. The clergy themselves, either from fear or conviction, now threw in their lot with the mob, and seizing on chairs, stools, thuribles, candlesticks, anything that came to hand, laid about them manfully. What did the provost mean by taking this step without consulting their wishes? Was not St. Donatian's as great as Blandinium, and were not the canons of Bruges as good men and true as the monks of Ghent? By God and His saints the body of Charles should never quit their cathedral! They would die first! In face of the opposition of his own clergy and the increasing fury of the mob, resistance was impossible, and Bertulph gave way, whilst Abbot Arnulph, giving thanks to God that he had escaped with a whole skin, was glad to go back to his monastery without the much-coveted treasure. This satisfied the people for the moment and they returned quietly to their homes, but in public estimation the crime of endeavouring to give Charles decent burial outside Bruges was as great a one as that of his murder, and in the sequel Bertulph had to pay dearly for it.

On the following morning (Friday, March 4), after a solemn Requiem Mass had been chanted for him in the chapel of St. Peter outside the Bourg, Charles was laid to rest in the place where he fell in front of the Lady Altar in St. Donatian's.

CHAPTER VI

Vengeance

MEANWHILE Charles's friends had been scouring the country far and wide, and wherever they went crying vengeance, and that not vainly. A bevy of thirty knights at once took up arms and swore they would not lay them down until they had washed them in the blood of the assassins, and—ominous note of warning—these men were all of them, or nearly all of them, partisans of the Erembalds. By common consent they chose Gervais Van Praet for their chief, and at once began to lay waste and plunder the lands and property of those who would not join them. Thus, gaining fresh recruits wherever they went, the little band rapidly grew into a vast army. Soon the town and fortress of Ravenschoot—a mighty stronghold of the Karls which, through some unaccountable blunder, had been left ungarrisoned—went up in flames; by the end of the week the smouldering embers of his brother Wulfric's palace, not a stone's throw from Bruges, warned Bertulph that the enemy was at his gates, and there was no sign of the reinforcements which William of Löo, who was perhaps in daily communication with the Provost, had promised to send from Ypres. Next morning, therefore, his nephews made a sortie beyond the ramparts, in the hope of putting the insurgents to flight, but after no little hard fighting they were smitten hip and thigh and forced to lead their shattered troops back to the city.

The burghers, however, still loyal to the cause of their châtelain, had been hard at work night and day strengthening the fortifications—old men, women and children, even the clergy themselves, had lent a willing hand—and the town was said to be impregnable. Perhaps it was, but for all that, on Wednesday the 9th of March, the enemy walked in at the Sablon gate. There was a traitor within the camp. May be one of the provost's own household. It was the hour of the evening meal, and so confident were the townsfolk in the strength of their walls that they remained quietly seated at table whilst the Isegrins[11] were marching through their streets, and the insurgents were already in the heart of the city before the news of their advent had reached Bertulph's palace. The Erembalds then were had at an advantage, and though they fought bravely—they always fought bravely—after a long and bloody conflict, the chief shock of which was on the *Pont de l'Ane Aveugle*, they were at last forced to retire to the Bourg, hoping against hope that they would be able to hold out until William of Löo should arrive.

As for the burghers, when they saw how the land lay, and that the insurgents would probably prove victorious, they either joined hands with them or endeavoured to maintain a neutral attitude, awaiting the issue of events—a prudent policy which their descendants have not unfrequently followed. Some ten days after the night of the great betrayal, the Isegrins approached their opponents with overtures of peace—offers of life and liberty for all within the beleaguered fortress who averred their innocence, if only they would come forth and prove it.

In the turmoil and confusion incident on the flight to the Bourg not a few of the attacking party were still within the fortress when the gates were shut, and many plain citizens, who perhaps had little sympathy with either side, but certainly had had no part in Charles's death, were in like predicament. It was on behalf of these men that the Isegrins now approached their foes. Still there is no reason to doubt that the offer was made in good faith. 'Many who were innocent availed themselves of it, and many also,' says Galbert, 'whose conduct was suspected. Of their ultimate fate we know nothing, nor what proportion the out-goers bore to those who remained behind. The number of these last, however, must have been considerable, and among them were Bertulph, Hacket and a nephew whom the contemporary chroniclers invariably describe as Robert the Child. Not that these three acknowledged themselves guilty—on the contrary, they stoutly maintained their innocence, nor had they any sympathy with the murder—but for them the bonds of kinship were indissoluble, and the guilt of Burchard and some other members of the family was notorious and avowed. 'Not one among ye,' cried Hacket, who was spokesman for the rest, 'not one among ye bewails this bloody deed more bitterly than do we. Send into exile, if ye will, all those who acknowledge their guilt. Impose on them what penalty our judges and our bishops shall deem fit, provided that life and liberty be respected, and that ye do them no bodily harm. Give us some assurance of this, and that we, who declare our innocence, shall be offered opportunity of proving it, each man as befitteth his state—clerk according to Church law, knight in accordance with the laws of chivalry—and we surrender, but if these conditions do not seem good to ye, then will we remain here and defend this fortress. It is better to live with our guilty kinsmen than to come forth and meet a dishonourable death at your hands.' This extraordinary speech is given by Walbert, who was at Bruges during the whole of this troublous period, and avers that he noted down on his tablets each night the events that had occurred during the day, but he adds that owing to the excitement and turmoil that prevailed in the city it is not unlikely that some of his statements are inaccurate.

Needless to say that the Isegrins turned a deaf ear to Hacket's proposals. In the deliverance of their friends they had obtained all that they wanted; the only answer they vouchsafed was from the mouth of the 'Winged Lie' and the 'Winged Lie' breathed out threatening, and slaughter, and curses into the bargain. All hope of conciliation was at an end, and, says Walbert, 'the belligerents went their several ways full of headiness and gall.'

All that day the fight continued without any marked success on either side, but towards sunset the attacking party were beaten back with great loss, and the Erembalds were left, as they fondly believed, at peace for the night.

Worn out with hard fighting, and filled with an overweening sense of security, inspired by their unlooked-for success, the whole of the little garrison had retired to rest, save only a handful of sentinels wearily straining their eyes over the dark city. All through the night these men were content to freeze on the ramparts, chilled to the bone by a cutting east wind, but towards the small hours of morning the icy breath of coming day drove them into the great hall of Charles's palace, where some one had kindled a fire. There they sat before the glowing logs, dozing and drinking and chatting together in a fool's paradise, and clean forgot the little western door by which their friends were wont to come and go, and that a rusty lock and half-a-dozen nails alone secured it. 'This one weak spot, when we were freezing on the battlements, some prowling Isegrin smelt out, and whilst we are rubbing a little life into our poor numbed limbs before Charles's fire, a host of them swarm round it. Some one suggests an axe, it yields at a blow, and the rabid pack rush in so swiftly and so suddenly, and with so little noise, that their cruel fangs are at our throats almost before we are awake. The whole Bourg is alive with men—they seem to spring up from the earth, every crevice and every corner bristles with them, and so dark is it that we cannot distinguish friends from foes. Panic lays hold of us, we lose our heads, turn cowards and sue for mercy, or leap in despair over ramparts as doth poor Giselbert, whose bruised and bleeding body they tie to a horse's tail and drag all round the market-place. The bravest of us take to our heels, and trampling one another down, crush through the narrow bridgeway which leads from Charles's palace into St. Donatian's church, determined there to make our last stand, and then, O wonderment! the howling pack draw off and leave us for a little space at peace.'

Such was the scene in the Bourg on this momentous night. All that was left of the Erembald host was huddled up in the cathedral, too much shattered in mind and body to be a cause of present disquietude; their opponents were free to do what they would, and they were more eager for plunder than revenge. They had come to a conglomeration of palaces, to a region abounding in treasure, to a place where much corn and wine and oil were stored up; their mouths watered for these things, and the word was given to plunder, and like a flock of locusts they carried off everything. Charles's palace, containing also Hacket's apartments; the provost's palace, and the palace of the canons of Bruges, all of them were stripped; from the bed and the underlinen in Bertulph's sleeping apartment to the gridirons and saucepans in his kitchen, and from the mead and ale in his cellar to the leaden gutters of his roof. Nor had they any greater respect for the property which had once belonged to Charles. They carried off even the meat hanging up in his larder, and the bed on which he had slept. Disappointed at not discovering the much-coveted treasure in his strong-room, they consoled themselves by wrenching off the wrought-iron doors, and bearing them away on their shoulders, nor did they despise the chains and manacles and other instruments of torture that they found in the dungeons under the palace, though the rich hangings and tapestry which they tore from the walls of his state-room, and the great store of wheat heaped up in his granary were doubtless objects more to their taste. The canons' dormitories in the cloister contained great treasure. So well stocked were they with rich and costly apparel, most likely ecclesiastical vestments, that though the marauders began to carry them off early in the morning, it was not until nightfall that the task was complete.

Galbert, who gives a detailed account of all this, concludes his observations with this quaint remark: 'Our citizens,' he says, 'in acting thus, were fully convinced they were doing no wrong.'

Meanwhile the men of Ghent were secretly negotiating for Charles's body; it was arranged that it should be handed out to them through one of the windows in the choir, and early next morning they proceeded to put the plan in execution. 'Our burghers, however, got wind of it, and they being as keen to retain the relics as the Ghenters were to carry them away, infinite tumult ensued, which was only quenched by the stones and arrows and boiling pitch which the Erembalds, who had by this time shaken themselves together, were hurling down from the battlements. Thus rudely brought to their senses, the contending factions came to terms, joined forces, took the church, and drove their opponents into the tower. Fortune had once more almost smiled on the Karls, and again that day the cup of hope was destined to be dashed from their lips. It happened thus:—

When the Bourg was taken, Bertulph's palace had been allotted to the Stratens as their share of the plunder, or rather they had allotted it to themselves, and that very morning had 'insolently and vauntingly and vaingloriously' run up their standard over the roof, at sight of which all were filled with disgust, for the provost and his household, before the betrayal, were in sooth devout and courteous men, held in high esteem by the whole city. 'The hearts of our burghers swell against them and we lust for their blood, the more so as they are actually carrying off corn and wine which is our property, for it was we who bore the brunt of the battle whilst these men were snoring in bed. At all costs this pilfering must be stopped. We break into the courtyard, and one of us with his sword staves in a cask of wine—signal for infinite uproar. The Stratens take to their heels. Our men outrun them, and slam the gates of the city so that none shall escape. Hacket rushes out on his tower and frenziedly exhorts the mob to slay his foes—calumniators for whose sake Count Charles was slain. The market-place bristles with armed men, a waving forest of spears. All Flanders is in town to-day. Greed, vengeance, lust for relics, itching ears—a hundred wayward impulses have drawn them here, but one are they, at least, in this one sentiment—old Tancmar and his nephews merit hemp. Of all the blood and all the tears which have been shed these scandalmongers are the cause, these backbiters, these intriguers, these liars, who, with false, foul tongues, for sordid ends, moved Charles to spurn our noblest men and stung them on to slay him. Thus we murmur, thus we declaim, and the whole town roars with the thunder of our indignation, until pressing onward to the Bourg, where rumour says young Walter lies concealed, for we would fain have him out and hang him, there at the very gates, upon the bridge which spans the Boterbeke,[12] we meet our new-made châtelain Gervais Praet, who with his ready tongue doth still the storm. 'Yon vaunting ensign shall be furled—see, friends, it is even now furled—nor shall this Tancmar lord it in your provost's house; he and his kith and kin shall forthwith quit the town. I pass my word, and as for the liquor and the grain, the men who took the citadel shall have the eating and the drinking of it.' So we disperse, and whilst old Bertulph's choicest wine is gurgling down our parched-up throats or we are hurrying on to grab what share we may of his great store of wheat—in this pinched time of dearth no little boon—the trembling Tancmar and his nephews skulk away, each one of them empillioned behind a stalwart knight, so timorous are they of the men of Bruges; and darkness falls upon the town, shrill with the blaring trumpets of the Erembalds, who all night long sound signals of distress, for this day arrows winged with lying script have brought to them assurances of help.

The day before the Bourg was taken Bertulph managed to effect his escape. He was let down by a cord from the battlements, and safely conducted by a friend in the Isegrin camp, whom he had heavily bribed, out of the town and three leagues further into the open country beyond. Here left to his own devices, walking by night and sleeping where he could by day, he at length reached the manor of Alard van Woesten, who had married one of his nieces, and was lord of the little town of Woesten on the French frontier in the neighbourhood of Ypres.

In this stronghold he lay in hiding for about three weeks, after which time, the rumour of his arrival having somehow or other leaked out, it presently reached the ears of William of Löo, who was keeping his Easter in the city hard-by. Upon receipt of this important news William at once took horse, and with 'much noise and great expedition' began to make inquiries concerning the provost's whereabouts.

Having searched Alard's house, and the house of his daughter hard-by, and not finding the object of his quest, he was beside himself with rage, fired both houses, seized the girl, swore that he would put her to torture if Bertulph were not produced before the morrow, and rode off. Alard, therefore, having to choose between his daughter and his uncle, revealed the place where Bertulph was concealed, and he was at once taken prisoner by William's officers.

Well knowing that his days were numbered, and that he had nothing to hope from the gratitude of the man for whose sake he had risked so much, and at whose hands he had received so little, the aged prelate prepared himself to face death with what courage he could. He was a dying man, he said, and he wished to see a priest. His captors granted the request, 'and there, in the sight of all men, he confessed his sins, and prostrate on the ground smote his breast and prayed God to have pity on him.' Next morning they would have taken him on horseback to Ypres, but he refused to ride, and though it was freezing hard persisted in walking there barefoot. 'This soft, luxurious prelate,' comments Walbert, 'who in the days when fortune smiled on him used to shrink from a flea bite as from a dagger thrust!'

A certain priest from whose lips Walter learned the details here noted down, walked by Bertulph's side and, as they went, they intoned alternately verse by verse the Lady Office and the *Te Deum*. Thus, martyr-like, with a song of triumph on his lips, this staunch old man went forth to die. 'As they drew near to the gates of the city a great multitude came forth to meet them, crying aloud and clapping their hands and leaping for joy, and they struck the provost with their fists, and beat him with staves and pelted him with the heads of sea-fish (of which very many are taken in these parts), and heaped every kind of insult upon him, all of which he bore with patience, speaking never a word.' This was all the more remarkable, says Walter, because the provost was naturally a proud man who could ill brook ridicule or insult of any kind; and he adds:—*Apropos* of this, I remember a story which was told me by one of his own servants. Upon a certain occasion when the provost was seated before the fire in his great hall, with his household around him, the discourse turned to the Passion of Our Lord, and of the insults which He suffered with so much meekness in the house of Caiaphas. 'For my part,' quoth the provost, 'I can never understand that portion of Scripture. If low fellows of that kind had struck me I would at least have spat in their face.'

The remaining portion of the story of Bertulph's execution is told for us by Walbert. It reads like some breviary legend of a martyr's death.

There he stood in the midst of the market-place, surrounded by a ribald, jeering throng, with countenance unmoved and eyes turned heavenward as though invoking God's pity. Then one of those who were standing by struck him on the head, saying, 'O thou proud man, why dost thou not deign to sue for mercy, seeing that thy life is in our hands?' but the provost opened not his mouth. And for his greater ignominy they stripped him of his clothes and hanged him naked on a cross in the midst of the market-place, as if he had been a thief or a robber.

Then drew nigh unto him William of Löo, and thus addressed him, 'Tell me, O provost, I conjure thee, on the salvation of thy soul, in addition to those whose names we already know, who are they who are implicated in Count Charles's death,' and Bertulph made answer, and said before all those present, 'Thou knowest, O Burgrave, as well as I.' William, hearing those words, was transported with fury, and commanded stones and mud to be cast at the provost and that he should be put to death. Then those who were assembled in the market-place to sell fish, tore his flesh with their iron hooks and beat him with rods, and thus they put an end to his days.

'William at once sent a herald to Bruges to inform the Isegrins of what he had done, and we in our turn,' says Walbert, 'handed on the news to the Erembalds in their tower, whereat terror and despair pressed them closer than the generals of our army, and naught was heard but the sound of their lamentations.' Thus Walbert. Nevertheless, they held out bravely until the 20th of April, and that, notwithstanding that they were besieged by Louis the Fat and a great army of French knights; by William Cliton, the newly-elected count, and a horde of Normans; by almost all the chivalry of Flanders, and a host of burghers from Ghent, who still hoped that they would be able to obtain Charles's body for Blandinium.

The great army, which six weeks before had taken refuge in the Bourg, was now reduced to a mere handful. Of the rest not a few must have died in battle, others perhaps of wounds and wretchedness and want, but in all probability the vast majority had made their escape, hoping perhaps that they would be able to raise a sufficient force to effectually succour those of their comrades who remained in Bruges, and afterwards place on the throne a sovereign who would respect their liberties. Be this as it may, by the 20th of April but thirty worn-out men remained in St. Donatian's, who continually straining their eyes over the vast expanse of flat country surrounding them, descried there no token of hope. Moreover, the Isegrins were battering in the tower—at each thrust of the ram it trembled to its base. Instant surrender or instant death was the only alternative, the Karls chose the first, and young Robert cried out, in the name of the rest, that if his personal liberty were guaranteed they would lay down their arms. Louis accepted the condition and they prepared to descend. One brave fellow indeed, preferring death to disgrace, would have leapt over the ramparts had not his comrades held him back. 'At sight of which,' says Walbert, 'our burghers shed tears,' but their sympathy led them no further.

One by one the little band of heroes came forth, the lean men through a narrow aperture giving on the stairs, those who were too corpulent through a larger window near the summit of the tower, and these men let themselves down by ropes.

'Pale they were,' says Walbert, 'and livid and ugly with hunger, and they bore on their faces the stigma of their crimes; but our citizens wept when they saw those who had once been their leaders led away to prison.' No wonder; the dark fetid hole into which they were huddled was of such narrow dimensions that the inmates were not even able to sit down, and after a few days' detention there, only three or four of them had strength to stand.

From this wretched fate young Robert alone was exempted, but Louis thought that his promise not to cast him into prison was sufficiently respected by giving him into the custody of a citizen of Bruges. Of Robert's entire innocence there can be no doubt. Even Walbert, the enemy of his race, bears testimony to his noble qualities. He was most popular, not only in Bruges, but throughout Flanders. Again and again the burghers had petitioned Louis in his favour. Even some of the Isegrin leaders had followed their example, but for all of them the French king had one answer. He had sworn to take no step without the consent of his Council, and Robert remained in custody.

As to the other prisoners, their captivity lasted only a fortnight. It was then (4th May) determined that they should be thrown from the tower which they had so bravely defended, and the same day the sentence was carried out.

The soldiers entrusted with this odious task had received strict orders to complete it with as little noise as possible, and with brutal levity they told their victims that the King was about to give them proof of his mercy.

The prisoners were then led one by one to the scene of execution, not by way of the *Place du Bourg*, which then, as now, was open to the public, but secretly through the Loove and across the covered bridge uniting it to the cathedral.

On more than one occasion the townsfolk had shown marked sympathy for the Erembalds, and Louis feared that if his project was generally known, or if the victims were afforded an opportunity of appealing to them, an attempt at rescue might be made, which would perhaps end in revolution.

The first to suffer was Wulfric Cnopp, the brother of Bertulph and Hacket. Until a few moments before his death he was ignorant of the fate in store for him. He had just time to take one last look at his beloved city, and then with a mighty effort, for Wulfric was a man of gigantic stature, the executioners threw him over the ramparts. There is reason to believe that this man was really guilty of the crime imputed to him.

Then came young Walter, the son of the Châtelain of Ardenburg, a noble and a comely youth. 'For the love of God,' he cried, when he reached the summit of the tower and the executioners were about to complete their task, 'for the love of God let me say a prayer first.' They granted him a moment's respite, and then like a flash of lightning he fell down headlong and dashed all the life out of his beautiful body.

The next to die was one Eric, a knight of noble birth. Though he had been hurled from so great a height, and though in the fall his body had crashed against a wooden staircase with such violence that a step secured by five nails had been thereby wrenched off, he was still breathing when he reached the ground—had strength even to make the sign of the Cross. Some women of the people would have staunched his wounds, but one of the King's household heaved a great stone and drove them away. Better so—'the little life that was left in him was but a lingering and a cruel death.'

The rest suffered in like manner. Some were innocent, some were guilty, seven-and-twenty of them all told. Their names are not recorded— this only we know of them. They faced death without flinching, and died like Christian men. His Saviour's name was the last word which passed the lips of each of them, and each of them made the sign of the Cross before he fell. By a refinement of barbarity they were not permitted to receive the consolations of religion under pretext that they were excommunicated. This was in direct contravention of Charles's own ordinance concerning criminals. Their bodies were denied Christian burial. They were thrown into a marsh beyond the village of St. André, and for years afterwards no man after nightfall would willingly pass that way.

'On Friday, May 6, King Louis resolved to go back to France, and the same day he left Bruges, carrying away Robert with him.' Great was the lamentation of our citizens when they saw him depart, for this noble youth was beloved by all of them, and they knew he would never return. "Good friends," said he, on seeing their grief, "my life is not in your hands. Pray God to have pity on my soul." Louis did not dare to execute his victim at Bruges, nor indeed here offer him any indignity, but no sooner had they quitted the outskirts of the town than he gave orders that his legs should be tied under his saddle, and when they reached Mont Cassel he cut off his head.

Burchard too had paid the penalty of his crime. The Karls said that, having quarrelled with Robert, he had been slain by him in a duel, during the time when they were besieged in the tower, but Walter and Walbert affirm that in this they lied, and that in reality he had made his escape, and that he was afterwards captured and executed; and there is also a tradition that he succeeded in escaping altogether from his native land, and after many wanderings at length found refuge in the south of Ireland.

Be this as it may, he had disappeared from Flanders, and thus the great house of Erembald was all but wiped out. Of those who traced their descent in the direct male line to its mighty founder, only Hacket and his little son Robert, a child of tender years, remained alive. The châtelain made his escape from the tower a few days before the surrender. Whether he purchased the good will of one or other of the Isegrin leaders, or whether he had succeeded in hoodwinking them, is uncertain. All we know is that he escaped from Bruges, and, wandering alone across the great salt marsh at the north of the city, presently reached the impregnable stronghold of his son-in-law, Walter Cromlin, the mighty Lord of Lisseweghe, a mere village now, but in those days an important sea-coast town. Here he lay concealed until Dierick of Alsace, more than a year later, brought peace once more to Flanders.

Hacket was shortly afterwards placed on trial, and the fact that he succeeded in clearing his character is proof presumptive that Bertulph, who like his brother Hacket had all along protested his innocence and his capability of proving it, would have likewise been able to make his words good.[13] Immediately after the trial Hacket was restored to his former rank and possessions, we hear nothing more of the charge of serfdom, and for many generations his descendants were mighty men in Flanders. Amongst them note the magnificent Louis of Gruthuise, Peer of Flanders, France and England to boot—Edward IV. created him Earl of Winchester—who in the fourteen hundreds lived in royal state in the beautiful palace on the banks of the Roya, which still goes by his name.

Of Hacket's subsequent history little is certainly known, but if the conjectures of Olivier de Wree are well founded—and the evidence which he adduces in their support is surely worthy of consideration—the life and career of Desiderius Hacket was indeed a strange and chequered one.

Briefly the facts are as follows. In 1135 Rodolphe of Nesle, a scion of the house of Erembald, was appointed Châtelain of Bruges; the name of Hacket does not cease to appear at the foot of official documents until nearly fifty years later, but whereas previous to 1135 the writer of this signature invariably describes himself as châtelain, subsequent to that date he signs as Canon of St. Donatian's, later on as Dean of the same church, and later still as Abbot of Dunes.

Bearing in mind the uncommonness of the name, and the fact that we lose all trace of Hacket the layman when Hacket the churchman appears, it would seem in the highest degree probable that the signatures before and after 1135 were the handiwork of one man. That this was certainly the case after that date the testimony of the monastic chroniclers clearly shows. They also tell us something more. The ecclesiastic in question, before he was appointed Abbot of Dunes, for a short time governed a branch house which he himself seems to have founded at Lisseweghe.[14] He was reputed in his day a famous preacher; he was living and signing documents in 1183, and died at an advanced age and in the odour of sanctity. It would seem then that the bellicose Châtelain of Bruges ended his days as a monk.

Strangely enough Hacket's sworn enemy and rival, the man to whose enmity was due all the misfortune that befell his house, the treacherous Tancmar of Straten himself, towards the close of his life also donned the cowl. He became a monk in the great Benedictine house of St. Andrew hard-by his own estate, and tradition says that he too died a saint.

Surely it is not a little significant that three of the chief actors in this bloody drama should have been numbered by their contemporaries in the ranks of the blessed. Charles, that hero of blood and sentiment, of violence and delicate emotions, who firmly believed that he was dying for justice sake; Straten, the devotee, who for his own ends fanned the flame of his master's wrath—and poor Hacket, who was accused of murder, escaped by the skin of his teeth, and at length proved his innocence, most probably by the rite of ordeal. The age in which these men lived was an age of contrasts, an age of clashing tones and inharmonious tints. In those days it was the fashion to be devout, and the shibboleth of the fine gentleman was the fervent expression of his unwavering faith.

CHAPTER VII

Bruges in the Days of Charles the Good, etc.

OF the actual buildings of Charles's day only a few fragments remain: the Chapel of St. Basil, the lower part of the tower of the present cathedral, and perhaps some portion of the Church of Notre Dame; of those associated with his tragic end or the bloody scenes which followed, in all probability no stone is left.

His palace, called the Loove, which he himself had built, has long since been swept away; its site is now occupied by the Palais de Justice. The old Church of St. Peter, where his funeral Mass was celebrated, was pulled down at the close of the seventeen hundreds, of the church which took its place only the chancel now remains, and even this no longer serves its original purpose. Some years ago it was converted into a tavern, and it is now a warehouse. St. Donatian's, the scene of Charles's death, and of the Erembalds' last stand for life and liberty, was destroyed at the Revolution. It stood just opposite the Hôtel de Ville, on the site where now, under the shade of spreading sycamore and chestnut trees, the flower market is held, and the statue of Van Eyck in the centre of this square marks the spot where Charles is said to have fallen.

The débris of the cathedral was carried all over Flanders. A portion of it is said to have been used for the construction of a château which stands some little way off the high road on the right-hand side between Steenbrugge and Lophem, about three miles from Bruges. It is a pleasant enough place to look at in its beautiful wooded grounds, but the country folk will tell you that ill fortune has always followed those who have dwelt there.

Charles's name is also associated with the beautiful Church of Notre Dame. Here, in 1091, a chapter of secular priests was installed, Charles provided for the endowment of half the canonicates, and when, in 1116, the building was destroyed by fire, it was he who restored it.

Tradition says that the main portion of the present church was constructed in 1180 or thereabouts by Gertrude of Alsace, the widow of Rodolphe de Nesle, Châtelain of Bruges, and curiously enough a scion of the house of Erembald, but as Charles's church was only completed in 1120, and it is not likely that a comparatively new and probably magnificent structure would have been deliberately pulled down—and there is no record of its having been accidentally destroyed by fire or otherwise—it may well be that Charles in reality only built a portion of the new church, perhaps the nave and the adjoining aisles, and that what Gertrude did, sixty years later, was to complete his unfinished work. If this be so, the greater part of the present building owes its origin to Charles the Good.

In the Church of Notre Dame we perhaps also get a glimpse of the magnificent Bertulph himself. Of its chapter a certain Germanus was the first provost, who in all probability at the time of his appointment was quite a youth, for shortly afterwards he went to reside at Louvain, in order to complete his theological studies, and one Bertulph was appointed to act as superior during his absence. What we are told of the character and disposition of this ecclesiastic coincides so nearly with the character and disposition ascribed to the redoubtable Provost of Bruges, that, bearing in mind the identity of their name, not a common one in those days in Flanders, and the intimate connection which we shall see each of them had with Eeckhout Abbey,[15] it is difficult to believe that the Bertulph of Notre Dame and the Bertulph of St. Donatian's were different persons. In each of them we find the same fiery temper, the same overweening pride, and the same indomitable will, the same exaggerated devotion and the same harshness in their dealings with their fellow-men. Walbert has left us a graphic picture of the receptions this 'proud prelate' held in the great oak-roofed hall of his sumptuous palace on the Bourg. Swelling with pride, there he used to sit on a stately throne placed underneath the huge beam which broke and fell with a mighty crash on the throne itself three weeks before his death—portent of coming ill, had he but taken it to heart, but Bertulph was too stiff-necked for that, says Walbert. There a crowd of knights and clerks and burghers were daily wont to jostle one another in their quest to pay homage to, or perchance seek favour from, the great man who was all-powerful alike in Church and State. When any one approached whom this proud prelate knew quite well but did not wish to recognise, he made pretence that he had never seen him before. 'Who is this person?' he used to ask of one of his attendants, and then, when he had been informed of the name and rank of his would-be interlocutor, if he were in the humour to do so, he would vouchsafe to salute him. And, blurts out Walbert with much feeling and inappositeness, 'he was very hard on his clergy.' Walbert was one of them, and he, if any one, should have known.

The canons of Notre Dame would certainly have given their Bertulph the same character.

Hardly had he been installed provost than he sent them all about their business and filled their places with monks. The irregularity of their lives, he alleged, was scandalous. Irregular lives in those days, if we may trust Walter, were far from uncommon alike amongst layfolk and clerics, and that was one reason why men thought so highly of Charles. Amidst so much wood, hay and stubble, Charles appeared pure gold. It is not unlikely then that Bertulph's accusations were well founded. Radbode, Bishop of Tournai, presumedly thought so, for he had authorised what had been done. Not so Germanus. Immediately on his return to Bruges, he petitioned Bishop Baldwin, who meanwhile had succeeded Radbode in the See of Tournai, to revoke his predecessor's decision, alleging that the changes at Notre Dame had been made without consulting him, the lawful superior, and in opposition to the wishes of the secular canons, and thereupon the bishop gave orders for their reinstatement.

This was on March 31, 1101. Bertulph was furious and appealed in vain to Rome. By letters, dated April 1102, Pope Pascal II. confirmed Baldwin's decision, and presently Bertulph's monks were forced to quit the canons' cloister. After several peregrinations they at last built themselves a habitation hard-by the Church of Notre Dame in the great oak wood which at that time fringed the left bank of the Roya and stretched far away into the country beyond.

This was the origin of the Abbey of Eeckhout (oak wood) famous in the annals of Bruges.

This abbey was destroyed during the French Revolution, and only the gateway now remains—No. 40 *rue Eeckhout*. Part of the grounds are included in the gardens of the Convent of St. André in the same street; part in a lovely old kitchen garden and orchard at the back of the houses on the Dyver. As Eeckhout Abbey was associated at its birth with Notre Dame, so was it at its death.

THE PORCH OF NOTRE DAME

At the time of the Revolution Notre Dame was dismantled—the pavement was torn up, the stained-glass windows were broken, and every kind of havoc was made, but the bare walls were left standing, and presently, when more tranquil times came, the old church was restored to public worship. As the beautiful flamboyant stalls which had once lined the choir had ere this been sold and carried away, it is said to England, it became necessary to procure new ones. It so happened that just before the French came, the monks of Eeckhout had ordered a new set of stalls for their abbey church. These, owing to the fact that they had not yet been erected, had escaped destruction, and by Napoleon's orders they were set up in Notre Dame. The wood-carver, however, who had made them, had not received payment, and protested that the stalls were his, and by way of asserting his right, every Sunday and feast day, at High Mass and Vespers, until the day of his death some years after, persisted in seating himself in the choir stalls at Notre Dame. Matter of little moment; after the Revolution there were no canons to occupy them.

From an artistic point of view there is nothing very remarkable about the stalls in question. They are sufficiently mediocre work of the period, but the hand of time has mellowed them, and their associations make them interesting. The carving of some of the *miserere* seats is very quaint, and is certainly ancient. Whether these formed part of the lost stalls of Notre Dame, or whether the redoubtable wood-carver employed some of the old Eeckhout work for his new stalls, it would be difficult to say.

CHAPTER VIII

William Cliton

WILLIAM OF LÖO, as we have seen, was the legitimate heir to the throne of Flanders, and if, when Charles fell, he had acted with energy and determination, there can be no doubt that he would have been able to grasp the prize he so much coveted, and retain it in spite of his enemies.

Fortune had been singularly kind to him. He was the only representative in the direct male line of the dynasty of Robert the Frisian, he was the favoured candidate of the great house of Erembald; his aunt, the countess dowager, was his staunch adherent. He had the goodwill of her second husband, his next-door neighbour, the powerful Duke of Brabant, who had given him his daughter in marriage. In Henry Beauclerc, who had married his wife's sister, and whose Norman duchy adjoined the realm to which he laid claim, he had a friend who knew how to back fair promises with English gold; and lastly, when Charles was slain, he was within a stone's throw of the capital. But 'William saw a meteor on the horizon: the sword of Gervais Van Praet,' and he was too dazzled by it to summon up courage to help his nearest friends, and when the Erembalds fell, the grandsons and great-grandsons of Baldwin the Devout took heart to dispute his claim. The number of them was legion. There was Charles's nephew, Arnulph of Denmark, and his first cousin Dierick of Alsace; Baldwin of Mons, the representative of the dynasty of Baldwin the Good; William Cliton; Stephen of Blois, and perhaps too Henry of England himself.[16]

The Burgrave of Löo had sat with folded hands when the tide was at the flood, and in doing so he lost his one opportunity. In vain he now posed as Charles's avenger. All the world knew of his intrigues with the Erembalds, and it was more than suspected that his own hands were red with Charles's blood. His treachery gained for him no new friends, and disgusted the remnant which in spite of all still clung to him.

On the very day when he was busy hanging poor Isaac of Reninghe[17] whom, in spite of a monk's cowl, a long face and a book of psalms, his blood-hounds had smelt out the day before in the Abbey of Terouane, Louis the Fat disowned him.

'Have nothing to do with William of Ypres,' ran the French King's letter to the barons and burghers of Bruges; 'have nothing to do with William of Ypres, because he is a bastard, born of a noble father and a mother of vile birth, who all her life was a weaver of thread' (it was the same charge that had stung the Erembalds to revolt; William's mother was a Karline), 'but come forthwith to Arras, and there choose in my presence a prince worthy of Flanders.'

II.—Genealogical Table of the Counts of Flanders from Baldwin V. to Baldwin VII.

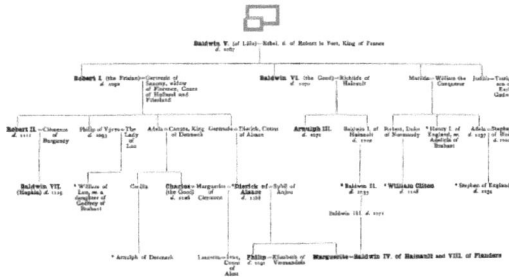

Louis had already determined who should be the new count, but he was wise enough to gild the bitter pill, and when the barons reached Arras he adroitly persuaded them to elect William Cliton, and to secure also the acquiescence of the burghers. William was only fourth in the order of succession, but he and Louis had married two sisters, and the French Queen naturally enough desired to befriend a kinsman on whom fortune had never yet smiled. Besides, the arrangement fitted in exactly with Louis's own views. The friendship of Flanders was to him a matter of far greater moment than the law of primogeniture, he had known William all his life, and he felt that he could trust him. His young favourite would doubtless, too, prove a dangerous rival to Henry Beauclerc, the one man whom Louis feared; with the aid of his Flemish vassals he would be able to wrest his Norman inheritance from the English King, and perhaps also the crown of England itself.

When the burghers of Bruges learned what had happened, they were cut to the quick. That Louis should have offered the communes of Flanders a voice in the election of their Count, and then presumed to foist on them the man of his own choice, was something more than injury—it was an insult. But the French King was backed by a great army; the burghers were shrewd enough to see that it was more politic to obey, and thus preserve the outward form of liberty, than to refuse to do so at a time when opposition was certain to be barren of profitable results, and on the evening of Tuesday (Easter Tuesday), the 6th of April, Louis and his nominee were permitted to enter Bruges.

Next day, says Walbert, the King and the Count, with their knights and ours, our burghers and the Karls of the seaboard, assembled in the Sablon Field, and there the Cliton solemnly swore to respect the privileges of the city and of the Church of St. Donatian, and to abolish the house tax and market dues, so that the citizens of Bruges should be for ever free. At the same time he acknowledged their right to modify and correct according to circumstances their own laws and customs. Then the vassals of Charles paid their homage to William, the mightiest putting their hands in his, and receiving in return the kiss of investiture, those of less degree simply bending while the Count touched them with his sceptre. All the great officers were confirmed in their rights and privileges, save only the Erembalds, who were declared incapable of holding office or property in the county.

Although William Cliton was thus legally invested with the sovereignty of Flanders, his right to govern that province was far from being generally recognised, and the whole land was rent by factions. William of Löo was still Count for the men of Ypres; St. Omer acknowledged Arnulph of Denmark; Audenarde, Baldwin of Mons, to whose standard had rallied Dierick of Alsace, who for the time being seems to have relinquished his own claim, whilst the Erembalds, as we know, were still holding out in their tower at Bruges and still receiving from the great freeholders of the seaboard assurances of support and help.

Nevertheless, if William could have given his subjects good government, if he had known how to exercise his new functions with a little tact and discretion, above all, if only he had been true to his word anent the abolition of taxes, in all probability things would have gradually settled down, and little by little men would have acquiesced in his rule. But William was a Norman, and the Normans had now become more French and more feudal than the French themselves. A man of this stamp was little likely to find favour with the Flemish people, who still retained, along with their rude Northern speech, their ancestors' love of freedom and justice, and the first incident of his reign was to them like salt on an open sore.

It happened thus. Shortly after the Count's arrival at Bruges, a certain citizen, who had married a sister of one of the Erembalds, crept up secretly, as he thought, to the tower of St. Donatian's, with a view to a little business talk with his brother-in-law, who owed him a considerable sum of money. One of Praet's men saw him, and, as all communication with the besieged had been strictly forbidden, the fellow was arrested and brought before the Count.

The news of what had happened spread like wildfire, the burghers flew to arms, and crying out that they would suffer tyranny at the hands of no man, that the prisoner was a free citizen of Bruges, and that it was for them to judge him, made a rush for the Loove. Fortunately for William the doors and windows were barricaded before the mob had time to reach the palace, and all their efforts to batter them in were fruitless. At length, when the burghers had expended something of their energy in red-hot threats and curses, that crafty old knight, Gervais Praet, went down amongst them, made them a speech, called them friends and fellow-citizens, bade them bear in mind that it was at their own request that the Count had appointed him châtelain, averred that in the matter which had called forth their wrath he had only acted in accordance with the law, but if they were not satisfied with what he had done, he had no wish to exercise authority over them, and was quite ready to resign his châtelaincy. In a word, the oil of his eloquence soothed the burghers for the moment, and they dispersed to their several homes.

Similar disturbances, arising out of incidents as trivial, occurred shortly afterwards at Lille and at St. Omer, and in each case they were with difficulty suppressed after much blood had been spilt, whilst the heavy fines in which William by way of punishment mulcted those towns altogether alienated the goodwill of the citizens.

But this was only a beginning. After the conquest of the Erembalds and the capture of William of Ypres, the Cliton grew bolder. On September 16, one hundred and twenty-five burghers of Bruges and thirty-seven of Ardenburgh were condemned as Burchard's accomplices. In vain they protested their innocence and demanded a legal trial before their own judges. William, in spite of his oath, refused to listen, and all who were suspected of having given assistance to Charles's murderers were treated in like manner. Stronghold after stronghold was razed to the ground, and the Karls of the country-side and the free burghers of the Flemish cities went forth from the land in thousands.

William's empty purse could not satisfy his rapacious followers. This was probably the cause of the violent measures he took to discover Charles's treasure, and of his attempt to re-impose the house tax and the market tolls. From time immemorial these dues had been granted in fief to sundry great nobles, who were now clamouring for compensation; and hence the oath, which he had too inconsiderately taken when first he undertook the government of the country, only gained for him the ill-will alike of the knight and the burgher. Thus was he set betwixt two foes, without the means or the ability to withstand them. At Ghent the citizens and nobles joined hands, and with stinging words the great imperial vassal, Ivan of Alost, voiced their common indignation. 'Sir Count,' he cried, 'if you had intended to deal righteously by this city and by us who are your friends, instead of authorizing the most odious exactions, you would have treated us justly and defended us against our enemies. But, on the contrary, you have violated all your promises and broken all your oaths, and every obligation arising from our common plighted troth is thereby cancelled. We know how you have treated Lille and we know how you have treated Bruges, and we know, too, in what manner you would like to treat Ghent. 'Let the barons and the burghers and the clergy of Flanders judge betwixt us, and if it be found, as we allege, that you are without faith and without loyalty, a perfidious and a perjured man, then renounce the office you now hold, and we will choose a worthier Count to govern us.' Cut to the quick, the Cliton sprang forward. 'Hold,' he cried, 'I free you, Ivan, from the homage which you have sworn to me, and with my sword I am ready now to prove to you, my peer, that in all that appertaineth to the government of this realm I have acted righteously.' But the voice of Ivan was the voice of the people, he refused the challenge, and it was at length decided that a great Council should be held at Ypres on the eighth day of the ensuing month, for the purpose of deliberating on the affairs of the country; and that all delegates should come unarmed. Meanwhile, determined to rid himself of his turbulent subjects by stratagem, William, before the appointed day, betook himself to Ypres accompanied by a large band of armed retainers, and an armed rabble of the lowest class, so that the town was filled with soldiers, purposing, when the delegates arrived, to take them all prisoners. But these last getting wind of the plot, halted at Roulers, and presently two heralds rode into the market-place at Ypres, and thus made proclamation:—

'Be it known to you, Sir Count, that Ivan of Alost and the men of Ghent by our lips proclaim that henceforth they renounce that homage which hitherto they have faithfully kept to you, because they are well aware that you have come hither to destroy them by ruse and naughtiness.'

From that moment William's cause was lost. On the 11th of March, Dierick of Alsace entered Flanders. The great imperial vassals, Daniel of Termonde and Ivan of Alost, at once rallied to his standard, Ghent received him with open arms; a little later (March 27), when he reached Bruges, Gervais of Praet declared in his favour, and three days afterwards the nobles and burghers assembled in the Champ de Sablon solemnly deposed William Cliton, and declared Dierick his successor, and he in his turn solemnly confirmed and increased the rights and privileges of the city, and made proclamation that henceforth no man should be condemned on suspicion and without trial for complicity in Charles's murder.

By this just and politic proceeding he gained the goodwill of the Karls, and thus supported alike by the nobles, the burghers, and what we should call the yeomen farmers of the sea coast, nothing could arrest his progress. Neither the threats of the French King, nor the spiritual thunder of Archbishop Simon of Tournai, not even the victory which William and his Normans gained at Axpoel Heath, where so great was the slaughter that on Dierick's return to Bruges the whole city was filled with lamentation.

Nothing shows more clearly the unpopularity of William than the barren results of this victory. Not a single city opened its doors to him. Presently, when he was laying siege to Alost, he received a mortal wound, and his death on August 4, 1128, left Dierick master of Flanders. The night that William died, says Ordericus Vitalis, Duke Robert (his father), who was in prison at Devizes, and had been there twenty-two years, felt in a dream his own right arm pierced with a lance, whereupon he seemed to lose the use of it, and when he awoke in the morning, he said to those about him, 'Alas! my son is dead.'

Walbert, though he enlarges at considerable length on the iniquity of 'our burghers' in rebelling against their lawful sovereign, gives William but a poor character. In my opinion, he says, the Almighty removed this man by death from the county, because he had laid waste all the land, provoked the inhabitants thereof to civil war, and set at naught alike the laws of God and of man. Nor did God suffer him to go the way of all flesh until he had first endured the chastisement due to his misdeeds. For in sooth Count William will confess amongst the shades whom he sent before him to the Infernal Regions that, of all those things he possessed in life, this alone now remains to him—his military reputation.

Ordericus Vitalis, who represents the Cliton in much more favourable light, bears witness also to his prowess in battle. 'Ad militare facinus,' he says, 'damnabiliter promptus.'

CHAPTER IX

Dierick of Alsace and the Precious Blood

IT was to the cities and to the people of Flanders that Dierick of Alsace owed his crown. When Ivan of Alost and Daniel of Termonde renounced their homage to William Cliton, they did so in the name of the burghers of Ghent. When Louis interposed on behalf of his kinsman, it was the burghers of Bruges who hurled back the proud reply,—'Be it known to the King and to all princes and peoples, and to their posterity throughout all time, that the King of France hath no part in the election of a Count of Flanders.'

When William persuaded Archbishop Simon to lay Ghent and Bruges under interdict, it was owing to the fear inspired by the people that 'no clerk was found hardy enough to proclaim it,' and when Dierick repaid him in his own coin by sentence of excommunication, the bolt was hurled by all the clergy of Bruges, assembled together in the Church of Notre Dame, in the presence of all the burghers.

The triumph of Dierick then meant the triumph of the people, the triumph of liberty, the triumph of nationalism as opposed to the centralizing and imperialist ideals of France. In a word, the triumph of all that was good in the great cause for which Bertulph and his comrades had died.

The new Count was a Fleming of the Flemings. He had been brought up amongst them; their habits and customs were familiar to him, his speech was their speech, his thoughts were their thoughts, and his ways were their ways. 'Men called him wise,' says an ancient chronicler, 'and he was all his life kindly, upright, loyal, brave, and great withal in the art of governing men.' Indeed, his whole career shows what skill and tact he possessed alike in conciliating the goodwill of his own opponents and in settling the disputes of others.

As early as May 31, Arnulph of Denmark resigned his claims in his favour (*see* Wegener, note on p. 169), later on he purchased the acquiescence of another rival, Baldwin of Mons, by giving him his daughter to wife. Even William of Ypres in the end acknowledged his right to the throne, and was content to end his days obscurely as simple Lord of Löo. His first act as prince was to bring about peace between the Isegrins and the free landholders of the seaboard, and by his reconciliation with Hacket, whom he again reinstated in the châtelaincy of Bruges, the legal right of the

Karls under his jurisdiction to the title of freemen was publicly acknowledged. Henceforth, until the Revolution, they were the *Francq Hostes* or *Francons* of the Liberty of Bruges. At his coronation, Dierick had solemnly sworn to respect the lawful rights and liberties of all his subjects, and he loyally kept his word. Throughout his long reign of forty years he always showed himself a good friend to commerce, a staunch upholder of popular institutions, and a generous supporter of the down-trodden and the oppressed. To him, says a Flemish writer, the greater number of the communes of Flanders are indebted alike for their origin and their development. During his reign were inscribed in the charters of the Flemish cities the germs of those rights and liberties which are to-day guaranteed by the Belgian Constitution.

Like all good and wise men of his day, Dierick was profoundly impressed with the truths of Christianity, and after the manner of his age, he on more than one occasion took up the sword of the Crusader. On his return from one of these expeditions, he brought back with him to Bruges a treasure which has had no little influence on the architectural, and artistic, and religious development of the city; a vial of dark, ruby-coloured fluid, which tradition said was some of the water in which Joseph of Arimathea had once washed the blood-stained body of Christ. The early history of this precious memorial of Our Lord's Passion is veiled in mystery, but from the day when Dierick of Alsace brought the famous relic to Bruges the thread of its story is unbroken. The circumstances which led to his possession of it are well known. It was the time of the second Crusade. Dierick, roused perhaps by the preaching of St. Bernard at Furnes, or possibly moved thereto by reason of his kinship with Baldwin, King of Jerusalem—they had married two sisters—resolved to serve under the banner of the Cross, and in the month of June 1147, along with the Emperor Conrad and Louis VII. of France, set out for Palestine; but the campaign was almost barren of results. What with the perfidy of the Greeks, and the pettiness and jealousy of the European leaders, it could hardly have been otherwise. The little that had been accomplished, however, was due to the courage and perseverance of Dierick, and by way of recompense King Baldwin bestowed on him the relic in question.

It was enclosed in a tube of crystal, with chains of silver and stoppers of gold, and Dierick received the gift on his knees from the hands of the Patriarch of

Jerusalem, but he said that a rough soldier like himself was not fit to be the bearer of so holy a thing, and hung it round the neck of his chaplain, Leo of St. Omer, who never parted with it, night or day, until on the evening of April 7, 1150, he returned with the Count to Bruges. Then, with much solemn pomp, the relic was consigned to the Court chaplains, who placed it in the old chapel which Baldwin of the Iron Hand had built, adjoining his palace in the Bourg, where it still remains, and is still preserved in the same crystal vial in which Dierick of Alsace received it. The burghers of Bruges have on more than one occasion been near losing their much-prized treasure, but somehow or other it has always come back to them.

During the troubles with Ghent in the days of Van Artevelde, the relic was one May morning being carried in solemn procession round the ramparts. Presently the band of monks and friars encountered a band of soldiers; the two processions became entangled, and during the confusion some one cried out, 'the Ghenters are upon us.' Panic followed, and when the panic was over the relic had disappeared. Three days later some nuns from the Beguinage saw something shining at the bottom of the stream which runs through their cloister. It was the reliquary of the Holy Blood. Then again, during the troublous times which closed the fifteen hundreds, when Calvinism triumphant held the town, and churches and monasteries were sacked, it was only through the prudence of Juan de Malvenda that the precious treasure was saved. Malvenda, who was one of the church-wardens of St. Basil's, secretly conveyed the relic to his own house—an old-fashioned, red-brick turreted mansion, still standing in the rue *aux Laines* (No. 18), where he concealed it in the cellar till the storm had passed. Again, for over twenty years, from October 13, 1799, till April 20, 1819, the relic was hidden in the houses of various citizens, in order to preserve it from the fanaticism of the Jacobins. For the same reason the annual procession on the Feast of the Precious Blood had to be discontinued, and it was only resumed in 1819. This procession was first instituted in 1303, in memory of the deliverance of the town from the French by Breidel and De Coninck. At first it was of a grave and solemn character, the faithful of both sexes following chanting litanies and psalms. Little by little it grew spectacular. In 1395 the apostles and evangelists were introduced, the next year King Herod and his Court, in 1405 the Nativity, the tree of Jesse, and so forth. At length, in the fifteen hundreds, the profane and the sacred were mingled together, giants, clowns, jugglers followed, the corporation of Bruges thinking by this means to give the procession a popular character, and thus to draw visitors to their town.

The great procession of the Holy Blood has long since resumed its decorum, and thousands of strangers from all parts of Europe annually throng the town to witness it.

Like the Sainte Chapelle at Paris, and the old city church of St. Etheldreda (Holborn), the Sanctuary of the Precious Blood at Bruges consists in reality of two distinct churches, one set over the other. The lower storey, dedicated to St. Basil, was founded, as we have seen, by Baldwin, Bras de Fer, and is in all probability the most ancient building in the city. There can be little doubt that this chapel was originally the private oratory of the Counts of Flanders, adjoining their primitive palace. The four great columns which support the vault, the western and southern walls, and the annex, erroneously called the Baptistry Chapel, with the adjoining buildings,

none of which were originally included in the chapel but formed part of the Count's palace—these are the oldest portions of this most interesting structure. In 1095 Count Robert of Jerusalem, on his return from the Holy Land, placed here the relics of St. Basil which he had brought with him from Cæsarea in Cappadocia; hence the dedication. Later on, his nephew, Dierick of Alsace, in gratitude for some marvellous answer to prayer obtained through the intercession of the saint, restored and embellished the church; hence the erroneous tradition which makes him its founder.

Such as Dierick left St. Basil's in 1150, so it is to-day. It has recently been carefully and conscientiously restored, and it is perhaps the most beautiful and perfect specimen of Romanesque architecture in Flanders. During the work of restoration, when the pavement was renewed, an interesting discovery was made:—the vault in which had lain, since 1412, the mortal remains of Ian Van Oudenaerde, the architect who restored the belfry in 1396 or thereabouts, and who added the four beautiful turrets at the angles of its second storey. The *Porte de Ste. Croix* and the *Porte de Gand* are also his work, as well as the massive round tower at the head of the Minne Water. The nave of St. Basil's has from time immemorial been known as the Masons' Chapel. Here, until the Revolution, the members of the Guild of Masons were wont to perform their devotions and to celebrate annually, with great pomp, the feasts of their patron saints, and it was doubtless on this account that Ian Van Oudenaerde, that great Master Mason, was laid to rest in St. Basil's.

The upper chapel, which is probably the place where Dierick enshrined his priceless relic, was almost entirely rebuilt towards the close of the fourteen hundreds, and of the original Romanesque structure little now remains save the two round-headed bays which separate the naves. The work of reconstruction was not yet finished in 1482, but as during the following year the first stained window was put in, it would seem that it was at this time approaching completion.

Both the upper and lower chapel suffered much during the religious troubles under Philip II., and again at the time of the French Revolution. Indeed, when the *Septembriseurs* had sated their fury on the old building, there was little left but the bare walls, and into such a state of decay had it fallen that when Napoleon visited Bruges in 1810, the civic authorities were thinking of pulling it down.

'That,' said the Emperor, 'shall never be,' when the question was mooted in his presence. 'When I look at those graceful minarets, I fancy myself in Egypt. To destroy a monument like that would be a sin crying for vengeance.' Thus the old church was saved. Presently it was restored to public worship, for from the time of the riots until 1818 the lower chapel had been used by the police as a prison for drunken and disorderly persons, and a place in which to confine stray

PORCH OF THE CHAPEL OF ST. BASIL

dogs, and during the same period the upper chapel, roofless, windowless, a veritable wreck, had served no purpose whatever. The present elaborate scheme of decoration was carried out in 1856 from the designs of two English architects, William Brangwyn and Thomas Harper King, and the old church is now gorgeous with colour and gold. But though the general effect is on the whole pleasing, the details are not happy. Thanks to the late Baron Béthune's *Lucas Schoolen*, native artists could by this time do something better, and it is much to be desired that the wealthy confraternity of the Holy Blood would undertake the redecoration of their chapel. The lower sanctuary was restored only two years ago and, as we have already noted, most successfully.

La Noble Confrérie du Précieux Sang consists of a provost and thirty titular members, all of whom must be Flemings of noble, or, as we should say, gentle birth, in memory of Count Dierick and the thirty Flemish knights who in 1150 brought the precious relic to Bruges. In addition to these there are a certain number of honorary members of other nationalities, for the most part great ecclesiastics, amongst them Pope Leo XIII., whose name was enrolled in the 'golden Register' on May 5, 1844, at which time he was Nuncio to the Court at Brussels. In addition to these, some thousands of persons of every nationality and of all classes are united to the confraternity under the title of affiliated members.

The management of the confraternity, the churches, and all that appertains thereto, is entirely in the hands of the provost and titular members, who are laymen, but other members, of whatsoever degree, participate equally in the Masses and devotions which are celebrated in the Chapel of the Precious Blood.

We are indebted for the above details to the kindness of Canon Louis Van Haecke, chaplain-in-chief of *La Noble Confrérie*. If any of our readers should desire to know something more concerning this subject we would refer them to his interesting work—*Le Précieux Sang à Bruges*.

CHAPTER X

Philip of Alsace and the Charter of the Franc

PHILIP OF ALSACE reigned over Flanders from 1168 till 1191, and notwithstanding his frequent wars the land prospered under his rule. In his method of government he followed the policy of Dierick his father. Like him he was a builder of cities—Nieuport and Damme, at least, owe their origin to Philip of Alsace—and like him he was a promoter of popular liberties and popular institutions. It seems to have been the mission of the princes of the House of Alsace, as Kervyn justly observes, to proclaim the rights of the communes of Flanders, and their fulfilment of it is their greatest glory. Bruges, Ghent, Ypres, Furnes, Gravelines, Nieuport, Dunkirk, Damme, are among the famous cities to which one or other of them granted municipal charters. But the charter which will interest the reader most was conceded to neither city nor town, but to the inhabitants of that vast irregular-shaped tract of country in the neighbourhood of Bruges which went by the name of its Franc, or, as we should perhaps say, its Liberty, and comprised within its borders no less than ninety-one parishes, and the towns of Ostend, Blankenberghe, Eccloo, Dixmude, Lisseweghe, Ardenburgh and Sluys—all of them in these days centres of no little importance. Though from time immemorial, as we have seen, the yeomen who inhabited this district had been to all intents and purposes a free and independent people, who elected their own chiefs and lived under their own laws, it was Count Philip of Alsace who first gave legal sanction to their political constitution, and the instrument by which he did so was the famous *Keurbrief* of 1190.

As with the first Flemings, with our own Saxon forefathers, and probably also with the ancestors of all nationalities of Teutonic origin, the Wehrgeld, or, as Green calls it, 'the Blood-wite,' or compensation in money for personal wrong, and mutual responsibility were the mainspring and corner-stone of the judicial code which Philip's charter sanctioned. Eye for eye, limb for limb, life for life, or for each its equivalent in current coin, this is the rough-and-ready theory which runs through the whole of this remarkable piece of legislation. But it was not only for personal injury that punishment in kind or an allotted fine was exacted; it was the penalty also attached to other offences. Thus the man who had been convicted of breaking down a dyke was condemned to suffer the loss of the hand with which he had broken it, and probably, by way of compensation for the damage which he had thereby entailed, to forfeit all his goods; and it was a penal offence in the Liberty of Bruges to marry an infant without the consent of her heirs-at-law. 'Whosoever,' runs this curious enactment, 'shall be convicted of wedding a girl who has not yet arrived at years of discretion, without the consent of those of her relations who are her heirs presumptive, shall be liable to forfeit all his goods, and if such an one shall have carried his infant bride out of the realm, her heirs may lawfully take possession of her goods; but if the aforesaid girl, repenting, shall presently return home, and be willing to quit her unlawful spouse, her property shall be restored to her; but if, on the contrary, she will not leave him, then shall she in no wise recover it.'

The life of each man had its allotted value, which varied according to rank and station, and curiously enough, in days, when throughout Europe the priesthood was held in high esteem, the clerk's life was valued at only one half the price of the life of the Karl. Just as the Salic law fixes the composition for the murder of a Roman proprietor at the half of that payable for the murder of a Frank, so the law of the Liberty of Bruges valued the life of a clerk, who was considered as a Roman, at only half of the value of the life of a Karl.

As to the fines imposed, the *Keurbrief* ordained that they should be levied in the first place on the property of the offending party, and if this were too inconsiderable to realise the required sum, that his fellow guildsmen should make up the deficiency.

Bearing all this in mind, Hacket's demand that the limbs and lives of Charles's murderers should be spared becomes intelligible. It simply meant that the usual fine should be imposed in lieu of the death penalty, which, under the circumstances, was not unreasonable.

Some of the enactments contained in this remarkable code are sufficiently curious. Take, for example, the following: 'Whosoever shall harbour a *scurra*[18] for more than one night, may lawfully duck such an one on the morrow if he or she refuse to quit his abode.' Others are no less remarkable for their practical common sense. For example the prudent regulation anent weights and measures. 'All weights and measures,' runs the article in question, 'shall be the same in the villages as in the towns. Any headman convicted of falsifying weights and measures shall pay a fine for each offence of three livres, any one found in possession of false weights shall forfeit a like sum, and double the damage caused thereby.'

The game laws of the Liberty of Bruges were singularly oppressive. Perhaps Philip stipulated for their insertion in the *Keurbrief* as the price of the large concessions he had made. In a country well-stocked with stags and boars, to say nothing of ground game, the following enactment must have been an intolerable burthen:—Whosoever shall be prosecuted for fencing in his property against game, if he refuse to undergo judgment by red-hot iron, shall submit to an inquiry by the Count, and if he be found guilty, all his goods shall be at the disposition of the Count and the châtelain, but his life and liberty shall be safe. The Flemish did not obtain complete redress of this iniquitous law until 1477.

If the reader should wish to know something more of this interesting document we would refer him to Gheldorf's *Histoire Constitutionelle de la Ville de Bruges*, where the original text is given, together with a French translation and explanatory notes, p. 465.

The magistrates of the Franc administered justice to those submitted to their jurisdiction in their *Landhuus* on the west side of the Bourg. The building of Philip's day has long since disappeared. It was replaced in the early fifteen hundreds by Van den Poël's sumptuous *Palais du Franc*, of which a remnant is still standing, and still forms one of the most picturesque groups in the city of Bruges. The most charming view of its quaint turrets and gables is from the great fish market along the Quai Vert.

Count Philip of Alsace was not only a builder of cities, a promoter of democratic institutions, the friend

THE PALAIS DU FRANC

of the manufacturer and the merchant, he ever showed himself a generous patron of letters and of art. So, too, his countess, Elizabeth of Vermandois. She delighted in the company of minstrels and troubadours, and herself presided over a Court of Love. To Bruges, in the days of Philip and Elizabeth, flocked half the literary men in Europe. Grave theologians like Andreas Silvius, or Philip of Harveng; historians like Lambert of Ardres, or Hugh of St. Victor; poets like Chrétien de Troyes, or Colin Muset, and a host of the most famous authors of the day. Here, in the Loove Palace, or in the pleasaunce of Winendael hard-by, they were wont to read aloud to the assembled Court the romances of chivalry then in vogue. *Erec, Enide, Clegès, Le Chevalier au Lion, Yseult, Tristan de Léonnois,* and the rest. The nameless authors of these two last dedicated their works to Philip himself, and Chrétien de Troyes wrote his famous *Saint Graal*—'the Church's counterblast,' as Green calls it, 'to the whirlpool of Arthurian romance'—

Por le plus preud homme
Qui soit en l'Empire de Rome
C'est le quens Philippe de Flandres.

That the Count himself was a man of some literary attainment, the following interesting letter seems to indicate: 'Knowledge is not the exclusive privilege of clerks,' writes Philip of Harveng to his friend and patron, Philip of Flanders. 'It is well to be able to lay aside strife and politics, and go and study in some book, as in a mirror. The lessons that illustrious men find in books, add to their nobility, increase their courage, soften their manners, sharpen their wit, and make them to love virtue. The prince who possesses a soul as lofty as his dignity loves to hear wise counsel. How thankful you ought to be to your parents that from your childhood they had you instructed in letters' (Epist. XVI., p. 81).

There is another circumstance in connection with Philip which it will be interesting to note. When St. Thomas à Becket fled before the fury of Henry II. he for a time found shelter at the Flemish Court. The memory of his sojourn there still lingers at Bruges. The chapel which he consecrated in Philip's château at Maele is still standing, and the well at Tilleghem, where legend says he once slaked his thirst, is still called by the country folk St. Thomas's Well.

CHAPTER XI

Baldwin of Constantinople

UPON Philip's death in 1191, without children, the country finally devolved on his sister Marguerite, who, as we have seen, had married Baldwin of Mons, the representative of the dynasty of Baldwin the Good. She only reigned three years, and was succeeded by her son Baldwin of Constantinople, who thus united the rival dynasties in his person.

The old Flemish chroniclers linger lovingly over the story of Baldwin of Constantinople, the last representative in the direct male line of the house of Baldwin of the Iron Hand, and the last Fleming who ruled over Flanders. They like to represent him as a prince of unblemished character, devout, austere, and adorned with all the virtues befitting his state. His figure is undoubtedly a picturesque and an interesting one. He was a man of brilliant parts—shrewd, quick-witted, eager, possessed of no ordinary mental activity and of a wonderful aptitude for business. During the short period of his reign he found time to reform the criminal procedure of his own patrimony—Hainault; to readjust the tolls and custom tariffs of Ghent and of Bruges; to abrogate in the latter city the iniquitous law '*de vino Comitis*,' which ordained that the town should furnish wine for the Count's household at a fixed price, often below the market value; to concede to Bruges, on August 14, 1200, the right to annually hold, during the month of May, a fair—a greater boon in those days than it is now; to busy himself with compiling sundry histories—really the chronicles of his native land—which afterwards went by the name of *Histoires de Baudouin*; to abolish many abuses; to cut the claws of usurers, and to purge, alas! by fire, his domain of heresy. He was not only a lover of learning and of learned men, but a ready writer himself, as witness the letters he addressed from Constantinople to the King of France and to the Pope—letters replete with valuable information concerning the Latin Conquest of that city.

His career as a soldier, too, was not inglorious. He made successful war on the French King and wrested from him the greater part of the province of Artois, and his brilliant action in the East led to the fall of Constantinople and to his own election to the throne of the Greek Empire; but the glory of his purple robe, and the glory of his sword, and the glory of his achievements as a citizen and a prince, pale before the weird legend of love and crime and Nemesis which chronicles his latter days. It reads like a fairy tale and comes to us on the authority of the last and greatest of our monastic historians: Matthew Paris, the famous scribe of St. Alban's.

On the morrow of Ash Wednesday, 1199, a great multitude thronged the Church of St. Donatian's at Bruges. Count Baldwin was to take the cross. The scene in the old church, old even in those days, was a solemn and a striking one. Within those walls which had witnessed so many tragedies and stirring deeds was gathered the *élite* of Flanders—the flower of Flemish chivalry was there, the household of the sovereign and of his consort, Marie of Champagne, and a host of wealthy citizens in holiday attire. Ranged on each side of the altar stood the famous canons of Bruges, in their long white linen rochets and purple veils, in front of them two choirs of singing boys from St. Donatian's school. The great bell tolled as if for a funeral, perhaps that same great bell which five centuries later fell from its lofty tower, and for fifty years lay buried beneath the débris of the cathedral, and now sends forth its melodious voice from the steeple of Notre Dame.

'O God, the heathen are come into Thine heritage, Thy Holy Temple have they defiled. Jerusalem is an heap of stones.... Help us, O God of our Salvation and for the glory of Thy Name deliver us, lest haply they should say among the Gentiles, where is now their God.'

Thus plaintively the first choir, and then with a shout of triumph the men and boys on the opposite side of the chancel made response:—

'Let God arise, and let His enemies be scattered, and let them that hate Him flee before His face. Like as smoke vanisheth, so let them vanish away, and as wax melteth before the fire, so let the wicked perish at the presence of God.'

'Receive this symbol,' murmured the Archbishop of Tournai as he fastened to Baldwin's breast a white linen cross embroidered with threads of gold, 'receive this symbol in memory of the Passion of Jesus Christ, and of the cross on which He died.' When Marie of Champagne besought the aged prelate to place also on her breast the Crusaders' sign, a shout of admiration, and perhaps too of dismay, burst from the crowd. Marie was so tender and so beautiful, and the way of the Cross was so hard—pray God that her end be not like that of the ill-fated Countess Sybil.

Baldwin set out for the East in the spring of 1203, Marie, who was then laid by in childbed, followed towards the close of the month, but she never saw her husband again. It happened thus. That shrewd old fox, Dandolo of Venice, taking advantage of the poverty of the Crusaders, compelled them to undertake for him a campaign against Zara, by way of payment for their transport to Palestine. Then came the conquest of Constantinople and the founding of the Latin Empire, and the elevation of Baldwin himself to the imperial throne (April 9, 1204). Meanwhile Marie had gone on to Syria and was there awaiting her lord. Presently, with the summer heat, plague swept the land, and Marie herself fell sick. When she was lying at death's door, the news of Baldwin's good fortune reached the town, and it was perhaps in reply to some inquiry of hers as to the cause of his long tarrying, that her attendants informed her that the erst Count of Flanders was now Emperor of Rome, and then the end came.

Baldwin was now at the zenith of his glory. From a petty tributary chief of a tribe of semi-barbarians, he had been raised to the throne of a great and civilized empire; but the tide of fortune was soon to turn, and Marie's death was the first drop in the bitter chalice that fate was mingling for him. In less than a year the discontent of the Greeks broke out in open rebellion. Joannice of Bulgaria had promised them help, and with a huge army, reinforced by a horde of Tartars, he laid siege to Adrianople. Baldwin marched to relieve the town, and fell wounded, perhaps slain, before its walls. Of what had actually befallen the Emperor nothing was certainly known. Some of his comrades were sure they had seen his dead body, others were equally sure that he had been taken alive. The Bishop of Soissons set out for France to gather funds for ransom. Henry of Flanders had recourse to the good offices of the Pope, who at once sent an embassy to Joannice to treat for Baldwin's release. Vain request. 'The Emperor,' averred the King of the Bulgarians, 'had paid Nature's debt—*debitum carnis exsoluerat.*'

Twenty years later some wood-cutters of Plancques, a village in the heart of the great forest which in those days stretched from Tournai to Valenciennes, discovered in an unfrequented glade, by the banks of a stream, a rude hut of osiers, thatched with turf, which they were sure they had not seen there before. It was the home of a long-bearded, white-haired old man, with a face covered with scars. Of his antecedents they could learn nothing. 'I am but a poor Christian,' he said, 'doing penance for my sins,' but there was something in his voice and bearing which belied his words. Not a few of the Crusaders, on their return from the East, had put on the black robe of St. Benedict or the brown frock of the poor man of Assisi— some of them were known to have chosen a solitary life, and to have hidden themselves in forests or caves, and the village gossips, over their ale, whispered to one another that of these the mysterious hermit was surely one. The peasant folk from the neighbouring villages flocked out to visit him; some of them had in their youth set eyes on the hero of Constantinople, and these men were convinced that, in the garb of a poor recluse, they now beheld him again, and presently it was noised abroad that Baldwin had come back to Flanders. At length the rumour reached the ears of a former comrade-in-arms, a friend who had known him well, Everard de Montagne, the powerful Lord of Glançon. He at once set out for the hermit's cell, saw the old man, and was convinced of his identity—so too

Sohier of Enghien, Arnulph of Gavre, Bourchard d'Avesnes (the ill-fated husband of Baldwin's daughter, the future Countess Marguerite), and a hundred others who had been intimate with him. But the hermit would vouchsafe no answer, and when they pressed him, returned only evasive replies. 'Are ye, then, like the Breton folk,' he said, 'who still look for the coming of Arthur?' Presently a deputation of citizens went out to the hermitage from Valenciennes; they greeted him with shouts of acclamation. 'Thou art our Count, thou art our Count!' they cried, and, in spite of the old man's protest, they carried him back with them to the city. Then at last Baldwin declared himself. They had rightly divined his secret; he was indeed the Count of Flanders.

The story of his adventures is a strange one. Wounded at the siege of Adrianople and sick almost to death, he had been taken prisoner by the Bulgarians. During the early days of his captivity a lady of the Court chanced to see him, perhaps the King's daughter herself. She was interested in his story, he was still young and handsome, and she gave him her heart. The Emperor feigned to reciprocate her passion, and her devotion knew no bounds; to save him, and, for his sake too, his comrades, she was ready to risk her life. A plan of escape was devised. By her aid it was successfully carried out and they all fled together.

Baldwin, however, did not marry the Bulgarian princess. The heroine who had rescued him was a Pagan woman, he was a disciple of Christ; but before they fled they had mutually plighted their troth—she to receive baptism at the first opportune moment, he, when this had been accomplished, to make her his wife.

When the time for fulfilling their pledges came, it found the infidel true to her vow, the Christian eager to be quit of his.

Was there no loophole? He took counsel with his Flemish friends. The Emperor was bound, they said, by his oath, but there was a gleam of hope; haply this Gentile woman would go the way of all flesh before she had accomplished hers.

Baldwin took the hint. On the eve of her intended baptism the hapless princess died. Retribution quickly followed. The murderer was presently entrapped by barbarians, who carried him off for a slave. Seven times he was sold from hand to hand, kicks and blows were his portion and indignities of every kind.

One day, when he was harnessed to a cart like some beast of burthen, he fell in with a company of German merchants who, learning his tale, had pity on him, and purchased his release. Filled with remorse at what he had done, he at once set out for Rome and confessed his sins to the Pope, who imposed on him a life-long penance. He then made his way back to his native land, and went and hid himself in the forest of Glançon.

Strange as it may seem, the knights and burghers of Valenciennes believed the old man's tale, and stranger still, in their pity for his great misfortune, they forgot his great crime. They put on him a purple robe and thrust a sceptre into his hand, and called him father and chief. For them he was the hero of Constantinople, the sovereign who had showered blessings on them all, the Christian who had suffered long years of anguish at the hands of heathen men. In their eyes, the red aureole of martyrdom already glowed about his head, and they begged locks of his hair for relics, and treasured up the water in which he had bathed.

It was the same throughout the realm. The men of Flanders everywhere remembered that they had loved Baldwin and they all knew that they hated Jeanne, and now Baldwin the beloved was in the midst of them again. The evil days of his daughter had become as a tale that was told. Wherever he went he was greeted with wild demonstrations of joy. The great towns of Flanders received him with open arms. His journey from city to city was one long triumphal progress. Presently he reached Bruges, and here at Pentecost he held his Court, and, clad in imperial robes, with his own hands armed ten knights.

But this was not all. The neighbouring sovereigns acknowledged his claim. The ambassadors of the Duke of Limbourg and the Duke of Brabant waited on him in the capital, and Henry III. of England (April 11, 1225) sent to 'his very dear friend Baldwin' letters of greeting, of congratulation, and of sage advice. 'Remember,' he said, 'that the King of France hath despoiled both the one and the other of us; let us therefore make a league together against him.'

If Baldwin had taken up the thread of his old policy, and allied himself with England, his course of action would probably have been crowned with the success of former days, but he was now a broken-down old man, cowed with long years of servitude and the memory of a great crime, he had neither the courage nor the energy to do so, but fatuously threw himself into the arms of the very man against whom Henry had warned him.

In the midst of the unlooked-for good fortune which had up to now attended the enterprise which the hermit of Plancques had been so loth to undertake, one circumstance was a cause of no little grief and disquietude; his daughter had refused to recognize him, and had fled to France, and though the cloud on the horizon was no bigger than a man's hand, it presaged, he foresaw, a deluge which would perhaps sweep him away.

In his trouble and confusion he turned a willing ear to the false counsel of his sister the Lady of Beaujeu,[19] who urged him to take the wind out of Jeanne's sails by himself confiding in the French King, who, thanks to her good offices, was disposed in his favour. Baldwin fell into the trap. Louis sent him a safe conduct, and towards the close of June he set out for Péronne, where Louis was at that time holding his Court.

His entry into the city on the evening of July 4 was a vision of Eastern splendour. All glorious in purple and gold, with his crown on his head, and a white wand in his hand, they bore him aloft on men's shoulders in a comely litter. Before him was carried the imperial cross, and a retinue of over a hundred gorgeously-attired knights followed in his train. At the palace gates Louis himself came out to greet him. 'Welcome, sire,' said the French King, 'if thou art indeed mine uncle Baldwin, Count of Flanders.' 'Fair nephew,' quavered the old man, 'such in sooth am I, but my daughter doth not know me, and would fain take away mine heritage; prithee help me to keep it.' Louis had already decided on the course he would pursue, and already agreed with Jeanne as to the price of his championship, but he deemed it prudent for the moment to disguise his intentions, and the Emperor was soon entertained at a sumptuous banquet, during which he again recited the story of his adventures, and with such good effect that many of those who heard him were moved to tears.

Presently the royal Council was summoned, and Baldwin was invited to plead his cause. He consented to do so, and it became clear that the solemn reception accorded him had been from the first a solemn farce. In inviting Baldwin to Péronne, the French King had but one object in view—to separate him from his friends—and in now affecting the appearance of a serious examination of his claim, his only desire was to discredit it. At last, after having endured much brow-beating and hectoring speech, the Emperor refused to answer any more questions; the hour was late, he said, and he had that day been greatly fatigued; on the morrow he would be ready to converse again. But the wary old man had no intention of keeping his word; he now fully realized the danger of his position. In coming to Péronne he had made a false move; his liberty, perhaps his life, was in peril, and he cast about him for some means of escape. Fortune was once more kind to him, and that very night he took horse and fled the city.

When he reached his own dominions he was greeted with the same wild demonstrations of joy which had at first hailed his coming. But if the great heart of the people still throbbed for Baldwin, the classes were no longer with him. He soon learnt that the sheriffs of Bruges and of other great towns had accepted Jeanne's amnesty, and that even the picked knights who had accompanied him to Péronne had played him false, and he lost heart. There was no peace for him in this world save in a life of penance. He had slain the woman who loved him, the woman who had risked her life for his sake, and her shade would assuredly drive him back to his hermitage or to the gallows.

The cause of this sudden *volte-face* in favour of Jeanne is difficult to surmise, but corruption had not unlikely something to do with it, for we find in a treaty concluded, at Bapaume a few days later the Countess of Flanders acknowledging that Louis, whose soldiers had not once drawn their swords in her behalf, had expended ten thousand livres in reinstating her in her dominions. Meanwhile Baldwin had disappeared. Some of the few who still clung to him affirmed that he had fled to Germany and had been received with hospitality by Archbishop Engelbert of Cologne, who, they averred, had counselled him to go to Rome and lay his case before the Common Father of the faithful. Be this as it may, Baldwin was presently arrested by Baron Erard de Chastenay, at Rougemont in Burgundy, who sold him to Jeanne for four hundred silver marks, and she, filled with savage joy, hanged him in chains on a gibbet at Lille between two hounds.

'Many of those who knew his story,' comments Matthew Paris, in his delightful, gossiping way, 'were convinced that this lot befell the Emperor in consequence of his sin.' 'And all those who had promoted it by their advice,' he adds, 'in like manner came to a terrible end.' 'One of these men, when he returned home to his wife, and had been recognized by her, was cast headlong into a well. She privily procuring the same because in her lord's absence she had wedded another man, and had borne him children.' 'So too of the rest. By some mishap or other they all of them perished miserably, for the wrath of God, who willeth not that evil should be rendered for good, was fiercely enkindled against them.'

CHAPTER XII

The Love Story of Bourchard d'Avesnes

BEFORE proceeding further with the story of Bruges, it will be necessary to go back to the time when Baldwin first disappeared from men's view (1205), blotted out by the thick mist of conjecture which clung round the bastions of Adrianople, and to note the course of events in Flanders from that date until the day of his unlooked-for home-coming twenty years later (1225).

The mysterious exit of the Emperor had left his patrimony in hazardous plight. Jeanne, his heiress and eldest daughter, was not yet fifteen years old; her sister Marguerite was still in her cradle; Philip, Marquis of Namur, whom Baldwin before setting out for the East had appointed their guardian, was a man unworthy of trust, and the redoubtable Philip Augustus was shaping the destiny of France.

Too shrewd to let slip so favourable a moment for strengthening his hold on Flanders, the French King at once laid claim as suzerain to the wardship of the infant princesses, and the Marquis of Namur,[20] bribed by the promise of a royal alliance, fell in with his kinsman's designs, and presently dispatched them to France.

In face of the storm of indignation aroused by so flagrant a breach of trust, Philip was constrained to hand over the reins of government to his co-trustee, Bourchard d'Avesnes, the son of the illustrious friend of Richard Cœur de Lion, and the chief of the Nationalist or anti-French party. But it was only after five years' negotiation, and a threat to throw himself into the arms of England, that at length Bourchard was enabled to obtain his wards' release, and before King Philip would suffer their return to Flanders, he took care to bestow Jeanne's hand on his kinsman Ferdinand of Portugal, a prince whom he deemed would be wax in his hands.

Perhaps the French King was from the first mistaken in his man. Certain it is that when immediately after the marriage he seized St. Omer and Aire, and under pretext of hospitality forcibly detained the newly-married couple, *en route* for Flanders, at Péronne, until they acquiesced in this act of spoliation, Ferdinand showed no disposition to submit to the outrage tamely. He went forth from his prison at Péronne filled with projects of vengeance, and having concluded a secret treaty with John of England, he waited to see what would happen. For two years he was fain to possess his soul in patience, but everything comes to the man who knows how to wait, and at the expiration of this time Ferdinand's opportunity came. Philip Augustus was now gathering up his strength for a crusade against John, whom the Pope had declared to have forfeited his crown, and he had summoned his vassals to meet him at Soissons. Ferdinand alone refused help. St. Omer and Aire, he averred, must first be restored to Flanders. Philip offered a money equivalent; Ferdinand would not accept it. Nothing but the restitution of the ceded cities would content him. By taking possession of them Philip had violated his duty as lord, and henceforth he (Ferdinand) was in no way bound by his oath of allegiance.

'One of two things must needs come to pass,' King Philip had swore when he learned that Ferdinand had renounced his overlordship; 'France must be Flemish, or Flanders French,' and presently he led into the Netherlands the great army which he had assembled to fight King John, who had now made his peace with the Pope. On May 24 Cassel fell, later on Ghent was invested, by the close of the summer the French were at the gates of Bruges. Soon tottering walls and smouldering embers were all that remained of 'its famous seaport called Damme,' and the vast wealth of merchandise stored there, and thousands of homes had been reduced to ashes. The fertile country round was white to harvest, and Philip reaped it with sickles of flame. From Bruges to the seashore all the country-side was one great field of black stubble.

All through the autumn the French King harried Flanders; Lille, Cassel, Courtrai, and a host of smaller towns had shared the fate of Damme before the snows of winter drove him back again to his native land.

About this time too Ferdinand set out on a journey that he had long had in contemplation—took shipping for Dover, and in due course reached Canterbury and his friend John, nor is it unlikely that during this interview the allies broached for the first time the famous project for the partition of France between England, Flanders, Limburg, Holland, Namur and the Empire, and which, if fate had been kind, would have assured to Ferdinand the provinces of Artois, Picardie and the Ile-de-France, including that Paris where, in days of yore, he had been so diverted by 'les folles filles et les jongleurs.' Be this as it may, the Flemish Count was the moving spirit and instigator of the whole plot. The outcome of it was the battle of Bouvines, and the outcome of the battle of Bouvines was twelve years' captivity for Ferdinand, the French yoke more firmly riveted to her neck than ever for Flanders, and for England, as we all know, the Great Charter.

This, then, was the plight of Flanders at the close of the year 1214. For sovereign she had a young and tearful wife, casting about her for some means to obtain her husband's release, and ready, for the moment, to make any sacrifice to deliver him. On this weak, helpless girl Philip Augustus had imposed as chief counsellor a creature of his own, a degenerate scion of the house of Erembald—one Rodolphe de Nesle, Châtelain of Bruges. Added to this, fortresses had been dismantled, strongholds had been razed, and two-thirds of the chivalry of Flanders were languishing in French prisons. But there was a gleam of hope on the horizon; there was still one man left in Flanders, mighty enough, as every one believed, to save the fatherland from sinking into a mere French province—that same man who, in the days of Philip's treachery, had taken the reins of government into his own strong hands and forced the French King to release his master's daughters. So thought all Flanders, and all Flanders was doomed to disappointment. For, despite his noble qualities and his great parts—a brilliant knight, a ripe scholar, an accomplished diplomatist, and withal a shrewd, hard-headed man of business—Bourchard d'Avesnes was not able to work out his own salvation much less the salvation of Flanders. When in the year 1211 the Flemish princesses returned to their native land, King Philip Augustus had reluctantly confided the younger of them, Marguerite, then a child of some eleven years, to his care until such time as she should have attained marriageable age, and Bourchard had since prolonged the term of his guardianship to one of life-long duration, as he fondly hoped, by espousing her himself: a proceeding which in no little measure enhanced his prestige and influence for the moment. Bourchard had announced his marriage to his sister-in-law, who, at least, had shown no open disapprobation, and after the battle of Bouvines, and the capture of Ferdinand, his star was still in the ascendant. If aught should befall the childless Jeanne, now cut off from all hope of offspring, his wife would be Countess of Flanders, and, in accordance with the usage of the day, he himself would share her throne. If this were matter of no little rejoicing for the inhabitants of that country, it was no less a source of consternation to the French King, who foresaw in Bourchard, Count of Flanders, an emulator of Robert the Frisian, and from that moment he determined to crush him. It was owing to his influence that the Countess Jeanne first showed herself Bourchard's foe, and if Philip himself was not the fabricator of the rumours which blasted his after career, fortune had placed in his hands a deadly poison which he did not scruple to employ.

It was in the gossiping ante-chambers of the Lateran palace that these rumours first took shape, and whatever of truth or falsehood there may have been in them, they were credited by Innocent III., who on 19th January 1216 sent letters to the Archbishop of Rheims, bidding him proclaim Bourchard d'Avesnes excommunicated 'until such time as he shall set Marguerite of Flanders at liberty, and humbly return to the manner of life becoming his ecclesiastical state. The testimony of several prelates and other trustworthy persons had convinced him that Bourchard was a sub-deacon and that he had been at one time a canon of Laon.'

Of the circumstances of the marriage, which had been celebrated after the banns had been regularly published in the presence of all the great nobles of Hainault, Innocent was probably ignorant. Indeed, he seems to have been doubtful whether any marriage had taken place at all. 'Bourchard has not feared,' he says, 'to perfidiously conduct Marguerite, the sister of the Countess of Flanders, to one of the castles confided to his care, and there to retain her, averring that she is united to him in wedlock.' Great then was the surprise of the Papal legates when they presently approached the Château de Quesnoy, and Marguerite herself came forth to meet them with her beautiful face radiant with youth and happiness—she was only fifteen years old—nor did her words of greeting in any way lessen their amazement. 'Learn from mine own lips,' she said, 'that Bourchard is my lawful spouse, and know too that I have for husband a better man and a better knight than hath my sister Jeanne.'

The sentence of excommunication was not pronounced. Bourchard had lodged an appeal to the Pope, but for all that, Jeanne, entirely under the influence of her French counsellors, laid siege to the castle of Quesnoy. The Lord of Avesnes, so far from being in a position to fight for his fatherland, was hard pressed to defend his wife, and during two years an intermittent warfare continued between his vassals and the vassals of the Countess of Flanders. At the end of this period he seems to have been taken captive, and there is a tradition that he was at one time imprisoned at Ghent. What became of Marguerite during her husband's captivity does not appear, but certain it is that when he had obtained his release and had withdrawn to the Château de Houffalize, on the banks of the Meuse, she found means to join him, and that here she later on bore him two sons—Baldwin and Jean.

The birth of these children but increased the fury of their father's enemies. Jeanne's French counsellors were well aware that unless Bourchard's marriage could be shown to be null and void, one or other of his sons would in all probability succeed to the throne, and they feared that in that case vengeance would be meted out to the men who had persecuted him. Philip Augustus too was more than ever convinced of the necessity of annulling the marriage, which guaranteed the legitimacy of his offspring, and by making Jeanne believe that she could obtain the release of her own husband at the cost of her sister's shame, prevailed on her to re-open the case at Rome, and the outcome was a fresh sentence of excommunication which set under the Church's ban not only the Lord of Avesnes himself, but his brother Guy and the friend who had given him hospitality, Thierri of Houffalize.

In vain Bourchard journeyed to Rome, there to plead his cause in person. The Pope, instead of granting the dispensation he asked, imposed on him, by way of penance, a pilgrimage to Jerusalem.

It was about this time that Baldwin of Constantinople again returned to Flanders. Chief amongst those who rallied to his standard were the friends and supporters of Bourchard d'Avesnes (no small number), and so long as Baldwin prospered, Bourchard's hope rose high. By what means the Emperor of Constantinople fell a victim to his daughter and to Louis of France (Philip Augustus had died two years before) we have already seen, and when Louis crushed Baldwin, he at the same time crushed Bourchard. The last hopes of the Lord of Avesnes were buried in the grave of Baldwin of Constantinople. But Bourchard had not yet drained the cup of his humiliation. During the year 1226 he was destined to taste all its bitterness. Enraged at the support which he had given to the hermit of Glançon, Louis forced the Princess Marguerite to come forth from the retreat where she had remained since her separation from her husband, break her plighted troth, and take a new spouse in the person of William of Dampierre. In vain Pope Honorius charged the Bishop of Soissons 'to make diligent inquiry, lest haply there should be some impediment by reason of kinship.' In vain rumour said that William, like Bourchard, was a sub-deacon; the marriage was celebrated without delay, and it was not until four years later that a Papal dispensation was obtained from the impediment of consanguinity.

How Louis induced Marguerite to take the step in question we are ignorant, but about this time Ferdinand obtained his liberty, and it may well be that the French King made his release conditional on Jeanne's bringing her influence to bear on her sister, and we know by the testimony of Marguerite's own sons that it was 'chiefly through the evil counsel of her sister Jeanne that she at last consented to the marriage. The same witnesses inform us that Marguerite handed them over to the tender mercies of her new husband, who imprisoned them 'for ten years or thereabouts *et multa mala eis fecit cum non haberent custodem sen defensorem.*'

For the rest—when William died, the sons of the Lord of Avesnes at length obtained their liberty and returned to Flanders, and the last days of their much-tried father, now an old man tottering to the grave, were in all probability cheered and consoled by the presence of those sons for whose sake he had sacrificed so much.

INTERIOR OF NOTRE DAME

As for Marguerite herself, she never again saw the man who had served her so devotedly, and whom she had so deeply wronged. The child love of earlier and happier days had given place to hatred so unrelenting, so cruel, that when Bourchard himself had passed away she did not hesitate to visit it on his children. Indeed, after Marguerite had become Countess of Flanders, the one object in her life seems to have been to exclude them from all part in their inheritance. If she could have had her way, the issue of William of Dampierre would have been declared the only legal heirs, alike of Hainault and of Flanders. Again and again at Marguerite's instance the facts of this antiquated matrimonial suit, every one of which had happened fifty years before, were discussed by grave divines. Again and again the Countess of Flanders dragged her honour in the dust, and besmirched the memory of her dead husband, in the hope of proving the illegitimacy of the children she had borne him. The case was heard in the ecclesiastical courts of France; it was food for the delectation of imperial judges, and its merits were considered by the lawyers of the Roman Curia over and over again, but in spite of the pains which Marguerite had taken to blacken her own character, in each case she was declared innocent—the children of Bourchard d'Avesnes had been certainly born in wedlock. Marguerite, however, refused to acquiesce, and it was not until the land had been drenched with blood by the supporters of the rival claimants, and Guy and William of Dampierre had both fallen into the hands of their opponents, that at length this implacable old woman and all other parties concerned agreed to refer the matters in dispute to the arbitration of that marvellous peacemaker, St. Louis of France, who awarded Hainault to the heirs of Bourchard d'Avesnes, and to the Dampierres, Flanders. A decision to which each party was constrained to submit, and when Marguerite died, Guy de Dampierre became Count of Flanders, and Jean d'Avesnes Count of Hainault.

HOSPITAL OF ST. JOHN AND SOUTH AISLE OF NOTRE DAME

But how, it will be asked, does all this concern the city on the Roya? What has the love story of Bourchard d' Avesnes to do with the story of Bruges? This much. Bruges, as the chief place of residence of the sovereigns of Flanders, was intimately associated with the Court of Flanders and all that appertained thereto. Moreover, it was during this period that Bruges began to assume its present aspect. If old Provost Bertulph, or Dierick of Alsace, or even his son Philip, could again re-visit the scene of their sorrows and their triumphs, they would hardly recognize in the city of Bruges aught save the chapel of St. Basil; but if Marguerite, or Jeanne, or poor Bourchard, were to come back again, they would find there much that was familiar to them—the great nave and choir and transepts of Notre Dame, in spite of whitewash and Rococo ornament, and the scars of their conflict with time, would be easily recognizable. So too the Cathedral of St. Sauveur, part of it, the nave and choir of the Church of St. Gilles, and the northern aisle and the tower of the Church of St. Jacques.

If the ghost of Jeanne could come forth into the *Rue Ste. Cathérine*, there too she would recognize in the old brown hospital tottering into the water, in spite of mutilated statues, blind windows, bricked-up doorways and an abundant crop of golden wallflowers which have found a congenial home in the chinks and crevices of its crumbling façade, the stately building which she herself had founded six hundred years ago, the withered fruit of that grand design over which, along with the Master Mason who conceived it, she had no doubt often pored, and which, perhaps even, she had herself modified. Whilst if the Beguinage hard-by with its Renaissance church, its Renaissance porch, and its white-washed cottages of the seventeen hundreds; if the hospital of Our Lady of the Pottery at the other end of the town, with its flamboyant windows, its recently-restored out-buildings, and its modern gateway; if the Romanesque hospital of St. John at Damme, pitilessly scraped as to its stones, and with its time-honoured brickwork degraded by red paint, appeared at first sight unfamiliar to her, an arch here, a gateway there, a piece of rude carving a little further on, would soon convince her that she was in the presence of old friends whom she and her sister Marguerite had known six centuries before. And so too of others of the bricks and stones, and perhaps also even of the trees of Bruges or its neighbourhood, though, alas! it is too seldom the manner of the Fleming to cherish his timber after it has attained marketable value. He is indeed an indefatigable planter, but he plants for profit, and he is a no less indefatigable wielder of the pruning-hook and the axe.

THE BEGUINAGE, WITH TOWER OF NOTRE DAME

Nevertheless, here and there some stalwart stripling has escaped notice long enough to have attained such huge dimensions as to evoke even the respect of this hard-headed, matter-of-fact Saxon—such a one is still standing in a wood not far from Maele Castle, the former country residence of the Counts of Flanders. Maybe it was already a great tree when Marguerite and Jeanne were still children living under the guardianship of Philip of Namur and Bourchard d'Avesnes, and that when they went out from the sultry town in summer-time to the cool of Maele woods they played beneath its branches.

There is a still more famous tree a little further off, but within measurable distance of Bruges. The time-honoured yew tree of Löo is said to be more than two thousand years old. It stands beside an ancient gateway in the main street of this picturesque little town—once the home of Bertulph's murderer, the perfidious William of Löo, and is associated with the name of no less remote a personage than Julius Cæsar. The country folk will tell you he once tied his horse to it.

A fragment too of the primeval forest in which Robert the Frisian built Winendael is still standing, and here also there is some old timber.

Let the visitor to Bruges, when he has fatigued his eyes with the glory of man's handiwork in the city, consider awhile the handiwork of God in the flat country surrounding it. Let him go forth into the forest of Winendael, or the woods of Tilleghem or Maele, and he will see what he will see.

CHAPTER XIII

The French Annexation

DESCENDED from a poor but illustrious family of the best nobility of Champagne, and nearly allied to the royal house of France—a man of great natural abilities, no less courageous than capable, and withal an ardent lover and lavish patron of literature and the arts—it was no mere vulgar flattery when Jacques Bretex, the troubadour of Arras, averred that Count Guy de Dampierre was the most polished and learned and generous prince of his day. His Court was one of the most brilliant in Christendom; thither flocked musicians, artists, men of letters, from all parts of Europe. His chief delight was to while away his leisure hours with them—in summer-time in the woody glades of Winendael, and in winter in the halls of his sumptuous palace at Bruges. It was thanks to his generous patronage that in days when every French town boasted a poet, in an age that was the age *par excellence* of French minstrelsy, this gentle art shone with the greatest *éclat* in Flanders and in Artois. But if French songsters like Adenez Leroy and Jacques Bretex enchanted the ears of Guy's Court with pæans of his virtue and his glory, plain citizens relished more the rude Flemish verse of the poets of the people—verse bitter, caustic, passionate, instinct alike with their hopes and their aversions, verse which, scorning the art of flattery, did not hesitate to discover the source of all this magnificence;—burthensome taxes and forced loans wrung from a long-suffering people by a prince who contemned their liberties. The bitter irony, for example, with which William Uuitenhove in his *Reinœert de Vos* (Reynard the Fox) bewails the progress which Master Reynard has made in science, and the haste shown by men hungry for riches to follow no other rule than that which he preached in his den, or the no less bitter and energetic hymns in which Jacob van Maerlant bewails the lot 'of the sheep wandering among the ravening wolves who have become their shepherds now that pride and avarice have given to every man who possesses gold the right to speak in the council chamber of princes.'

Bred in the traditions of feudalism, Guy mistrusted Flanders, the land of all others where freedom had made most headway, and the Flemish in their turn hated him because his dynasty had been forced on them by France. These two circumstances hampered him at every turn, and there was yet another which indirectly aggravated all his difficulties: he was the impecunious father of seventeen children.[21] Sons had to be settled in life and daughters portioned and married, hence the arbitrary taxation, the fines and forced loans with which he so often vexed his subjects. This too was the fruitful source of foreign complications. Guy, considering above all things how to obtain rich partners for his numerous offspring, did not always take into consideration the political opportuneness of their alliances. From every circumstance he must needs draw some pecuniary advantage, and that without regard to his real and permanent interests. Every town and abbey in his domains lent him money, he had recourse too to the usurers of Lombardy and of Arras, and he was always ready to sell privileges to whomsoever could afford to pay for them. The money thus raised was in great part expended in endowing his progeny. Thus it was that he purchased the lordships and manorial rights of Dunkirk, of Baitlleul, of Cambrai, of St. Omer and Peteghem.

His endeavours to affiance his daughter Phillippine, and when this failed, his youngest daughter Isabelle, to the heir to the English throne, were in great measure the cause of his troubles with France. With what tenacity Guy clung to this project, and that it was not altogether inspired by mercenary motives, the memorial presented by his two sons Robert of Bethune and John of Namur to Pope Boniface, bears witness. The Princess Phillippine was at this time a prisoner at Paris, and one object of the memorial was to interest Boniface in her behalf. 'Holy Father,' runs the passage in question, 'your devoted son Guy, Count of Flanders, is grievously afflicted that the union of his daughter with the Prince of Wales, a matter which had been guaranteed by solemn oaths, is not yet accomplished. It were a fine thing for him to have for his friend and son-in-law the heir to the English throne, and his daughter one day queen, which was what, with God's blessing, he had ardently hoped would come to pass,—nay, what a grand thing it would be for his subjects that England and Flanders, countries which hitherto have been so often at loggerheads with no little detriment to persons and property, should at length be united in bonds of peace. For the inhabitants of these lands are neighbours and they are wont to have much commercial intercourse the one with the other, chiefly for the transport of wool from England, and cloth from Flanders, but also anent many other products found in one country or the other.'

A fourth circumstance hampered Guy. His nephew Jean II. of Avesnes never forgot that he was the eldest son of the eldest son of Marguerite of Constantinople, that the highest ecclesiastical tribunal in Christendom had pronounced in favour of his father's legitimacy, and that thus, according to the law of primogeniture, he was rightful Count of Flanders; hence he lost no opportunity of injuring his uncle, and was continually plotting against him. Moreover, Guy was at daggers drawn with several of his great vassals, such as the Lords of Audenarde and Gavre, and he was not beloved by the higher clergy, at all events by these of West Flanders.

Thus it came to pass, in spite of his brilliant qualities, in spite of his all-round capability, in spite of his courage, his perseverance and his *finesse*, he failed in the noble task which it was his ambition to fulfil—to break from off the neck of Flanders the galling yoke of France—that his most cherished personal hopes were never accomplished; that he had to stand by with folded hands whilst poor little Phillippine, the child of his old age, the apple of his eye, was slowly done to death by Philippe le Bel, and that he himself, an old man broken down by insults and tears, at length died miserably in a French prison.

It must not be supposed from what has been noted above that Guy was animated by the instincts of a tyrant; he had no wish to establish a despotism in Flanders—nay, he undoubtedly had the welfare of his country at heart, but self came first. When he was not blinded by his own personal interests, he showed himself a just and a benevolent prince, following in his methods of government the example of his predecessors, Jeanne and Marguerite. Like them he favoured industry and commerce, and to a certain extent the freedom of the towns, but he viewed with an evil eye the extreme independence of the great communes, the like of which existed nowhere else in Northern Europe, and he would have reduced their liberties to the same level as those obtaining in France.

The jealousy with which the upper classes viewed the increasing well-being of the people was another item in the political situation of the day, and Guy endeavoured to exploit it for his own ends. The quarrel was not, as has so often been represented, a duel between burgher and noble, it was rather a tug-of-war between men of wealth and men of moderate means.

On the one side were doubtless a certain number of rich feudal lords, but there were also allied to them almost all the great merchants and traders of the greater communes, and nearly all the higher clergy—in a word, the *majores et potentiores*, as Monachus Gandavensis calls them. On the other, the small traders, the lower clergy, and perhaps a sprinkling of the Court nobility.

The former class alone monopolised all municipal authority, every post of profit and advancement was reserved for them, and the latter viewed this state of things with great disfavour; and Guy, with a view to crushing the oligarchy which governed the towns, fomented and increased the quarrel, backing up the small men who were not strong enough to disquiet him.

The Flemish as a nation have never been renowned for loyalty to the princes who governed them, and the sturdy patriotism of this hard-headed race will most frequently be found to have been inspired less by motives of sentiment than by motives of self-interest. This was certainly the case with the '*majores et potentiores*' of Bruges and Ypres and Ghent in the days of Count Guy.

So long as their rights and privileges and monopolies were respected, so long as all political and municipal power was in their hands, it mattered little to them whether they were called Frenchmen or Flemings, whether their nominal chief styled himself Count of Flanders or King of France. Thus it came to pass that when Guy, in order to curtail their power, threw his weight on the side of the little men, the governing oligarchy appealed from their Count to the parliament of his liege lord, the King of France, and that when, thanks to their aid, that monarch had made Flanders a French province, and had then thrown off the mask, and attempted to deprive them of all they held most dear, they veered round to the side of their rightful government, united with the little men, and finally chased the French from Flanders.

'Philippe le Bel,' says Kervyn, 'represents in the thirteenth century the worst tendencies of absolute monarchy.' He was firmly resolved to gather up all power into his own hands, that he alone should rule France, and that in the domains of his vassals nothing should take place without his consent. And note this. He was the first French sovereign who used the formula— *Par le plenitude de notre puissance royal*, and the first too who styled himself *metuendissimus*.

Flanders was the first province to which he directed his attention. Her princes were amongst the mightiest and the most independent of his vassals, and behind them was the strength of their free cities. United, these two forces would have been invincible; in hurling himself against the bed rock of their omnipotence Philippe would have only dashed himself to pieces, but, unhappily, at the time of which we are treating, Guy and his burghers were at daggers drawn, and their mutual animosities—animosities which he made it his business to foment—afforded Philippe a favourable opportunity for crushing both.

From the commencement of his reign the French King had persistently worried the Count of Flanders with a policy of exasperation which culminated, in 1296, in the decoying and detention of his favourite daughter Phillippine. This it was which at length drove Guy to openly break with his suzerain, and on the 7th of January 1297, after signing on the previous day at Winendael an offensive and defensive alliance with Edward of England, he despatched the abbots of Gembloux and of Florceffe to

Paris to inform the French King that on account of his evil deeds and his perfidy, Count Guy of Flanders henceforth held himself to be quit, delivered and absolved from all bonds, alliances, conventions, obediences, and services by which he might hitherto have been bound to him.

Philippe replied by invading Flanders at the head of 60,000 men. The greater communes, of whose rghts and liberties he posed as the champion, received him with open arms, and so hard pressed were Count Guy and his allies that early in October (1297) they were glad to consent to an armistice which was afterwards prolonged to a truce of three years.

Having thus for the moment discarded the trade of war, Philippe busied himself with diplomacy; purchased the defection of Albert of Nassau; concluded a secret treaty with the English King, affiancing his daughter Isabelle to the Prince of Wales, and his sister Marguerite to Edward himself. Thus on the very day when the truce expired he was enabled to pour his troops into Flanders with every anticipation of a successful and speedy issue. Nor was he doomed to disappointment. What could Guy do? Betrayed by his burghers, without friends and without cash, by the end of April he had lost all heart, and presently he was on his knees at Ardenburg before Charles of Valois, the French commander, humbly suing for peace. Absolute submission to the King's mercy, total abandonment of the remnant of territory which he still held, and a journey to Paris along with two of his sons and fifty of his barons, there to treat face to face with the King—these were the only terms upon which Valois would consent to relinquish hostilities, but he guaranteed to Guy, in the King's name, that if he failed to obtain peace in the course of the year, he should be free to return to Flanders. Stern as the conditions were, Guy and his little following forthwith set out for Paris, but only on their arrival there to be thrown into prison. Philippe was not bound, he said, by a treaty to which he had never assented, and presently, having obtained judgment from his lawyers that Guy had forfeited his dominions by reason of felony, he took possession of the entire county, and declared it annexed to the French crown. This was early in the year 1300. 'The burghers of the Flemish cities,' says a German historian, 'had been all corrupted by the gold or the promises of the French King, who would never have dared to cross their frontiers if they had been true to their Count.'[22] The rest of this story is more intimately connected with Bruges, and it must be told at greater length.

CHAPTER XIV

Peter de Coninck

ALTHOUGH the city on the Roya had been in great measure responsible for the success of the French arms—at the very commencement of the war she had opened her gates to Philippe le Bel—she was destined to be the chief factor in the great movement which ended by chasing the French from Flanders.

Early in the spring of 1301 Philippe le Bel had resolved to make a triumphal progress through his new domains, and on the 18th of May, accompanied by his Queen, he arrived at Douai—having visited Courtrai, Audenarde, Peteghem, Ghent—where he was received with the greatest magnificence. Towards the close of the month he reached Bruges, and Bruges would fain have surpassed her rival in the cordiality and gorgeousness of her welcome. All the palaces and public buildings were hung with precious stuffs; on platforms draped with taffeta stood the wives and daughters of the burghers, arrayed in glorious apparel, and tradition tells us how the shimmer of their gems and the lustre of their silks aroused the envy of Isabelle of France. 'I thought,' quoth she, 'that I alone was Queen, but here I see six hundred.'

But if the *majores et potentiores* were exuberant in their manifestations of loyalty, the people were dumb. In vain Philippe called the sheriffs to him, and bade them proclaim public games; no man would take part in them. Indeed, these very games were destined to be the source of the ill-fortune which afterwards befell the French.

The sheriffs essayed to place to the cost of the city companies the price of the gala uniforms expressly manufactured for the occasion. The latter refused to acknowledge the debt, and riots ensued which presently culminated in successful rebellion. In those days there dwelt in the city of Bruges a little wizened, one-eyed man who loved the people. Speaking no language but his own rude mother-tongue, he knew how to infuse so much fire into it, and to mould it into such pithy sayings, and there was so much shrewdness in his speech, and so much sense in his ugly head that, in spite of his physical infirmities and in spite of his uncouth form, his influence with them was unbounded. This man was the dean of the great Guild of Weavers, Petrus de Coninck, or, in plain English, Peter King.

What his original station in life may have been, and what public offices, if any, he may have filled, are questions, perhaps, which will never be determined. May be, as Gheldorf thinks, he was a man of noble birth who had formerly occupied some position of trust at Guy's Court—it was by no means an unusual occurrence for Flemish noblemen in those days to become members of city companies. May be Kervyn is right in asserting that he was a son of the people; nor, if this were so, does it follow that De Coninck had not been attached to his sovereign's household; men of doubtful origin, before and since, have sometimes been esteemed by princes, and Guy is known to have favoured his lesser folk. Perhaps he was a Flemish Karl of the Liberty of Bruges, one of those sturdy yeomen whose ancestors for generations back had, each of them, cultivated his own plot of land and held it by the strength of his own right arm.

Be this as it may, neither the baseness nor the brilliancy of De Coninck's origin diminished or increased the esteem in which he was held by the people. They loved him for what he was, and not for what his forebears had been; and when, supported by the deans of five-and-twenty guilds, in the market-place of Bruges, beneath the shadow of the great bell tower which had just arisen from its ashes more beautiful than it was before, he thundered at the corruption and ambition of the city fathers and called them sycophants and knaves, the vast crowd which thronged the market-place rallied round him to a man, and swore to refuse the obnoxious tax—that not one groat of their hard-earned coin should find its way into the coffers of so corrupt a municipality. In vain the outraged sheriffs caused De Coninck and his comrades to be put under arrest; that very night the people burst open their prison and set them free, and when John of Ghistelle, the chief of the Leliaerts,[23] concerted with them a plot to fall on the Clauwaerts[24] unawares and cut down all their chiefs, the bell which should have signalled the work of destruction was for more than one of the plotters his own passing knell.

Somehow or other the Clauwaerts had got wind of the storm that was brewing, and as the first shrill cry of the tocsin clanged over the city, they flew to arms. Panic laid hold of the Leliaert host, and though the swiftness of their heels saved some, not a few of the leaders were reckoned amongst the slain, and others before nightfall were safely lodged in the prison which had so lately held De Coninck and his friends; but the measure of the great tribune's vengeance was not filled up yet.

Jacques de Châtillon, the King's lieutenant, had for days been encamped outside the city walls, but he deemed the force at his disposal too small to risk a conflict. Each day, however, was bringing him fresh recruits, and a bloody encounter was at hand, when certain men in whom each side trusted offered their mediation. Thanks to their good offices an arrangement was effected, and next day De Châtillon and his knights rode into the city at the same moment that De Coninck and his friends left it.

That a man of De Coninck's stamp should have consented to act thus is at first sight incomprehensible, but after events show that this seemingly cowardly and vacillating conduct was inspired by no mean or unworthy motive. So great were the odds against him that, if he had then hazarded an engagement, nothing short of a miracle could have saved his little band from being cut to pieces. He was well aware that if he surrendered unconditionally the best thing he could hope for would be a halter, and that with his life was linked at that juncture the liberty of Flanders. He knew, too, the man he had to deal with, and that if he gave him sufficient rope he would certainly end by hanging himself. In a word, Châtillon's narrow, arbitrary and exasperating policy would soon drive not a few of the Lily's staunchest supporters—for the greater number of them were only Leliaerts from self-interest—to throw in their lot with the Lion, and that then, with a united Flanders at his back, he might hope to accomplish something. These events occurred in the month of July 1301.

All this actually came to pass. No sooner had Châtillon entered Bruges and re-established his authority than he declared all its privileges forfeited on account of the late rebellion, and exacted, moreover, by way of further punishment, the fourth penny of every workman's wages, and to overawe the discontented, he began the construction of a great citadel on the banks of the Minne Water.

In vain the burghers sent envoys to Paris to plead their cause before the King. Châtillon's henchman, the Comte de St. Pol, had preceded them, and their prayer and humiliation only added to his triumph; and when on their return to Bruges they told the astonished burghers how during their visit to Paris the Bishop of Pamiers had arrived there, charged by the Pope to demand the release of Count Guy and of Phillippine, and how the King had received him with insults and cast him into prison, these men knew they had nothing to hope from the tender mercies of Philippe le Bel.

Meanwhile the discontent at Bruges was increasing day by day. So great was the indignation aroused by the governor's arbitrary conduct that numbers of those who had formerly supported Philippe had now returned to their allegiance to Guy, and by the month of November the Clauwaerts had grown so strong that when De Coninck, taking advantage of Châtillon's absence at Ghent, appeared once more in the market-place 'no man dared lay hold of him.' Indeed, so terrified were the Leliaert magistrates at his unlooked-for arrival that they fled the city, and, for the moment, De Coninck was master of Bruges. But the people are ever a timorous and vacillating herd, and when De Coninck failed in an attempt to win over the Ghenters to the national side, and news came that Châtillon, at the head of a vast host, was on his way to Bruges, so great was their terror that they forced him to quit the town. Indeed, if he had refused to do so he would have fallen a victim to their fury—and two days later Châtillon marched in.

De Coninck was in no way disheartened. He knew that the burghers would soon call him again to their aid. Moreover, during the period which had elapsed between his first and second exodus, the prospects of the little band of patriots had vastly improved. William of Juliers,[25] Provost of Maestricht, a grandson of Count Guy, aroused by the woes of his native land, had exchanged the cassock for the cuirass, and placed himself at their head; John Breidel, Dean of the Butchers' Guild, one of the richest men in Bruges, and perhaps, like De Coninck himself, in brighter days a noble of Guy's Court, had thrown in his lot with them, and by the united efforts of De Coninck and these men the standard of the Lion now waved over Damme, and Oostburg, and Ardenburg, and the castles of Sysseele and Maele, and if Bruges in her wild panic had thrust the great tribune from her doors, he was not doomed to wander shelterless and alone. Five thousand of her bravest sons were found ready to share exile with him, and all the country round was still staunch to the cause of freedom. And yet so unequally matched were the combatants that the final issue could hardly be doubtful.

On the one side was Philippe le Bel, the mightiest king of his day, with all the chivalry of Navarre, and all the chivalry of France, and whatever knights he had been able to recruit throughout the Continent of Europe; and on the other, the tradesmen of Flanders, headed by an exiled priest and a handful of outlawed nobles who had been driven from their native land.

But De Coninck regarded the matter from another point of view. On the one side he saw tyranny and injustice, and on the other liberty and right, and he knew that though sometimes these champions have the air of feeble folk, in the long run they are bound to conquer; and perchance too William, calling to mind the words which in the old church at Maestricht he had so often chanted at Vespers:—*Deposuit potentes de sede et exaltavit humiles*, felt confident with a confidence not of earth that that God who chooses the feeble things of this world to confound the strong would surely fight their battle for them.

Be this as it may, on May 17, Châtillon marched into the city, but instead of bringing, as he had promised the burghers, only a small escort, two thousand well-armed knights marched in with him. Forthwith all kinds of rumours filled the air—Châtillon had brought great coils of rope to hang the chief citizens, there was to be a general massacre of Clauwaerts not even the women and children were to be spared. One French knight had been so sickened at his leader's wholesale project of vengeance that, rather than have a hand in it, he had made good his escape from the city.

Next day the kennels of Bruges were red with blood, but it was not the blood of her burghers. In their fear and their misery these weaklings bethought them of the man whom they had turned from their doors. 'If you have any pity for your fellow-citizens, if the bowels of your compassion are not shut up against our women and our little ones, come over and help us.' Thus they sent word to De Coninck at Damme, and before daybreak he was at Ste. Croix, and with him was John Breidel and a host of stalwart Flemings. A handful of burghers went out to confer with them, and presently with a great cry the exiles burst into the city. '*Schilt end vriendt*, for the lion of Flanders,' re-echoed through the narrow streets, and all those who could not pronounce this shibboleth, impossible of articulation for Gallic lips, were forthwith put to death. So stunned and confused were they by the suddenness of the attack, and the darkness of the night and the uncouth words of greeting which burst from the lips of their foes, that the Frenchmen hardly showed fight at all, but considered only how best they might quit the city, a matter not easy of

OLD HOUSES ON THE ROYA

accomplishment, for a strong guard of Flemings was posted outside each gate. All day long the work of destruction continued, and when at last, worn out with slaying, the Flemish sheathed their swords, the streets and lanes of the city were red with blood and filled with dead men, and so great was the number of corpses that it took three whole days to cast them into the adjoining fields, and there give them burial. And yet fortune had been kind to some of them; the lives of forty knights had been spared, and perhaps of three-score soldiers. These men had been cast into prison; others more fortunate still had saved alike their lives and their liberty. Amongst them note the authors of all the mischief, Jacques de Châtillon and Chancellor Flotte. The former, who, with all his faults, was no coward, at first essayed to stem the tide, but when his horse had been slain under him, seeing that resistance was hopeless, he endeavoured to slip away unobserved, and in the darkness and confusion succeeded in doing so. Presently, wandering about the mazy byways in search of some refuge, he fell in with Pierre Flotte in like predicament with himself. At last they discovered the place they were seeking, perhaps the garret or the cellar of some warehouse giving on one of the canals. Here these two friends, the one a prince of the blood royal and the other the bastard of a courtezan, each of them men of wealth and might, without victuals and without drink, lay huddled up in a frowsy corner, expecting each moment would be their last, until once more the shades of night fell on the town.

Then slinking forth, not without trepidation, Châtillon in the garb of a clerk, Flotte disguised in some other fashion, each of them presently made good his escape, and found an interval of breathing time, the first at Courtrai, the second at Lille, during which to recruit themselves for the great contest so soon to follow.

Truly the fourteenth century was a century of noise and adventure, and yet somehow or other in those days, so we are told, men had no nerves.

CHAPTER XV

The Battle of the Golden Spurs

THE victory was not yet won, Flanders was not yet free, but the massacre which took place at Bruges on Friday, May 13, 1302, and which the burghers for centuries after with brutal irony delighted to call their 'good Friday,' was the beginning of the end.

A few days before that event, William of Juliers had sought out the Lord of Moerseke and demanded of him the sword which Guy had entrusted to his keeping when he set out for France. At first the knight refused, but the war-like prelate seized it roughly from his hands, saying, as he did so, 'This is now my pastoral staff; henceforth the battlefield shall be my school, and soon Philippe le Bel shall rue his treachery to Guy of Dampierre'; and William kept his word. Remaining at Bruges for a few days to recruit his forces, he sallied forth into the country round, and soon Ghent alone of all the towns of Flanders was in the hands of the French; and early in June Guy of Namur, a younger son of Guy of Flanders, reached the capital, where he was welcomed with costly presents and garlands and clashing bells, and appointed Commander-in-chief of the Flemish host and Regent of the county.

Meanwhile Châtillon had brought to Paris the news of the Bruges massacre, and by the end of June Philippe had gathered together an army to be wondered at. 'So great was the number of chariots and horsemen,' says Matthew of Westminster, 'that the surface of the earth was hid by them.' Every baron in France who could take the field was there, and mercenaries from Spain and Italy, and Hainault and Brabant. Their leader was the Count of Artois. Presently they set out for the Netherlands, and towards the close of June they reached Lille.

Nor was the army of resistance which the Regent had assembled one worthy of contempt. In addition to his own German auxiliaries and a handful of volunteers from Zealand, he had collected recruits from every commune and châtelaincy in Flanders. Even from Ghent, the only town which still held to France, came seven hundred men headed by two sheriffs. In the foremost rank were the burghers of Bruges, each man ranged under the banner of the guild to which he belonged and gorgeous in its rich livery—purple, blue, gold, or white embroidered with crimson crosses. Their leaders were Breidel and De Coninck and the redoubtable Provost of Maestricht. Hard-by, under Eustace Sporkin, one of the last of the old

Saxon chiefs, stood the yeomen of the Liberty of Bruges; half naked, bare headed, sinewy of limb, carrying no weapon but the rude *scharmsax* of their ancestors, but for all that a force not to be contemned. From time immemorial the fathers of these men had borne the brunt of every foreign invasion and of every native tyranny. 'So far as they are concerned,' as Kervyn notes, 'the history of the fourteenth century is the history of every century which had preceded it.' Jacques de Châtillon, like so many tyrants before him, would fain have reduced them to slavery, and they had sworn to prevent it.

The Count of Artois set out from Lille during the early days of July, and, leaving behind him a long red streak, for in order to terrorize the peasant folk he had spared neither women nor children, he presently pitched his silken tents on a knoll of rising ground about two leagues from Courtrai. Before that time this hill had been called *Mossenberg* (the Mossy Mount), but on account of the revelry which then took place it has since been known as the *Berg van Weelden*, or the Mount of Feasting.

It took two days for the French force to assemble, and meanwhile the scouts, whom Artois had sent out to ascertain the position of the Flemish, brought back word that they were spread out in a single phalanx in the plain before the Abbey of Grœninghe, to the east of the town on the road to Ghent; that the river Lys on the north covered their rear; that on the west they were protected by the entrenchments of Courtrai, and on the south and east by the river Grœninghe, and that their position was impregnable; that, so far from showing fear at the approach of the enemy, as Artois had confidently expected, 'they were drawn up man to man with their arms raised above their heads like valiant huntsmen awaiting the charge of the wild boar.'

Those of the French knights who best knew Flanders besought their chief to put off the battle till the morrow. The Flemish, they urged, were not accustomed to remain long in camp, and want of supplies would soon disperse them; but Artois rejected the counsel with disdain. 'What!' he cried. 'We outnumber these men by half as many again; we are on horseback, they on foot; we are well armed and they are without weapons; shall we remain, before such a foe as this, rooted to the ground in terror?'

The decisive contest took place on Wednesday the 11th of July. The Flemish began the day with fasting and prayer. 'Behold before ye,' cried that militant prelate William of Juliers, 'behold before ye men armed for your destruction! Our hope is in the name of the Lord, invoke His aid.' Then, when a priest had raised the Sacred Host high above the kneeling throng, William of Renesse made known the battle cry—'Flanders for the Lion,' and then each man took up a handful of earth and pressed it to his lips, by way perhaps of spiritual communion, perhaps to testify their love for the soil of Flanders and that they were sworn to defend it.

Before the battle commenced, a frugal repast was served out to the men. The town archives of Bruges have preserved for us the bill of fare—fish, eggs, mustard and sorrel. Nor were omens lacking which presaged the fortune of the coming fray. A flock of doves hovered about the heads of the Flemish host, whilst over the French squadrons there wheeled ravens. Rumour said too that the Count of Artois had risen from his bed full of evil forebodings, that his favourite hound had attacked him and almost fastened to his throat, and that when he sprang into his saddle, his charger had reared three times before he would start. A more certain augury of misfortune was the impatient ardour which fretted his soul, and some grey-headed knights called to mind that fifty-three years before his father's impetuous temper had, at the battle of Mansourah, wrecked another French host.

Amongst the mercenaries whose assistance the French King had bought was a band of famous archers recruited in Genoa. These men at the opening of the conflict, stealthily advancing along the road to Sweveghem, presently espied on the other side of a thick hedge which skirted the banks of a stream a company of Flemish bowmen, and in less than the twinkling of an eye the arrows of the Italians were playing havoc with them. But if the foreigners' sharpshooting discomfited their opponents, it afforded no consolation to their French paymasters, and one of them appealed to Artois. 'Sire,' he burst out in the bitterness of his soul, 'sire, if these villains do so much, the day will be theirs, and what share will the nobles have in the glory?' 'Then let them charge,' was the reply. In vain that shrewd old fox Flotte pointed out that when once the Italian archers had broken the Flemish ranks and constrained them to quit their entrenchment, the nobles alone would have the glory of putting the enemy to flight. Artois refused to hear him. 'By the devil,' he cried, 'Pierre, you have still the wolf's skin,' and the knights rushed forward, trampling under their horses' hoofs the Italian archers, and even cutting their bow-strings with their swords.

There is some consolation in the thought that the littleness of these fine gentlemen was the cause of their overthrow. The marshy land—the *Bloed Meersch*, as it was afterwards called—in the foreground of the Flemish camp was everywhere intersected by streams, and deep and broad dykes, with hedges on their banks thick and high. (Such is still the character of the landscape in many parts of Flanders). These the Flemings had cut down, and with the felled brushwood they had concealed the water. The Frenchmen, unacquainted with the nature of the country, failed to perceive the trap which had been laid for them, and in an instant hundreds of men and horses were struggling in a watery grave, and the few who succeeded in reaching land were received by their opponents on the points of their spears. Then followed a hardly-fought contest, for though the knights who had first charged had been nearly all slain those behind them were legion, and the streams, now choked up with dead bodies, no longer barred the way. For a moment the Flemish were driven back and for a moment panic was imminent, but Guy of Namur, turning round to the great Abbey Church of St. Mary which towered behind him, cried out with a voice which echoed over the battlefield, 'Great Queen of Heaven, help us,' and with that cry he so heartened his wavering forces that they returned with renewed courage to battle.

During the *mêlée* which followed, Rudolphe of Nesle was struck down—a three-fold traitor this man; a traitor to his country, for he was a Fleming of pure blood; a traitor to the traditions of his own house, for in his veins flowed the blood of Dierick of Alsace, and the nobler blood of Erembald; and a traitor to his wife, for she was a daughter of the Count of Flanders. But in spite of it all he was a brave knight; he had gone farther that day than any Frenchman, and he preferred to die rather than to yield up his sword. By a strange coincidence, Jacques de Châtillon, who had been Rudolphe's successor in the government of Bruges, was fighting by his side when Rudolphe fell, and he too was cut down by the Flemish pikes. Not far off an old man was seen to throw himself on his knees. He had that day put on mail for the first time, thinking when he did so, not to take part in the conflict, but to have his share in the triumph which every Frenchman believed that morning would be its issue. Somehow or other he had been drawn, in spite of himself, into the thick of battle, and now loudly cried to his friends to carry him out, but no man had pity on him, and he was presently trampled to death by his own comrades.

Thus perished Chancellor Flotte, the foremost of Philippe's law lords, of that new *noblesse de robe* which he had raised up to counterbalance the might of the old *noblesse d'épée*, of that band of *chevaliers ès lois*, as they loved to style themselves, by whose astute aid he was gradually changing monarchy into despotism, and who, as Kervyn notes, 'under the grandson of St. Louis, became the tyrants of France.' Philippe had found him on the dunghill, and he made him to sit among the princes of his people. He was a shrewd, hard-headed man of business, and of good qualities, at least, he possessed these: fidelity to the cause he served, and loyalty to the man who made him. He had sworn not to return to France until he had wiped out the indignity which had been put on him by Bruges, and, as we have seen, he kept his word.

On the other side it had gone hard with the Provost of Maestricht, who was carried out of the battle with his temples streaming with blood. If it had not been for the presence of mind of his esquire, this circumstance would perhaps have caused a panic. He, swiftly buckling on his master's armour and galloping into the thick of the fight, cried out, 'It is I, William of Juliers, come back to do battle,' and so saved the situation.

It was not yet noon when the Count of Artois dashed to the front, crying out as he did so, 'Let those who are faithful follow.' Presently he came to a great dyke. Digging his spurs into his horse's flanks, he cleared it at a bound, and was alone in the midst of the Flemings. In an instant he had seized the banner of Flanders and torn it to shreds, but in bending forward to grasp it, his foot slipped out of his stirrup, and William Van Sæftingen, a monk of Hacket's abbey at Lisseweghe, who had fled from his cell to join the fight, dragged him from his saddle, and at the same moment someone wrenched away his sword.

'I surrender, I surrender,' he cried, but with brutal irony his assailants feigned not to understand, and before Guy of Namur could interfere to save him, the Count of Artois was dead.

Although deprived of their leaders, the French knights fought with their wonted valour, but amid the slime and dykes of the *Bloed-Meersch* cavalry was worse than useless, and before nightfall the first and second lines of the great army of invasion were cut to pieces. The third battalion— the reserve force—had taken no part in the engagement, and a handful of the men who formed it succeeded in making their escape, but they fled in the greatest disorder, and their retreat was nothing less than a rout.

For the rest, seventy-five noblemen, a thousand knights and three thousand esquires were among the slain, and the sum-total of the French losses are said to have amounted to twenty thousand, whilst the Flemish estimated theirs at a hundred all told.

So great was the number of the golden spurs which the conquerors wrenched from the heels of the French knights who had fallen that they measured them by the bushel, and be it noted that the cavaliers of the period in question wore but one spur. Some of these trophies William of Juliers sent to his church at Maestricht, and the rest were hung up in the Church of St. Mary at Courtrai.

This brilliant victory which the tradesmen of Flanders had gained over the flower of French chivalry made such an impression on the hearts of the people that to this day there is hardly a Fleming who is ignorant of the battle of the Golden Spurs. Nay, at the news of the victory of Courtrai, on all sides hope was re-born in the breast of the people, and the cry of liberty resounded throughout Europe. In France, at Toulouse and Bordeaux, the citizens took heart and drove out Philippe's officers. In Italy, while Florence showed signs of restiveness, Bologna, Mantua, Parma and

Verona made solemn treaty together to defend their rights. In Switzerland the echoes of Morgarten responded to the shout of triumph which had gone up from the battlefield of Grœninghe. In Hainault, at Liège, in Brabant, in Holland, a like enthusiasm was shown, and it was the same elsewhere. Thus Kervyn poetically,[26] and it is worthy of note that at Rome Pope Boniface VIII., who seems to have held the Flemish in no little esteem, caused public rejoicing to be made in honour of this triumph of democracy.

Breidel and De Coninck are said to have been knighted on the field of battle—a tradition which hardly supports that other tradition which makes them men of noble birth. Be this as it may, the men of Bruges have not forgotten them, and some ten years since they were sufficiently ill-advised to set up beneath the shadow of their historic belfry a statue in honour of these heroes, which in no way harmonizes with its surroundings, and every year since its erection it has been their wont to deck it with garlands, and, grouped around its base, to sing hymns in honour of the men who rescued their city from tyranny and drove the French out of Flanders.

Notwithstanding her enormous losses at the battle of Courtrai, France had not yet disarmed, nor was it until July 1303 that Philippe le Bel, in order to save Courtrai, which was at that time being threatened by the Flemish, at last consented to liberate their Count as a preliminary to negotiations for peace, but on condition that if terms were not agreed on by the following spring, he would again yield himself prisoner.

Great was the joy of the men of Bruges when, towards the close of October, their Sovereign returned to Winendael. They had forgotten the evil things which they themselves had endured at his hands in the days of his prosperity, and were mindful only of his own suffering during his long imprisonment, and many of them, says the Friar of Ghent, when they saw him once more amongst them, were affected to tears. Guy's sojourn at Bruges was not destined to be a long one. The negotiations with France fell through, and he scorned to break his word. When in the month of June (1304) the appointed day arrived, he quietly went back to his prison at Compiègne, and Philippe once more led his troops into Flanders, and with some measure of success. But the French King was in reality weary of the conflict. If the campaign should be prolonged, experience told him that in all probability fortune would favour the Flemish, and he again consented to treat with Guy and his burghers. Early in the new year terms had been practically agreed upon, and a treaty of peace was on the point of being signed when, on the 7th March (1305), the old Count died. The negotiations, however, were not broken off. Robert of Bethune was at once released from prison, Philippe acknowledged his right to the county of Flanders, by May he had reached his dominions, and early in June a definite treaty of peace was at length signed. Robert, however, was now an old man enfeebled in health and broken in spirit by the hard captivity he had so long endured, and the treaty to which he had set his hand, behind, it would seem, the backs of his burghers, was presently found to contain conditions to which they had never assented—conditions so disastrous to the interests of Flanders that they refused to ratify it. Then followed fresh negotiations

III.—Genealogical Table of the Counts of Flanders from Baldwin VIII. to Guy de Dampierre.

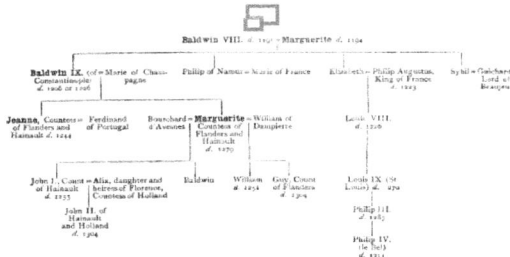

which dragged on for fifteen years, during which time Philippe himself was gathered to his fathers, nor was it until May 20, 1320, that terms of peace were at length agreed upon.

CHAPTER XVI

The Great Charter—The Belfry and the Tower of Notre Dame

STRANGE as it may seem, not only during the civil conflicts in the early days of Guy's reign, but during the turmoil and warfare which succeeded them, Bruges increased alike in prosperity, and comeliness, and might. True, she lost her charters when the belfry was burned down in 1280. Some said that the Count himself had fired it with a view to their destruction, and the new law which Guy had promulgated on May 25, 1281, as the burghers bitterly complained to the French King, was not worthy of the name of law, 'seeing that amongst other errors it ordained that criminals, in certain cases, should not be served with notice of trial nor suffered to state their defence, and that all the ancient rights and liberties of the city were either abrogated or curtailed.' Nevertheless, when Guy was hard pressed by Philippe le Bel, in order to conciliate the burghers he had re-established the ancient charter, and when in 1297 Philippe annexed Flanders, he, in his turn, confirmed it. Finally, after the expulsion of the French in 1304, one of Guy's sons, Philip of Thielt, who was at that time carrying on the government in the name of his captive father, filled with gratitude at the part which Bruges had taken, granted her a new and most liberal charter, in which all her old liberties were confirmed and even extended. This charter was probably drawn up by the sheriffs of Bruges themselves. When Robert of Bethune ascended the throne, in 1305, he at once confirmed it. Every succeeding Count, when he first entered the city, solemnly swore to maintain it intact, and it remained the fundamental basis of the civil and criminal law of Bruges until 1619.

The charter in question contains seventy articles, forty-eight of which deal with criminal law, and the remainder with civil law. Many of them express a breadth of view and liberality of spirit which, considering the epoch at which they were drawn up, is not a little surprising. Gheldorf in his *Ville de Bruges* (p. 321, etc.) gives the whole document in the original Flemish.

Note, amongst not a few prudent enactments, Article 33. It is so interesting, and denotes so clearly what progress Bruges had now made in the paths of law and order, that we cannot pass it over in silence. By it the citizen of Bruges was entirely set free from the superstitious and barbarous obligation of trial by battle. Henceforth, any man convicted of sending a challenge to a burgher was liable to a fine of sixty livres, in these days no small sum.

If such challenge had been accepted, half of the fine went to the Count, and half to the town, and the challenged burgher was also mulcted in a similar sum; if, however, he had refused the challenge he himself received a quarter of the fine, and, in that case, the Count received his full thirty livres, and the town only fifteen. Any man amenable to the city magistrates, who had lived for a year and a day within the limits of the city franchise and paid his taxes, was considered a citizen.

There were, no doubt, a number of persons living in Bruges who were not amenable to the city magistrates. The feudal lords, for example, though it was open to them, if they would, to enrol themselves as citizens, and not a few availed themselves of the privilege; persons submitted to the jurisdiction of the Franc; perhaps also the members of the Count's household, and the members of religious communities; and we know that from time immemorial there had been a large colony of foreign merchants in Bruges.

The municipal machinery by which the city was governed seems to have been, at this time, at all events, of a somewhat complicated nature. There were two distinct corporations, each presided over by its burgomaster.

The first consisted of the *écoutète*, or representative of the Count, the burgomaster and thirteen *Echevins*, who, according to Gheldorf, were the sole judges in Bruges. The manner of their appointment is uncertain; but we know that, save in the case of their having been convicted of felony or of having falsely administered justice, they were irremovable during the single year which they held office, and that convicted criminals, artisans who had not abstained from manual labour for a year and a day, and the *Echevins* of the preceding year, were ineligible.

The second corporation consisted of its burgomaster and thirteen town councillors. It is doubtful what were the functions performed respectively by these corporations. Perhaps the first, in addition to its judicial functions, was a legislative assembly, and the second administered the affairs of the town.

Curiously enough the original Flemish version of the charter of 1304 is mute as to the method of election alike of the college of *Echevins* and the town council, but Gheldorf has discovered among the archives of Bruges another version containing an article which gives minute directions on this head.

It was evidently drawn up in the interest of the members of the great city guilds, and awards to them the lion's share of all the appointments in question, viz.: the right to name absolutely all the town councillors and five of the thirteen *Echevins*, as well as a voice indirectly in the election of four others and in the nomination of each of the burgomasters. It allots to the burghers generally the right only to present eight persons to the Count in order that he may select from among them four more *Echevins*, and ordains that the members of the city council, and the nine *Echevins* thus appointed, shall elect the remaining four, and furthermore that the *Echevins* shall elect their own burgomaster, and the *Echevins* and councillors together, the burgomaster of the city council. Gheldorf conjectures that the charter which he discovered among the archives of Bruges was only a rough draft of the charter of 1304; that for some reason or other the clause anent elections was omitted from the fair copy, but that the method of procedure therein ordained was later on sanctioned by Philip of Thiette in a separate charter. If this be so, the document in question would seem to have disappeared.

It has been conjectured above that the *Echevins* of Bruges were not only magistrates, but also legislators, but even if this were so, the power which they wielded was less than it at first sight appears, for overshadowing the might of the *Echevins* was the might of the Colossus which appointed them, and the trade guilds had a practical veto over all their acts. These to be legal and valid must first have been stamped with the city seal, and the city seal was stored up along with the city archives in a strong chamber in the thickness of the belfry walls, secured by four wrought-iron doors with ten locks and ten keys, eight of which were in the hands of the guildsmen. Butchers, bakers, shoemakers, tailors, weavers, brokers, carpenters, smiths, the deans of each of these companies possessed a key without which it was impossible to open the doors of the municipal treasury, and these were the men who in reality governed Bruges when she was at the zenith of her power, and who continued to do so until her glory had faded away and she

THIRTEENTH-CENTURY IRON GATES IN BELFRY

was rapidly sinking to the position of a second-rate provincial town. To-day the old archive chamber is without its rolls, and without its great seal, but it is still closed by the wrought-iron gates which once secured them, though they are now seldom locked, and whosoever will may come and go at pleasure. It will be interesting to note anent these gates that the town accounts for the year 1290 has the following entry: *Item, Erembaldo fabro, pro januis ferreis ad thesaurarium in Halla, lxxxi. lb.* The name then of the smith who forged them was Erembald, and he received for his labour the sum of eighty-one livres, not on the whole an exorbitant fee.

The mention of the archive chamber brings us naturally enough to the great tower which contains it, to that belfry of Bruges which had just risen from its ashes more beautiful than of yore, the belfry of Bruges as it is now, without indeed its crowning glory, the octagonal lantern of the later fourteen hundreds, but without also the sorry disfigurements inflicted by the hand of the restorer a hundred years after.

The original structure was built in the days of the first Counts of Flanders, perhaps before the close of the eight hundreds, not of wood, as was formerly supposed, but probably of rough *velt* stone, the material employed for nearly all the buildings of that period. Whether any portion of the first belfry was left standing after the great fire of 1280 is a moot point, but maybe the foundations of the lower portion of the walls were spared, and that these were incorporated into the new building. Monsieur Gilliodts, who at present holds the office of city archivist, and probably knows more about his native town than anyone else, is of this opinion. Whether or no it be well founded is a question for experts to decide, if they can. In any case there can be no doubt as to the appositeness of the learned archivist's remark anent the present building. 'For six hundred years,' he says, 'this belfry has watched over the city of Bruges. It has beheld her triumphs and her failures, her glory and her shame, her prosperity and her gradual decay, and, in spite of so many vicissitudes, it is still standing to bear witness to the genius of our forefathers, to awaken alike memories of old times and admiration for one of the most splendid monuments of civic architecture which the middle age has produced.'

The other great tower of Bruges dates also from this period. It equals the first in comeliness and, calmly rising into the heavens some hundred feet above the highest point of the Bell-tower, surpasses it in the unadorned majesty of its grand proportions, for the sublime steeple of Notre Dame is in itself beautiful, and neither possesses nor requires embellishment. It is the first object which meets the eye of the Ostend fisherman as he nears his native coast, and seems more completely to dominate the old Flemish city, and the fair emerald landscape which surrounds it, than does the Belfry itself.

It took the men of Bruges, it is said, a hundred years to pile up this huge mass of tawny stone and golden-hued and blushing brick, and so marshy and unstable was the site on which they placed it, that as much material was needed for the foundations as is contained in that portion of the structure which rises above the soil, and the tower of Notre Dame, be it noted, measures from base to weathercock no less than four hundred and eleven English feet. It is said to be slightly out of the perpendicular, and a story is told—it is probably only a story—that the architect, on its completion, perceiving this defect, in despair threw himself from the summit and so was dashed to pieces; but for all that they buried him in consecrated ground, and his mausoleum was the splendid monument which he himself had erected.

The Church of Notre Dame was without the city boundary until the year 909. Up to that date it formed part of the domain of the lords of Sysseele. This ancient manor was submitted to the jurisdiction of Bruges towards the close of Guy's reign. The great square tower which was formerly the home of the lords of Sysseele is still standing, pleasantly situated on the outskirts of Maele Woods. With its Gothic gateway, its corner turrets, and its high-pitched roof it still forms a sufficiently picturesque group, but alas! it has recently been restored, and has thereby lost all trace of its conflict with time.

Bruges obtained also during the reign of Guy of Dampierre recognition of her disputed right to exercise jurisdiction over Sluys and Damme, and in 1289 a concession of less moment, but nevertheless one not to be despised. At the instance of his Countess, Isabelle of Namur, and 'in consideration for services rendered,' Guy made over, at this time, to the city for ever his right to succeed to the property of bastards dying without issue.

CHAPTER XVII

Louis of Nevers

LOUIS OF NEVERS, the eldest son of Count Robert of Bethune, inheriting from his grandfather Guy alike his brilliant qualities and his grave defects, was destined, like him, to be crushed by the weight of two overweening passions: love of gold, and love of self.

At first an ardent patriot, he had set himself at the head of the communes of Flanders in their struggle against his father's misgovernment—a misgovernment brought about first by fear of France, and later on, in his old age, by the spectre continually before his eyes of the fortress in which he had been so long immured at Compiègne; but what threats and force and a French prison could not accomplish in Louis of Nevers, was afterwards effected by hard cash, and presently Prince Louis the Patriot, his pockets well lined with French gold, so played on the terrors of his old father, a dotard of eighty-two, that he compelled him to acquiesce in a treaty with France, which his better judgment told him would be disastrous for the future of his realm (May 5, 1320).

Perhaps Louis would have gone further still, perhaps he was plotting even now the immediate destruction of Flanders.

Towards the close of the year 1320 when Robert, after signing at Paris the treaty in question, once more returned to his native land, thinking to obtain some little breathing time before he set out on the last dread journey, his chamberlain introduced to his presence a young man, who, in a voice broken with tears, avowed that he had been commissioned to poison him. 'And wherefore didst thou think to commit this crime?' said the old Count. 'Sir,' replied the youth, 'I was driven to it by the Prince of Nevers, who bade me follow the instructions of Brother Walter the hermit'—a monk whom Robert loved well—and little by little he learned that his death was to have been the signal for an outbreak which was to hand over all Flanders to the King of France.

Whatever may have been the truth of the mysterious youth's story; Robert believed it, presently Prince Louis was arrested and thrust into prison, and it was probably owing to the intervention of the burghers, who either did not credit the charge against him, or were still influenced by feelings of regard for their old champion, that his life was spared. Be this as it may, the Count of Nevers was shortly afterwards set at liberty on his undertaking to leave Flanders within eight days. This was on the 6th of April.

No sooner was Louis a free man than he set out for the French capital, where, three months later, on July 6, 1322, his inglorious career came to an end, and only two months afterwards Count Robert himself paid the debt of nature.

Rumour said that both Robert and Louis had been poisoned by Robert of Cassel—a younger son of Robert of Bethune—and that he had driven his elder brother out of Flanders with a view to his own succession.

Certain it is that the Lord of Cassel at once set claim to the throne, and at first it seemed probable that he would obtain it. He had for a long time past been mustering his forces, and now he had at his disposal a considerable army; all the stronghold in Flanders were in his hands, his father's ministers were his staunch and devoted friends, and so redoubtable did he seem that the French King refused to accept the homage of Louis of Nevers' eldest son, who also claimed the throne, and was now in Paris, alleging that it was for the Court of Peers to decide who was the rightful heir to the county of Flanders.

If Robert had been able to gain the support of the burghers, his triumph would have been assured, but they knew him to be a proud and ambitious man; the crime of parricide was associated with his name, and in spite of his professed devotion to the popular cause they profoundly distrusted him. More than a year before, Bruges and Ghent had made a solemn league and covenant together to defend their rights and liberties against any man who should attempt to infringe them, and had appointed a committee of ten burghers to watch over their common interests. These men, convinced that the feeble hands of a youth would lightly hold the reins of government, without waiting for the decision of the peers, invited the Count of Nevers to Flanders, proffered him their homage, and shortly afterwards informed the French King that if he should any longer delay to acknowledge Louis's right to the throne, they would themselves undertake the administration of the county.

King Charles submitted the more easily because he too saw in the youth of the burghers' candidate a guarantee of his own influence, but before he would consent to receive Louis's homage he exacted from him a secret promise that as soon as he should have consolidated his power, he would choose for his advisers the men whom he (Charles) should select.

Louis's first act upon taking possession of his dominions was one calculated to cause profound irritation to the citizens of Bruges. His uncle, Count John of Namur, had thrown in his lot with Robert of Cassel, and in order to purchase his support, Louis appointed him warden of Sluys, an office which had hitherto been held by the burghers of Bruges and Damme. Whereupon the committee of ten began to tremble for their commerce. Soon a mob of angry citizens, headed by Louis himself, who hoped by his presence to keep them in hand, were on the road to Sluys, and presently they returned to Bruges with the Count of Namur in chains. Louis had just succeeded in saving his life (July 1323). In vain his wife besought the intervention of Charles le Bel. The time-honoured rights of the citizens of Bruges must be maintained—thus the committee of ten, and Louis retired in dudgeon to France, and his uncle into the burghers' prison.

Although John grumbled not a little at the restraint, and especially that his gaolers would not suffer him to hear Mass at St. Donatian's, his life in the Steen was not without compensations. The beds there were good, prisoners were permitted to receive their friends, on festivals his rooms were decked with flowers, and the burghers supplied him with good cheer in abundance. Singing and music beguiled the day, cards and dice the night, and it was owing to the disorder consequent upon these revels that he presently made his escape. When, at length, the news leaked out, Bruges was in consternation. In the midst of it, Count Louis returned, and not alone. The burghers noted with indignation that he had brought with him as chief Minister a Frenchman, and a Frenchman who bore a name of evil repute—Chancellor Flotte's son William, the lordly Abbot of Vezelay—and worse still, that he shunned the counsel of those of his own race.

For the moment, however, Bruges had nothing to fear. Her rights over the port of Sluys were acknowledged, and John of Namur publicly forgave the burghers for his arrest and imprisonment. But Louis of Nevers was no longer the ingenuous orphan who in days of yore had sought the protection of his faithful commons. If he were lacking in strength of will, it was not the committee of ten, but the King of France who knew how to manipulate him. But in reality he was no weakling. True he was the tool of Charles le Bel, but in favouring his interests he was playing at the same time his own game. He was a voluptuary, if you will, and a voluptuary who found pleasure in low company and unrefined vice. He delighted in the buffoonery of dwarfs and jesters, whom he enriched at his subjects' cost. His chief favourite was one John Gheylinc, a groom whom he calls in his charters his counsellor and his friend, and if he had had his way he would have given him his daughter to wife. Added to this he was proud and revengeful, devoid of pity, and not only an unfaithful husband, but a cruel one into the bargain.

But for all that Louis was no fool; he had inherited alike the perverse humour and the brilliant intellect of his father and his great-grandfather. With consummate skill he played Ghent against Bruges, and Bruges against

Ghent, and Edward of England against Charles of France; and though the chief object of his life was the gratification of his wayward impulses, in his efforts to attain it he showed no little ability.

Such was the prince whom the communes of Flanders had set over them, but Louis rarely honoured the Netherlands with his presence. The dissipation of his Court at Nevers was more to his taste than the humdrum respectability of his burgher nobles, and his vicious life was there less *en evidence* and less criticised than in the democratic towns of Flanders. His absence, however, was a greater cause of embarrassment to his Flemish subjects than his presence in their midst would have been, for his lieutenant, the Lord of Aspremont, vexed them with oppressive taxes to enrich foreign favourites, and though in the great towns the influence of the burghers was powerful enough to hold him in check, in the country he had a free hand. Here dominated great Leliaert lords who had been for years past in the pay of France: the Moerkerkes, the Praets, the Ghistelles, and the rest, men who had fought, or whose fathers had fought, at Courtrai, and mindful how many of their kinsmen had fallen beneath the rude battle-axes of the Saxon Karls, thought only of vengeance. These men were wont to sally forth from their castles to take fines from those whom they feared most, and if their victims resisted, they put them to death.

'Intolerable are the manners of the Karls: with dishevelled beards, garments in tatters, and shoes in shreds, they would fain tame knights. With their knotted clubs and their long knives thrust into their girdles they are as proud as lords, and think that all the universe is theirs—God blast them! But we shall know how to chastise these men. They shall be drawn on hurdles and hanged on gibbets. The Karls must bend before us.'[27]

Thus the Leliaert nobles; but they reckoned without their hosts. The spirit which animated the Saxons of Flanders in the fourteenth century was the same which had hurled their ancestors against the tyranny of Richilde in the twelfth; which had driven the Erembalds to dash themselves to pieces rather than submit to Charles the Dane; which had inspired the Blauvoets in the eleven hundreds to resist the exactions of Mathilde, and which only yesterday had nerved their fathers to withstand and conquer the armies of France.

And, as in those days, there was no lack of leaders—a Bertulph, a Wulfringhen, a Sporkin was always at hand when he was wanted—so now, in the time of their extremity, captains were found. These men led their ragged hosts against the castles of their oppressors, and soon the land was filled with smouldering ruins. Aspremont, unable to quell the storm, summoned the Count from Nevers, who entered Flanders early in 1325; but Louis had no army to curb his turbulent subjects and was thus compelled to treat with them. Philip of Axel, a citizen of Ghent, was appointed Governor of Flanders in place of the Lord of Aspremont. Fines were imposed, promises of amendment were made, but the armed bands were not dissolved, and no sooner had Louis turned his back than the trouble began again, whilst the efforts made to extinguish the conflagration only increased it. Here and there a homestead razed, some stray farmer kidnapped and perhaps hanged or broken on the wheel; these things but nerved the Karls to greater efforts, for every man believed that his turn would come next. Their chief leader was one Nicholas Zannekin, the richest and the mightiest of them all, a man of the same class as Bertulph, who, like him, despised the nobles of the Court, and, like him, was regarded as a slave.

During the temporary lull of hostilities at the opening of the year, he had deemed it prudent to seek refuge in Bruges, the only town in Flanders where a man obnoxious to the authorities had some chance of saving his head, and there he soon obtained as much influence with the burghers as he had hitherto exercised over the country-folk of his own race (the men of Furnes). Nor did he cease to remind them, ground down as they were by odious and illegal taxes, of their rights as free citizens and the duties which their station imposed, and when Sohier Janssone (another popular leader) who had taken possession of Ghistelle Castle, presently appeared before the city walls with booty and captives, Bruges flew to arms. Zannekin soon rallied to his banner all the neighbouring communes. Thorhout, Roulers, Poperinghe, Nieuport, Dunkirk, Cassel, Bailleul, Furnes, threw open their gates at his approach, and wherever he went he was hailed as his country's saviour. 'The men of Furnes,' says the Flemish chronicle, 'received him as the angel of the Lord, and showed more submission to him than to any other man, and gave him greater honour than if he had been Count or King.'[28] Robert of Cassel, who had gathered together a small band to oppose him, withdrew when he saw how matters stood, but Zannekin, backed as he was by the communes, had little fear of him, and it was, moreover, bruited abroad that Robert himself was not hostile to the insurrection.

Louis was now in Flanders; sometimes at Courtrai, sometimes at Ypres, often at Ghent, lavish in flattering promises to the burghers, holding out to them bright hopes of new liberties and larger privileges than any yet accorded to Flemish towns.

Presently the French King sent them gold, and passed his word that no treaty should be made with the insurgents without first taking the advice of the burghers of Ghent. From all which politic proceedings came this result—the Ghenters forgot their compact with Bruges of 1321, at first posed as mediators, and then openly went over to Louis's side and aided him with cash and men. At this juncture Louis attempted to treat with the insurgents. Let the points at issue be submitted to the arbitration of Robert of Cassel and the sheriffs of Ypres and of Ghent, and no sentence of death (this he guaranteed), or banishment, or mutilation, should be pronounced on any of the rebels. Bruges and her allies consented, and the arbiters made it known that they would receive a deputation of the insurgents on the 11th of June ensuing, at the great Abbey of Dunes. But meanwhile a Karl of Furnes was slain by a knight. This incident sufficed to throw the whole country round into uproar, and when, on the appointed day, Zannekin and his friends, all armed to the teeth, reached the abbey, not one of the judges was there to meet them—fear had kept them away—and the flame of rebellion waxed fiercer than before. Louis, at his wit's end, grew doubtful of his uncle's good faith. The Lord of Cassel, he thought, was secretly allied with his enemies to wrest from him his crown. Why not make away with him? and soon letters were dispatched to the bailiff of Warneton to keep a watch on Robert's movements, and when an opportunity offered, to cut off his head. This sentence was never executed. Louis's own chancellor warned Robert of his danger, and himself informed Louis of the motive which had impelled him to do so. 'I wished,' he said, 'to save the honour of the Count of Flanders in the eyes of men, and his soul from the vengeance of God.'

More hated than ever by reason of this odious attempt, and filled with fear at the news that Bruges had already garrisoned all the principal towns of West Flanders, Louis, at the head of four hundred knights, marched into Courtrai, prepared to renew hostilities in good earnest. It so happened that six burghers of Bruges arrived there at the same moment, and Louis forthwith put them under arrest. Thereupon Bruges made ready for battle, and sent messages to Courtrai that five thousand staunch men and true were on their way to rescue the imprisoned burghers. Louis, filled with consternation, broke down the bridges over the Lys and fired the *faubourgs* along its banks. There had been no rain for weeks, and the thatched roofs on the opposite side of the stream had been baked by a blazing sun. A strong wind was blowing in the direction of the city, and soon Courtrai itself was in flames. Meanwhile Louis was stationed in the market-place, and with him were the six merchants from Bruges. Perhaps he had intended to cut off their heads, perhaps to carry them with him to Lille, but the sight of their prince standing there surrounded by the Leliaert counsellors, by whose advice he had fired the town, and now preparing to seek safety in flight, so worked on the men of Courtrai that they forgot their burning homes and thought only of vengeance. The very women took part in the combat which ensued, and their sobs and cries excited their husbands yet more than the tocsin which all this time was shrieking over the city. Presently Louis was left alone. Some of his knights had fled, some had been taken prisoners, not a few had been slain, and when next day the men of

Bruges reached Courtrai, her citizens delivered him bound into their hands. They placed the Count of Flanders on a sorry steed, and loaded his counsellors with chains, and thus conducted them all to the capital, where the sheriffs at once proceeded to try them, for they had murdered, it was alleged, the peasants of Furnes, and reduced Courtrai to ashes—with this result: Louis was retained a prisoner in the Halles, and his counsellors were hurled from the windows of the Steen.

Never had the citizens of Bruges been so mighty as they were now. On the 30th of June her sheriffs had met in the Halles, and, in union with the Franc, the city of Ypres, of which town Zannekin was now governor, and of the other confederates, had appointed Robert Regent of Flanders. Louis from his prison had issued a charter approving what had been done, and the ambassadors of the French King, who on the 15th of July had reached Bruges with offers that the charges against Louis should be submitted to his judgment, were present to witness their triumph.

True, Ghent was still loyal to the captive at Bruges, but Ghent had been humbled in battle, and even Ghent was not united. Three thousand of her weavers had fled for refuge to the camp of Robert of Cassel, and Bruges replied to the French ambassadors that Louis could not be set free until Ghent had renounced her treaty with him, and had frankly joined hands with her. The ambassadors were disposed to agree to these terms, even though they knew that this meant all sovereignty in the hands of Bruges, but Ghent was too proud to submit. Though Louis had oppressed and misgoverned the rest of Flanders he had showered blessings on Ghent, and now that the worm had turned and conquered, and Louis was in prison, she would never consent to enter into an alliance with her hated rival. Far better that all the Karls should perish, far better that Flanders should become France.

In face of this opposition the French King cited Robert to Paris to justify his conduct in supporting rebels. The citizens of Bruges received the bearers of the summons 'with horns raised and dire threats,' and Robert refused to comply. Then came interdict and excommunication (the French Kings claimed the right to direct these ecclesiastical thunders); a few days later, in their conflict with Ghent, a check; presently, in consequence of the rigour of winter, the forced raising of the siege of that town; and lastly, rumours of a French invasion.

To retain Louis longer in prison were to risk, thought many, all that had been gained. Better release him now of their own free will, and when they were in a position to make terms, than be compelled to do so six months hence unconditionally at the point of the sword, which, seeing the trend and conjunction of events, would probably be the case.

Thus argued Bruges, and presently Louis went forth from the Halles to the Chapel of St. Basil, where he swore on the Holy Blood that he nourished no resentment against his captors, and that he would do his utmost to ward off the threatened invasion. This done he was once more a free man, and forthwith, after a hurried visit to faithful Ghent, hastened to Paris, where his patron assured him that as long as he followed his counsel, he could count on his friendship (this was in the month of March 1325), but that he was not in a position to help him for the moment, as he had other business in hand. Then once more Louis returned to Flanders, and after much confabulation, terms were agreed upon. The burghers were to build a monastery, and to send some hundreds of pilgrims to sundry shrines, to rebuild the churches destroyed during the recent tumult, to pay their just debts to the King and to the Count, and to swear fealty to the latter. Louis, on his part, undertook to respect their liberties, the King to re-establish free trade betwixt France and Flanders and to silence the thunder of the Church. Towards the close of April 1326 this convention was ratified, though, in all probability, none of the parties signing it had any intention of observing its terms. The burghers retained their former leaders, Louis refused to enter the town where he had lived eight months a captive, but neither party was at present in a position to recommence hostilities; for two years matters dragged on, and then the storm broke.

On February 1, 1327, King Charles le Bel had died, leaving an only daughter, a child of tender years, and a widow who was expecting some two months hence the hour of her delivery. France at this time was divided into two great parties. On the one side were the feudal lords, who, since the days of Philippe le Bel, had seen their power gradually passing from them into the hands of the King, and on the other, the citizens, who, during the same period, had witnessed their privileges daily contemned, their rights trampled on, and their trade threatened by the avidity of royal harpies. Each of these parties, then, was equally discontented with the present state of affairs, and each of them found the present moment a propitious one for changing it. The barons turned their eyes to Philippe of Valois, the next heir in the direct male line to the throne of St. Louis. The burghers hoped when the old King died that his Queen would give birth to a son, and failing this, they wished that the crown should devolve on his eldest daughter. Their hopes, as we know, were dashed to the ground by the birth of a second princess and the succession of Philippe of Valois. But they saw the finger of God in the extinction of the house of Philippe le Bel; they felt that the time had come to strike a blow for freedom, and they were only waiting for the Flemish burghers, who during thirty years had lavished blood and treasure in behalf of this sacred cause, to raise the standard of revolt.

'If once these Flemings cross our borders,' the barons had warned the new King, 'all France will join them.' Philippe determined to take the bull by the horns, and at Rheims on the day of his coronation he made his purpose known.

On the Count of Flanders devolved the duty of bearing the King's sword, but although he was present, with four-score knights, when the royal heralds called on him to perform his duty, he made no sign. Thrice they summoned him, and still he was silent. All men were filled with wonder, and the King demanded an explanation. 'Sire,' he replied, 'they 'summoned the Count of Flanders; I am Louis of Nevers.' 'What,' said Philippe, in feigned astonishment, 'art thou not also Count of Flanders?' 'Such men call me,' was the reply, 'but I hold not this office in fact. In no Flemish city save Ghent do I dare show my face.' 'Fair cousin,' replied the King, 'by the Holy Unction which hath this day flowed on our head, we will not go back to Paris until we have established thee in the peaceful possession of thy realm.' Some of his counsellors would have persuaded him to defer the expedition. France, they said, was unprepared, and to invade Flanders in the autumn was to risk disaster; but the King, who saw the importance of himself beginning the campaign, refused to hear them. He consulted Gauthier de Châtillon, who had served seven kings in their wars in the Netherlands. 'For the man who has a stout heart,' he answered, 'this is no inopportune season for battle.' 'Good,' replied the delighted King, as he embraced the old soldier. 'Let those who love me follow.'

With all speed he set about his preparations, and the great army which two months later (August 1328) assembled at Arras, collected from all parts of Europe, was such that the like of it had been never seen there before, and Arras had beheld the armies of Philippe IV. and Louis X.

Nicholas Zannekin, with ten thousand Karls, occupied Cassel, a fortified town some six miles inland from Dunkirk, perched on the top of a hill which rises well-nigh a thousand feet above the level of the sea, and stands solitary in the midst of the low land which surrounds it. Sohier Jansonne had brought him reinforcements to the number of six thousand men, and though messengers had been despatched to Bruges, to warn them of the French invasion, these men believed themselves strong enough to alone save Flanders.

During three days the French King sat down before Cassel awaiting the retreat of his foes. His knights' heavy chargers, weighted as they were with their own trappings, and the armour of the men who bestrode them, were unable to climb the steep sides of the mountain, and thus the cavalry were forced to remain idle spectators of the skirmishes which succeeded one another without ceasing. In vain the footmen multiplied their efforts;

they were in each case driven back, till at length Philippe in despair gave the word to burn the surrounding country, and presently the fertile plain was filled with flames and desolation, and all the land re-echoed with the wailing of old men and women and the shrieks of frightened children; but the Karls in their lofty fortress were as stable as the hill on which they stood, and at last, weary with slaughter, the French returned to camp, took off their heavy armour, and gave themselves over to revelry.

Whilst these things were going on at the foot of Mount Cassel, the Karls at its summit were holding council of war. The wisest of them would have waited until the Bruges burghers had had time to bring them help, others would have gone down under cover of night, and surprised the French in their tents, but Zannekin dismissed their words with disdain. 'What,' he cried, 'with the French King before us, not fight! Shall we, then, who know not what fear is, tremble at this man's fierce looks? Let us rather thank God that the foes we have so long waited for are now here, and profit by their confusion to slay them forthwith.' 'Ay, ay,' answered a thousand voices, and the Karls made ready for battle. 'They were brave men and free,' notes Villani, 'and they feared not to assail this most redoubtable host.'

The long summer's day was mingling with night when the Karls went down into the French camp, and before any one was aware of their presence they were in the midst of the barons, who, 'without armour and arrayed in gorgeous apparel, were going from tent to tent to gossip together of the day's doings.'[29] Presently a knight, one Rénaud of Loire, came forth to upbraid them for thus 'presuming to disturb the privacy of gentlemen.' He had taken the intruders for a company of his own troops returning late to camp. In less than the twinkling of an eye Rénaud was a dead man. Some of his comrades had essayed to defend him, but they shared his fate, and the Flemings marched on, not far now from the object of their quest—the royal pavilion. Philippe, like his knights, had lately dined, and now, replete with rich dishes and strong drink, he was dozing in his tent. Suddenly his chaplain plucked his sleeve. 'Mark ye, sir,' he whispered, as he peeped through the curtains, 'the Flemings are upon us.' 'A monk's nightmare,' muttered Philippe, and he was turning again to sleep when Miles of Noyers rushed in and confirmed the chaplain's fears. In a moment Philippe had buckled on his mail, and almost alone, for the greater number of his attendants had fled, went out to face the foe. The first man he met was Zannekin. His battle-axe was raised to strike, and in another moment it would have split open the King's skull had not Miles dexterously drawn Philippe aside. Then the tide of fortune turned, and soon all that was left of the Saxon host were three great heaps of corpses.

Zannekin was the last to fall, 'and his death cry was mingled with the voices of the royal chaplains intoning the antiphon of St. Denis.'

Of the sixteen thousand Flemings slain not one had attempted flight, not one of them had budged an inch. Each man fell where he had stood at the beginning of the conflict. If courage could have given the Karls victory, the day would have been theirs, but so great were the odds against them, that from the first they had but one ground for hope—that panic inspired by the suddenness of their coming would fight for them. On this poor chance Zannekin had ventured his all, and he paid the price of his temerity.

If the townsmen of Flanders had been made of the stuff of their country cousins disaster might have yet been averted, but these latter were full-blooded Saxons, and in all the cities, save haply Furnes, the burghers' power of resistance was in some measure rendered nugatory by their grandams' Celtic nerves.

So was it at Ypres. When the news of the disaster reached them the burghers were for instant submission if only Philippe could be prevailed on to guarantee their lives and their limbs. One man alone kept cool, and strangely enough that man was a clerk. From the pulpit of his own church (he was parish priest of St. Michael's) this sturdy representative of the Church Militant implored his fellow-citizens, 'for God's sake and the sake of the fatherland,' to show fight. But it was too late. That very day Miles Noyers entered the town with an overwhelming force, and the handful of labouring men who had been moved by their priest's appeal were cut to pieces.

So too was it at Bruges. When the news of the disaster reached them, the women went into hysterics and the men lost their heads, and in less than the twinkling of an eye, the lilies of France, run up by their own hands, were proudly floating over the belfry.

In spite of their pusillanimity, the reckoning which the burghers had to pay was a sufficiently onerous one: humiliation unspeakable, the city fathers on their knees suing for mercy in the dust of the Maele road, and worse—the charter of their liberties cancelled, their ramparts broken down, and a fine so heavy that they were never able to pay it; and worse still—not a few of their leading citizens, men of substance and renown, tortured to death, and all their wealth confiscated.

Amongst these note Lambert Bowine, captain of the Franc, and Willem de Deken, town burgomaster. His fate was the cruellest of all. He had fled to Brabant in the hope that the burghers there would protect him, but they showed themselves as craven as their fellows in Flanders. They handed him over to the French King, and poor Deken was carried to Paris, where he was mutilated, pilloried, put on the wheel, taken off again for fear he should die too soon, and bleeding, broken, in pitiable plight, but still alive, set in gaol till the morrow, when he was torn to pieces by wild horses. They gathered up the fragments of his poor mangled body and hung them on the great gibbet of Mont Faucen, by way of object lesson for the citizens of the capital.

These items made up the sum-total of the burghers' bill of costs, and it was the same all over the country. Not a town save Ghent preserved its liberties intact, and even beloved Ghent saw not a few of her burghers driven into exile. In less than three months ten thousand Flemings were done to death.

The Abbot of St. Martin's at Tournai explains how this came about. 'Louis's keen appetite for gold,' he says, 'increased in a marvellous manner his suspicions, and consequently the number of his victims. And the most galling part of it was that all this untarnished gold was squandered on harlots and on favourites, men too of mean estate some of them. His lackeys, his grooms, and even his barber were at Bruges installed in palaces which had once been the homes of honourable burghers.' The city archives bear witness to it.

At last, after long years of waiting, salvation came from England, at first indirectly, and afterwards through the active co-operation of Edward III. with the communes of Flanders.

Of course England acted from self-interest. She had no more love for the down-trodden burghers of Flanders than they had for the comfortable yeomen on the other side of the channel; and even if her sympathy had been ever so great, she could not have raised a finger to help them unless she had been likewise impelled by some less ephemeral motive. Individuals may sometimes indulge in the luxury of pure benevolence; trustees, in justice to their clients, can rarely afford to do so. Occasionally the interests of the latter may go hand in hand with their own charitable inclinations, and then they may pose as philanthropists, and if the pit applaud their seeming generosity, so much the better

In the case before us, however, no such protestations were made. The freedom of the Flemish communes was vital to the prosperity of England, and the motives which inspired the respective parties were avowedly motives of mutual accommodation. In those days the wool growers of the island kingdom had but one customer, the mammoth guilds of Flemish weavers, and they, in their turn, could nowhere find such famous wool as in the English market.

'So fine was the breed of English sheep at this period,' notes Green, 'that the exportation of live rams for the improvement of foreign wool was forbidden by law, though a flock is said to have been smuggled out of the realm shortly after, and to have become the source of the famous merinos of Spain,' and the magnitude of the wool trade between England and Flanders may be estimated from this fact. In a single year Edward received more than eighty thousand pounds from duties levied on wool alone.[30]

When, therefore, in the autumn of 1336, hostilities broke out between Edward III. and Philip of France, and Louis of Nevers, at the instigation of the latter, caused every Englishman in Flanders to be put under arrest, and Edward by way of reprisal forbade the exportation of English wool, all Flemish looms ceased work, and the towns were filled with misery. But the sheep-farmers of England suffered equally with the weavers of Bruges, and soon the English King was forced in the interests of his own subjects to attempt negotiations, first with Louis of Nevers, and when this failed, directly with the burghers.

It was in consequence of Edward's efforts to attach the communes to his interest that the Count of Flanders about this time entirely reversed his home policy, essaying by the largeness of his promises and concessions to induce the communes to side with France, and among the cities which most benefited by his changed humour Bruges stood first. She was permitted to deepen and widen her moats, to reconstruct her ramparts, and by a charter, dated April 14, 1337, all her ancient rights and liberties were re-established and confirmed.

This then was the first boon which Bruges received from England's intervention—a boon, in truth, conferred indirectly, but no small one for all that.

Ghent was the only city which did not participate in Louis's favours. Of the cause of this, of Louis's relentless persecution of the town he had once held dear, of her heroic resistance and ultimate triumph, thanks to the patriot Van Artevelde and the support of Edward III., it is not here the place to treat in detail. These things belong to the story of Ghent. Suffice it to say that Bruges, which for a time had supported Philippe and Louis in a half-hearted way, at last, seeing how matters stood, and that Ghent was conquering all along the line, joined hands with her; that at a solemn assembly of the representatives of the city and the Liberty of Bruges, and the cities of Ypres and Ghent, held under the presidency of Van Artevelde at the Abbey of Eeckhout early in the spring of 1337, and only a few days after Louis's re-establishment of the Bruges charter of rights, their alliance was solemnly proclaimed; that at this assembly it was furthermore enacted that each of the three *bonnes villes*—Ghent, Ypres and Bruges—should choose three deputies to watch over their interests and administer the country; that on the 29th of April a deputation from all the towns and communes of Flanders, headed by Jacob van Artevelde, waited on Louis at Maele, and there recounted to him all that had taken place; and that he, finding submission the only course open to him, consecrated the acts of the burghers with the seal of his approval, and, once more burthening his soul with perjury, solemnly swore to maintain intact all their rights and liberties. From that moment until his death Van Artevelde was ruler of Flanders. Essentially a man of peace, in face of the great conflict raging between England and France the main object of his policy was to keep Flanders out of the fray, and for some time his efforts were successful. So much so that he even accomplished the difficult task of negotiating treaties of commerce with each of the belligerents.

It was only the perfidy of the French King which at length drove him to take sides with England. Philippe and Louis had broken their most solemn engagement before he determined to seek out Edward III. at Bruxelles and in the name of the communes of Flanders solemnly recognize him as the successor of St. Louis.

During the nine years of Van Artevelde's government Flanders prospered exceedingly, and during all that time, thanks to his consummate abilities and Edward's generous support, she held her own. At length, when the fear of her enemies was taken away by too much prosperity and an overweening confidence, the besetting sin of the Flemish people wrecked all.

The country-side had grown jealous of the city, the lesser communes of the three *bonnes villes*. The canker had spread further still; town suspected town, guild was at loggerheads with guild, and even individual citizens began to cast evil eyes on one another; and, added to this, there was the hatred of rivals jealous of Artevelde's great position; and Louis, who was now residing in France, through his agents blowing the fire.

Presently the crisis came. Early in July the representatives of the communes had met at Bruges for the purpose of electing a regent, and Sohier of Courtrai, Artevelde's brother-in-law, with King Edward's consent, had been chosen to fill the office. On his return to Ghent after this conference the great tribune was besieged in his house by a mob of small tradesmen and street roughs in the pay of his rivals and of Louis of Nevers.

He had been plotting, they said, to hand over Ghent to the tender mercies of the English, who were going to pillage the town; he would make the Prince of Wales Count; he had taken advantage of his position to heap up a vast fortune, and had sent his treasure to London. In vain Van Artevelde tried to appease them; the sound of his voice but increased their fury, and his servants, who knew the risk he was running, dragged him from the window and would have had him seek refuge by a back way in a neighbouring church. Too late; the mob had by this time broken into the house, and a cobbler felled him dead on his own threshold. Thus perished the noblest man of his century, and with him too fell the grand edifice he had reared. The besetting sin of his people had once more shattered the mansion of Freedom.

The Count of Flanders did not long survive his illustrious victim. When the English victory of Cressy gave feudalism its death-blow, he fell fighting for the French King, and note this fact—Philippe of Valois was the one man to whom Louis had ever been faithful.

CHAPTER XVIII

Louis of Maele

LOUIS OF MAELE, the eldest son of Louis of Nevers, so called from the place of his birth, was a beautiful stripling of sixteen years when the old Count died. He too had fought at Cressy, had received honourable wounds there, and had been knighted on the battlefield. But if he possessed his father's courage, he was heir also to his inclination to crooked ways, as the communes of Flanders soon learnt to their cost. Immediately after the great defeat he had set out for Paris, where he did homage to Philippe of Valois, and from thence sent envoys to Halwyn to negotiate with the Flemish burghers, who, strangely enough, consented to accept him for their prince. Perhaps they thought that Louis's youth would render him manageable, perhaps inherent jealousy prevented them from agreeing on anyone else, but for all that, the long-headed Flemings deemed it expedient to make their own conditions—conditions which, whatever they may have been, Louis seems to have had no hesitation in accepting, for, by the end of November, we find him installed at Bruges, and—presage of his future policy—surrounded by the Leliaert nobles who had been his father's friends. Presently he publicly proclaimed the first part of his programme, and vehemently urged the communes to renounce their allegiance to Edward III. From this moment men had little doubt that the ultimate goal of his ambition was to crush the strength

MAELE CASTLE

of the towns. For generations the Kings of France had endeavoured to enslave them, and Philippe of Valois himself had broken his most solemn pledges, whilst the English monarchs, from time immemorial, had shown themselves their friends, and for fifteen years King Edward III. had backed fair promises with blood and sterling gold. Interest and inclination alike, then, resolved the burghers to stand by him, nay more, to draw the bonds of union closer by marrying his daughter to their Count. Louis, when the matter was first broached to him, refused to listen. He would never wed, he plainly told them, the daughter of his father's murderer, but when the burghers persisted, no less dogged than they, he resolved to cut the knot in true Flemish fashion. Not strong enough to risk a contest at Bruges, the chief centre, for the moment, of nationalism, he feigned acquiescence, and presently, along with the city fathers, set out for Bergue, where Edward was holding his Court. The meeting took place towards the middle of February, at the Abbey of St. Winoc, and Edward received the Flemish Count with every token of affection, solemnly assuring him, as he took him by the hand, that he was a stranger to his father's death, and presently Isabelle of England and Louis of Flanders mutually plighted their troth.

It had been arranged that the marriage should take place in the middle of April, and a fortnight previous to the appointed date Edward's ambassadors waited on Louis, who had meanwhile returned to Bruges, and besought him to take command of the English forces.

Next day he planned for their entertainment a great hunting party in Maele Woods. No sooner had the hawks been loosed than, feigning great zest for the sport, he set off at full speed and was soon out of sight of his companions, nor did he rein in his horse until he had crossed the French frontier and reached Lille.

Edward was furious when he learned what had happened, and Isabelle cut to the quick. She was in sooth, she said, Countess of Flanders, and until the day of her death she continued to wear the Flemish arms embroidered on her gown. As to the burghers, they at once took up arms, and it was only the mutual jealousy of Ghent and Bruges that saved the truant Count. His policy was to favour the latter town, in order that he might thereby hold in check alike her great rival and the other cities of Flanders.

Throughout his long and tumultuous reign of well-nigh forty years, by his lying, his meanness and his chicanery, Louis of Maele showed himself the worthy son of Louis of Nevers.

He made Bruges the seat of his government and his chief place of residence, and here he squandered in riotous living the gold which he everywhere extorted throughout the rest of his domains.

Embellished by splendid monuments, enriched by the presence of a lavish and luxurious Court, her trade fostered by privileges innumerable and concessions without end, the city on the Roya prospered marvellously during the reign of Louis of Maele. Advancing from day to day in comeliness and wealth and renown, she, during this period, attained the acme of her greatness. Merchants from every country in Europe bought and sold in her markets, ships from all parts of the world brought rich cargoes to her wharves. No less than twenty foreign Consuls occupied palaces within her bounds, and her population is said to have numbered two hundred and fifty thousand souls. But if Bruges now shone resplendent in a golden halo of magnificence, the moral squalor of her citizens equalled only the meanness of spirit of the man who had done such great things for her. Fickle, selfish, cowardly they had ever been, and they now only showed themselves grateful to their benefactor so long as it was in his power to help them, and, when they had gone over to the national party, only supported their new friends whilst their star was in the ascendant.

In 1379 Louis of Maele had granted them permission to construct a canal for the purpose of bringing the waters of the Lys to Bruges, doubtless with the object of preventing, by means of a greater flow of water, the silting up of the Zwyn, which even at this early period had already commenced. During four months, from the 19th of March to the 23rd of July, the men of Bruges were busy at this undertaking, and then a great army of Ghenters, fearing for their own commerce, went out and put them to flight. Louis was unable to afford protection, and the burghers threw open their gates and made common cause with his enemies.

Presently they prepared a sumptuous banquet in honour of their new friends. Among the guests who sat down to it was the Ghent leader, Jean Yoens, dean of the great guild of watermen. That night he died mysteriously of a malady which no physician could diagnose, and the gossips on 'Change shrugged their shoulders and whispered poison.

But though Bruges had allied herself to the city on the Lys, and a great army of Ghenters was, with her consent, encamped in her midst, her soul was rent with envy, and on May 13, 1380, her citizens surprised and slew no small number of them in the Friday Market, and then these sturdy burghers, still smoking with the blood of their guests, went and sought out Louis of Maele, and demanded from him fresh privileges by way of recompense for their devotion. Just two years later, on May 3, 1382, retribution followed.

For years past Louis had oppressed and persecuted the men of Ghent 'even as Pharaoh of old had persecuted the children of Israel'; of late fortune had singularly favoured his efforts; he had cut off all their supplies, and the town was sick with hunger. Such was the misery of the people that for a fortnight—we have it on the testimony of Philip van Artevelde—thirty thousand of them had not tasted bread. At length, driven to it by wretchedness, they determined to go forth and beard the lion in his den, and presently Philip van Artevelde and a handful of half-starved burghers set out for Bruges. He had called to his standard all men who were able to take the field, but a bare five thousand of them had answered his summons—to such pitiable plight had famine reduced the strength of the city of Ghent, one of the most populous towns in Europe.

When they reached Oedelem, in the neighbourhood of Maele Castle, Philippe sent envoys to Bruges to make one last effort to negotiate an honourable peace, but the guildsmen remembered their bloody triumph of two years ago, and boasted that in less than an hour they could easily cut to pieces this puny band of Ghenters; and presently Louis, at the head of eight hundred knights and forty thousand tradesmen—tailors, butchers, fishmongers and the like—unarmed and half drunk, in spite of his better judgment was compelled to go forth to battle. With such an auxiliary force behind him the issue was a foregone conclusion. At the first discharge of their opponents' artillery, the drunken rabble made for Bruges. The Ghenters gave chase, and ran so swiftly that they reached the city gates almost at the same moment as the men they were pursuing; one of the foremost of them was in time to thrust his pike between the doors at the moment the Bruges men were closing them, and soon Van Artevelde and his comrades were thronging into the city.

Louis, who had been unhorsed at the commencement of the stampede, had somehow or other managed to remount, and along with some thirty or forty knights had the good fortune to reach his palace in safety. From thence he sent out heralds to summon all his burghers under pain of death to assemble in the market-place. Hardly had he done so when Robert Maerschalck, the husband of one of his natural daughters, came in hot haste to the palace with tidings that Van Artevelde was now in the heart of the city. Night had already set in, and his counsellors, trembling for the safety of his person, would have had him remain indoors, but Louis refused, and accompanied by a handful of serving men, and crying, 'Flandre au comte au lion,' rushed out into the darkness. When he reached the Grande Place he knew that his cause was lost. It was filled indeed with armed men, but it was not the burghers of Bruges who had assembled there. Flaunting over the seething throng, he could distinguish the banner of Ghent. 'Put out your lights,' hissed the Count to his lackeys, 'and let each man think of himself.' Alone, under cover of the darkness and a buttress of St. Amand's Church—long since demolished—he unbuckled his coat of mail and put on the clothes of one of his serving-men.

About midnight he summoned up courage to knock at the door of a wretched hovel hard-by, and recognizing in the person who opened it a poor widow to whom he had often given alms, appealed to her generosity. 'Woman,' he whispered, 'save me; I am the Count of Flanders.' She pointed to a rickety ladder, and bade him go up to the garret. There, under a heap of straw, he lay all that night and all the next day. When darkness had again set in he made his way out of the city, and, after a host of hairbreadth adventures, presently reached Lille. 'Now mark,' comments wise old Froissart, 'all ye who hear this tale, consider what marvellous changes of fortune God in His good pleasure bringeth about. In the morning the Count of Flanders had thought himself one of the mightiest princes in Christendom, and in the evening he found it convenient to hide himself in the mean home of a poverty-stricken woman.'

As for Van Artevelde, he treated the conquered town with no little generosity. By the small hours of the morning he had completely gained the upper hand, and his first act was to forbid further slaughter, and all looting, and every kind of outrage under penalty of death. He next summoned the burghers of Bruges to a conference in the Grande Place. Hardly had they assembled than a member of Van Artevelde's own family was led bound into his presence. He had been taken red-handed in some act of violence. 'What,' exclaimed the great tribune, 'you, who should have been a pattern of obedience, the first to break my commands!' and he ordered that he should be flung headlong from one of the windows of the belfry. As he fell some men-at-arms caught him on the points of their spears, and a cruel shout of approbation welled from the throats of the Bruges men—'Behold a just judge, a man cut out for captain of Flanders!' and they swore that henceforth the burghers of Bruges would live in brotherly love with the burghers of Ghent.

But Van Artevelde, knowing the men he had to deal with, required something more tangible than their bare word, and the burghers were compelled to deliver into his hands a goodly number of hostages; to witness the destruction of three city gates:—the *Porte Ste. Croix*, the *Porte Ste. Cathérine* and the *Porte de Gand*, and thirty feet of wall around each of them; and lastly, to submit themselves to the two Ghent captains, Peter Van den Bossche and Peter de Wintere, whom Artevelde appointed governors of the town. For the rest he contented himself with requisitioning an ample supply of provisions for the famine-stricken town of Ghent, and for three whole days the high road from Bruges to that city was crowded with carts and waggons groaning under the weight of food stuffs.

At the expiration of that time, thanks to the energy and prudence of Van Artevelde, the markets were peacefully re-opened, and the town assumed its wonted aspect. During his short rule—it only lasted six months—trade revived, justice was rigorously administered, and peace reigned throughout Flanders. Then came the French invasion, the Flemish defeat at Rosebeke, and the great tribune's untimely death (November 27, 1382). The conquerors found his mangled body on the battlefield amongst a heap of slain, and they hung it in chains on a lofty tree, and the birds of the air devoured it.

Never had Flanders suffered a defeat so disastrous. 'Sixty thousand of her sons had perished,[31] the land was deluged with blood.'[32] A blow had been hurled at communal government from which it never really recovered.

Thanks to the intervention of Louis of Maele, and his son-in-law the Duke of Burgundy, backed by the support of certain great nobles whose goodwill the burghers had purchased with heavy bribes, Bruges suffered less at the hands of the French than the other communes of Flanders. She was not handed over to pillage, but the Breton mercenaries, disappointed of the rich booty which they thought to have obtained there, scoured the country round with fire and sword. 'The French,' says the monk of St. Denis, 'cut the throats of all whom they met, sparing neither rank, nor age, nor sex, and thus it may be truly said of them that they slew the widow and the orphan, the youth and the maid, the old man and the suckling at its mother's breast.' As for Louis of Maele, he approved what he could not prevent. 'Some people ask, most redoubtable lord,' said he to King Charles VI., 'how may best be crushed the turbulent spirit of this race—by sparing the land or by reducing it to a desert. As for me, I can only say: deal with the county of Flanders according to thy good pleasure, and whatsoever thou shalt deem fit to ordain I shall be contented.' In truth Louis's influence in the counsels of the French King was almost a thing of the past, and what little influence he still possessed was diminishing day by day. The campaign against Flanders had, indeed, been undertaken ostensibly for his behoof, but its real object was to deal a blow at England and to shatter the forlorn hope—the Flemish communes—of the restive communes of France; and when two years later (January 26, 1384) a truce was concluded between Richard II. and Charles VI., what Louis deemed his interests were wholly disregarded. In spite of his opposition—on this King Richard had insisted—the communes of Flanders, who had not even laid down their arms, were included in the truce of Lelinghem.

An exile from the rich land which he had once tyrannized over and exploited—for Louis no longer dared show his face in Flanders—without influence and without means, literally a homeless, impotent, poverty-stricken old man, dependent for his daily bread on alms which France begrudged him, so mean a creature did the once magnificent Louis appear in the eyes of the Duke of Berri that during the discussion of the terms of truce he had not hesitated to answer his vehement protest with insolent and contemptuous speech. *Cousin,* he said, *si votre imprudence vous a couvert de maux et de honte, il est temps de renoncer à vos fureurs et de suivre de meilleurs conseils.*

Cut to the quick by the insult, and powerless to resent it, Louis did not wait for the negotiations to be terminated, but withdrew in dudgeon to St. Omer, and here it was that he presently learned that the treaty in question had been signed. It was the last straw. The hand of death was upon him, and he knew it.

Louis was lodging in the great Benedictine Abbey where lay the bones of the founder of his house, Baldwin, Bras de Fer. Thither he summoned his companions in misfortune—the Dean of St. Donatian's, the Lord of Gruthuise—founder of the Gruthuise Palace—John of Heusden, his physician, who was also Provost of Notre Dame, and Robert, his natural son, and in their presence he dictated his last will and testament. 'Be it known to all,' said the dying Count, 'that I, mindful of the great honours, wealth and possessions, which Jesus Christ of His pure grace hath bestowed on me, unworthy, in this world, the which I have not used in His service and honour but for mine own vain glory, commend my poor sinful soul, as humbly as I may, to Him, to the Blessed Virgin, fount of mercy, and to all the saints in Paradise, whom I humbly beg to obtain for me forgiveness of my many and great sins.' Then, with his own hands, he wrote to the Duke of Burgundy, conjuring him to repair the wrong which he had done to Flanders. He was sore grieved, he said, at the destruction of his people, who had been punished at his request.

On the night of the 30th of January 1384 a mighty hurricane swept over the land of Flanders. It was as though the four winds were blowing together, and yet neither tree nor steeple was touched by it, but the skeletons of Louis's victims swayed to and fro on their gibbets and trembled in their chains. The spirits of darkness, said the people, were whirling his soul to hell.[33] '*Ce dont plusieurs gens disoient ce que bon leur semblait,*' comments shrewd Juvenal des Ursins, which is as much as to say the wish was father to the thought.

A splendid specimen of civic architecture, perhaps the most perfect building of its kind in Northern Europe, still bears witness to poor Louis's generosity to his beloved city Bruges. The present *Hôtel de Ville*

THE HÔTEL DE VILLE

was his gift. He laid the foundation stone during the heyday of his magnificence, on January 14, 1376. In May 1379 the building must have been nearly completed, for about this time we find one Gilles de Man, a name still common in Bruges, busy gilding and colouring the statuary and niches of the façade, and the municipal accounts inform us that he received seven *livres* and fourteen *escalins* for his labour. Early in the following year the work was suspended on account of the trouble with Ghent, in all probability it was not resumed during Louis's lifetime, and it was perhaps only completed in 1420.

Who the original architect may have been is a matter of conjecture. Monsieur Verschelde, the founder of the Archæological Society of Bruges, and for many years city architect, suggests Jean de Valenciennes, the artist whom we know designed and in great measure himself executed the sculpture which adorns the edifice. If this conjecture be warranted, Jean was, indeed, a creator of no ordinary talent, but of his story no vestige has come down to us, save only this: a man of the same name, perhaps his father, perhaps Jean himself, was *vinder* of the Bruges guild of painters in 1364.

It will be interesting to note that the façade of the Hôtel de Ville is the earliest structure in which appears an architectural arrangement which seems to have originated at Bruges, and which is perhaps the most distinguishing feature of its civic architecture. We allude to the long panels or arcades in which windows placed one over the other are frequently enclosed in such a manner as to give them the appearance of a series of long single windows ascending from the basement to the topmost storey.

Amongst the other remarkable structures of this period, note the nave and aisles and the upper portion of the transepts of the present cathedral, which replace work of an earlier date destroyed by fire on April 9, 1358, and were probably completed some two years later. If we can judge from the remnant still standing:—the choir ambulatory and the lower portion of the transepts, the old Church of St. Sauveur was far superior, both as regards design and execution, to the present edifice.

The great northern outer nave to the Church of Notre Dame dates also from this epoch (probably 1360). Here we have a striking example of the persistence of a feature rarely if ever met with in Gothic architecture either in England or in France, and which is, perhaps, so far as Northern Europe is concerned, at all events during the period in question, peculiar to Flanders—the semi-circular arch. The architects of Bruges seem never to have entirely abandoned it, and hence in that city its presence does not necessarily indicate that the building in which it is found is of Romanesque origin. Thus we find it in the tower of Notre Dame, which, as we have seen, dates from the close of the thirteenth century; in the northern transept of the cathedral of the same date; in the windows of the *Porte de Gand*, and of the *Porte Ste. Croix* of a century later; in the great porch of the hospital of St. John, and in the western façade of the Church of Notre Dame, and in domestic architecture of every period, over and over again. Sometimes it is used alone, sometimes in conjunction with the pointed arch. In the case of the northern nave of Notre Dame, it is employed for the vaulting, for the huge doorway at the western end, now bricked up, and for the five small bays of the outer arcade which connect it with the main building, whilst for the windows, for the bays of the inner arcade, and for the great opening at the east end which gives access to the tower, pointed arches are used.

For the rest, the building in question is characterised by its great height, the magnificent span of its vault, the grandeur of its proportions and the general simplicity

IV.—Genealogical Table of the Counts of Flanders from Guy de Dampierre to Marguerite of Maele.

Matilda of—**Guy de Dampierre**—Isabel of
Bethune   d. 1304   Namur

Robert III. = Yolonde of Bethune) of d. 1322 Nevers	William, mar. Adela daughter of Rodulph of Nesle	Marie = William of Juliers	Philip married Matilda of Thiette	5 other children		John of = Marie of Namur Artois d. 1331	Guy	Philippine	Isabel	4 other children

Louis Count = Jeanne, daughter of Nevers and heiress of d. 1322 Hugo IV., Count of Rethel	Robert of Cassel	William of Juliers, Provost of Maestricht	John II. of Namur d. 1335

Louis I. = Marguerite, daughter
d. 1346   of Philip (the Long
                of France)

Louis II. (of = Marguerite
Maele)   of Brabant
d. 1384

Marguerite = **Philippe
of Maele**   **le Hardi,**
d. 1405   Duke of
                Burgundy
                d. 1404

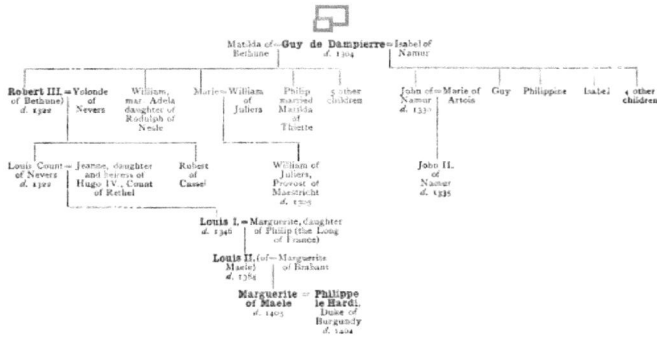

of its design. There is an unusual dearth of sculptured ornament, but what little there is, is happily conceived and delicately carried out.

As the building now stands, with its once glowing frescoes blotted out with white-wash, with its windows bereft of their painted glass and even of their tracery (this is now being replaced), with its cold, dismantled altars, and its chilling eighteenth-century pavement of marble, black and white, its general appearance is sufficiently bleak, and we were going to say sufficiently uninteresting, but that, no part of Notre Dame can ever be. The old church is too irregular, too picturesque, too mysterious. The incense of a thousand sweet memories still clings to its columns, the music of a thousand noble deeds still re-echoes in its vaulted roof, and in weird nooks and corners the red lamp of tragedy still burns. Something of its glory we have already noted, and we shall tell something more in its proper place.

Reader, make a pilgrimage to Notre Dame in the gloaming, and if thou art one of the initiated thou shalt haply learn the rest.

CHAPTER XIX

Bruges under the Princes of the House of Burgundy— Philip le Hardi and John Sans Peur—1385-1419

THE advent of the House of Burgundy found the communes of Flanders crippled and humbled by the disasters which had recently befallen them— disasters which, as we have seen, were but the natural outcome of their own domestic feuds. But though the battle of Rosebeke, and the events which followed, left Flanders bleeding, exhausted, almost dead, the dire calamity which had befallen her had in it this element of strength—it had brought about a reconciliation between Bruges and Ghent; the feuds which had so long neutralized their endeavours were for the moment laid aside, and when in December 1385 the new Sovereign deemed it politic to come to terms with the latter city, it was doubtless this consideration which prompted him to concede to the rebel Ghenters, whom he had defeated again and again, terms hardly less advantageous than they themselves would have exacted had they been in a position to dictate the conditions of peace.

By this treaty Philip confirmed all the time-honoured rights and privileges and franchises of Ghent and of her allies; granted a general amnesty to all who had taken part in the recent rebellion; guaranteed the release of all prisoners of war, and the restitution of all confiscated property.

Had the communes remained united they would probably have been able to successfully withstand the craft and perseverance of their Burgundian chiefs, whose policy, no less than that of their predecessors, was to convert their limited rights over Flanders into a complete and absolute sovereignty. But if strife weakened the resisting power of the burghers, the terrific and magnificent princes who were striving to enslave them were deprived of one element of strength which was never lacking to the puny Lords of Nevers—the assistance and support of France. Harassed by England, rent by internal factions and with a lunatic for king, France was in no position to help anyone during the first half of the period we are now considering; and when, later on, under Louis XI., she had at last recruited her strength, the ambitious designs of the Dukes of Burgundy had forced her to become their bitterest foe. For not only would these men have welded into one vast independent state the conglomeration of fiefs in France and in Germany, which, by inheritance, by marriage, by conquest, by haggling they had gradually gathered into their maw, but their insatiable lust for dominion prompted them to meddle also with the private concerns of France—to essay to direct alike her domestic and foreign policy. Hence the memorable quarrel between the Dukes of Burgundy and the French princes—a quarrel which, notwithstanding the disasters it brought on their chiefs, was no little advantage to the Flemish race.

But there was another circumstance which in no small degree favoured the cause of freedom.

To carry out their vast enterprises the Dukes of Burgundy were constantly in need of the sinews of war. They wanted men to do battle for them, and they wanted money to further their political schemes. In each of these commodities Flanders was rich, and in spite of her recent enfeeblement, and in spite of internal divisions, she was still strong enough, and shrewd enough, to withhold her aid on each occasion that it was asked until she had first some substantial *quid pro quo*.

The necessity then of their Sovereigns was the burgher's opportunity, and whenever they implored their assistance the answer, whether from Ypres or Bruges or Ghent, was invariably one—they were prepared to sell at a reasonable price, provided prepayment were made. Some grievance must first be redressed; some large charter of liberties granted; some obnoxious tax abolished, or some new treaty of commerce signed. But for all that the burghers knew very well that when their lords made concessions it was in spite of themselves, and when they curtailed their liberties, which they invariably did whenever they could safely do so, it was with a view later on to their total annihilation.

At the close of the reign of that magnificent ruffian, John the Fearless, the communes had thus achieved no small measure of success, whilst the progress which their rulers had made towards the goal of their ambition, at least so far as Flanders was concerned, was *nil*. For every two steps forward the exigencies of circumstances had forced them three steps back, so that, when John the Fearless died, Flanders was freer than she had ever been before.

This is all the more remarkable from the fact that Ghent, the mightiest of the Flemish cities, had of late shown herself but half hearted in support of the popular cause. It was the old story. Jealousy of her great rival, Bruges, and the national inability to withstand corruption. Philip the Rash and his morose son had alike favoured Ghent.

The vicissitudes of Bruges during the whole of this season were marvellous in the extreme—a continual alternation of peace and warfare, of merry-making and tumultuous frays, of luxury and pinching need, of honeyed speech and dire threats, for Philippe and John alike carried two faces under their hoods. When they wanted anything they could smile sweetly enough, and when they felt themselves independent they were wont to terrorize with fierce looks, and bloody deeds too, for the matter of that.

Hardly had the echo of the *Carillon* died away, which had swung out the joy of the burghers at the great pacification at the opening of Duke Philip's rule, when hostilities broke out again. Philip was in no way sincere in signing that treaty which Ghent had so proudly negotiated with him, more like an independent sovereign state than a conquered rebel city, and presently he conceived a diabolical plot to slay all her burghers by means of Breton mercenaries whom he would secretly have brought into their midst. This fell design having been happily discovered, the agents who were to have accomplished it, disappointed of the rich booty they thought to have obtained at Ghent, turned their attention to Bruges, and soon began to break into the houses of sundry honourable burghers there, and to insult and molest their women. Whereupon tumult unspeakable, and in the midst of it all the Duke of Berri was descried riding towards the *Pont des Carmes*. This man was the most hated of all the French knights, for his hands were red, every burgher believed, with the blood of their favourite Louis of Maele. In a moment he was surrounded by the howling mob, unhorsed, wounded almost to death, and 'if it had not been for the intervention of the Sire de Ghistelle—a man of weight, at Bruges—he would not have escaped with his life.' Thus Froissart; and he adds, 'Nor would a single knight or squire of France have been left alive in the town.'

Meanwhile Philip's affairs had prospered in France. He was now practically regent of the kingdom. His wife, *'une creuse et haute dame,'* was installed at Paris, and had undertaken the administration of the Queen's household. The King's counsellors were in exile; the Bishop of Laon was dead—poisoned, it was thought by many—and others would have probably shared his fate had not Philip's hand been restrained by a passing fear that the King's reason was returning.

Things then were going well with the Duke of Burgundy. He had time to turn his attention to the taming of the Flemish burghers, and amongst other regulations and proceedings, in direct contravention of the treaty of Tournai, he began to fight against the popular conscience.

It was the time of the great schism. From Rome and Avignon rival claimants to the Papal throne were hurling anathemas at one another. All Europe was divided as to who was the rightful Pope, and since it suited Philip to support Clement, of course his burghers felt bound in conscience to acknowledge Urban. Thanks to a gift of sixty thousand francs, the Ghenters had obtained permission to remain neutral, but hardly had three months expired when the Bishop of Teruanne went over to the side of Avignon, and at the same time all Antwerp followed his example. A favourable moment, thought Philip, to commence proselytism, by corruption, by violence, by any means at hand; and presently he formally forbade any of his subjects to obey the Pope of Rome. Then throughout Flanders all public worship ceased. Here and there, in the chapel of some great castle protected by high walls and a double moat, a Clementine priest would occasionally say Mass, but the boldest of them would not celebrate in public. If they had ventured to do so, the people would have dragged them from the altar. Bruges was beside herself. From the pulpit of St. Walburge the curate proclaimed the curse of Heaven on all who should recognize the Pope of Avignon, and forthwith fled the country. So too the Abbot of St. Peter's and the Abbot of Bandeloo, and a host of monks and burghers, not a few of whom took refuge in England, where they obeyed the Pope of Rome. One of these last was not so fortunate. Petrus van Roesclare, a civic dignitary of great wealth. He was arrested and carried to Lille, and there they cut off his head. John van der Capelle, the patriot whom Philip had appointed High Steward of Flanders, after the pacification of Tournai, was for the same motive deprived of his office. So too John of Heyle, whose good offices had greatly contributed to the settlement of Tournai. He was loaded with chains and cast into prison, where shortly afterwards he died. 'Men called him a martyr, for during the two months previous to his death he had tasted no solid food, and all that time he had passed in prayer.'

Philip, who was not ignorant of the rebellious spirit which his religious policy had aroused, about this time came to Bruges, hoping that his presence would frighten the burghers into submission. He had brought with him the Clementine Bishop of Tournai. On the following Sunday an ordination took place at St. Sauveur's, and the next day at Sluys, but on neither occasion was a single burgher present, nor would any of them avail themselves of the ministrations of the newly-ordained clergy.

But though the Bruges men grumbled and stayed away from Mass, their religious convictions were not sufficiently strong, or they were too much awed by the presence of Philip, to attempt any overt act of opposition. Not so the men of Ghent. As soon as the obnoxious edict had been published, a riot ensued which was only with difficulty calmed by the Urbanist clergy themselves. Whereupon Philip, perceiving that the burghers had made up their minds, permitted them to follow the dictates of conscience, and Ghent then became a place of pilgrimage throughout Flanders. It was the only town in the country where men could worship as they would, and all Bruges went out there at Easter-time to receive Holy Communion (1394).

The death of Duke Philip, ten years later, afforded no little consolation to his subjects, but the advent of a yet sterner ruler soon taught them to regret the old man's decease, for if Philip had beaten the Flemings with rods, his son John scourged them with scorpions.

As is the wont of most men when first they are invested with authority, during the early days of his reign he had been all smiles and condescension. At Ghent he had sworn on the true cross to 'respect the rights and liberties of the communes and to do by them all that a righteous Lord and Count of Flanders should do.' When a deputation of huffy burghers from Bruges and the other *bonnes villes* came out to greet him at Menin and showed themselves more eager to make known their grievances than to bid him welcome, he smoothed their ruffled feathers with soft words. He was ready, he said, to do anything they wanted; and when, a few days later, a second deputation waited on him at Ghent to complain of the commercial depression caused by the war between England and France, his answer was all that could be desired. He had already done his utmost to effect a reconciliation, but was prepared to try again, for no one, he added, with a touch of humour, was more interested in the prosperity of Flanders than he, for the richer she was the more she could afford to give him.

It was not until John had been thwarted that he showed of what stuff he was made. Opposition first came from the burghers of Bruges, and the burghers of Bruges were the first to experience the sting of his lash. It happened thus.

When in 1414 an English fleet of a hundred vessels sailed up the Zwyn and was threatening the fortress of Sluys—evil reminiscence of the conquest of Charles VI.—the burghers of Bruges refused to defend it, notwithstanding their Sovereign's earnest entreaties. 'It did not behove them,' they said by the mouth of their burgomaster, Lievin van Schotclaere, 'to protect a citadel which threatened the English less than their own liberties,' nor was it until the invaders had taken Sluys and burnt the castle that, at last, the Bruges men consented to arm, and perhaps even then there was some secret understanding between them, for the English retired at the approach of the burghers, 'slowly and without any sign of disquietude, rather after the manner of friends and allies than foes.'

As for John, he withdrew to Ghent disgusted; made it known that henceforth he would reside in that city; with a lavish hand scattered gold there; succeeded in corrupting not a few of the leading burghers, and at length conciliated the goodwill of the whole town by concluding a commercial truce with England, which by putting an end to the mutual piracy of the belligerents was intended to pave the way for a regular commercial treaty. Being thus in a position to act without hindrance, he turned his attention to the truculent burghers of Bruges, and presently the watchers on the belfry—for then, as now, night and day, there were watchers on the belfry—descried slowly winding its way through the woods of Maele, like some huge silver snake, and drawing nearer and nearer to the city, a troop of armed men. In an instant the tocsin was swinging, but the signal had been given too late, and when the breathless citizens reached the market-place, they found it filled with the Duke's guard, and there on the Halles balcony was John himself with a rod in his hand—symbol of coming chastisement. Sixteen great city officers were deprived of their appointments and condemned to exile or mulcted in heavy fines, and their places were given to certain obscure citizens on whose subservience John could rely. It was gall and wormwood to the burghers, but they bent their heads to the storm, nor did they refuse to set their seal of acceptance to the humiliating *Kalfvel* which the Duke imposed on them in place of their time-honoured charter, nor to thank him for it into the bargain, and that, though it wounded alike their pride and their pockets, curtailed their liberty, and imperilled their necks, by putting burthensome restrictions on the use of guild banners, by utterly suppressing the *maenghelt*, or monthly subsidy, which from time immemorial the corporation had granted to each of the trade guilds, and by making all kinds of vexatious enactments which were sanctioned by pain of death.

Note amongst the banished, Nicholas Barbesaen, erst burgomaster and city treasurer, who had been in former days a devoted adherent of Louis of Maele, and on more than one occasion, as he himself recounts in a memoir still extant amongst the archives of Lille, had risked his life to save him. He was also a man of much public spirit, and at his own cost had rebuilt the town gates which had been destroyed by the Ghenters in 1382. Two of them, the *Porte Ste. Croix* and the *Porte de Gand*, are still standing. 'I showed great diligence,' he says, in the document above referred to, 'anent the public buildings of the town, such as bridges, fountains, gates, towers and the like, the greater number of which were rebuilt during the time that I was burgomaster and treasurer of this city.'

THE PORTE DE GAND

But the meed of John's vengeance was not yet complete. Emboldened by the ease with which he had obtained the burghers' acceptance of the *Kalfvel*, he imposed by means of the new corporation a host of onerous taxes which had never been heard of before, notably a heavy duty on wheat, and obtained from his subservient magistrates a legal decision that the seventh *denier* in all town revenues belonged by right to the Sovereign.

To every honest burgher submission meant sorrow and bitterness of heart, but with their town in the hands of foreign mercenaries, Ghent bound hand and foot with golden fetters, sycophants and traitors in their own camp, they could but lie low and wait, and they waited for four years, and then their hour of triumph came.

It was the fall of the year 1411. The strife between the Burgundians and the Armagnacs was at its height. John was encamped in the plain of Montdidier waiting for Orléans to give battle. With him was an army of Flemings recruited from all the towns in the county. Their services, for a limited period, had been purchased by means of concessions—according to one account at the cost of a commercial union with England consecrated by an acknowledgment of the suzerainty of Henry IV. Each city was to fight under its own banner and be commanded by its own elected chiefs; on these conditions only had the burghers consented to leave their homes, and so eager was John for their services that he had made no protest even in the case of the Bruges men who had chosen Lieven van Schotclaere the burgomaster, whom he himself had deposed in 1407.

Presently the allotted term expired, the French had made no sign, and John could only prevail on the burghers to remain with him one week more by granting them fresh favours 'on account of the good, agreeable and notable services which they have rendered us, do render us, and will, we hope, continue to render us.' But when the week had passed and still Orléans tarried, neither prayers nor promises could induce them to further prolong their soldiering. At daybreak a mighty roar went up from the Flemish camp—*Go go, wapens wapers, te Vlaendren waert*, and they went. John rode out to confront them, and, with his hat off and his hands clasped, very humbly begged them to remain only four days longer; they were his brothers, he said, his comrades, the dearest friends he had; he was ready to renounce in their favour all the taxes of Flanders. But they were deaf to all his prayers; their only answer was to show the letter which limited the duration of the expedition, and to point to the ducal seal with which it was stamped.

Perceiving that it was useless to insist further, John the Fearless accompanied the Flemings as far as Péronne, where, having thanked them for their services and commissioned the Duke of Brabant to conduct them to the frontier, he bade them farewell, and almost alone set out for Paris. Thus ended the famous expedition to Montdidier, and thus did Bruges obtain her first instalment of vengeance. She had wrung from John undoubted favours, refused the only boon he asked, and received from him into the bargain a sufficiently humble acknowledgment for the 'good, agreeable and notable services which she had daily rendered,' but the hated *Kalfvel* was still in force; she was still governed by the creatures of the man who had wronged her, and of both the one and the other she was determined to be rid.

On the evening of the 6th of October, 1411, the Bruges men with Schotclaere at their head, and accompanied by the soldiery of eleven other towns, reached the great plain of Ten Belle, three leagues from home. Here they encamped for the night, here too they took counsel together, and next morning when Baldwin de Voss came out to greet them and to learn the hour of their arrival at Bruges, they replied that the *Kalfvel* must first be cancelled, and all grievances redressed. Whereupon the wily burgomaster with much plausible speech essayed negotiation. He would make known their wishes to the Duke, who would doubtless give favourable ear to them, but meanwhile they must lay down their arms and return peaceably to their homes. *Sils ne veulent perdre, he added, la bonne grâce de mon dit seigneur, en lequelle ils estoient sur tous autres qui l'avoient suivi de son pays de Flandres.*

These specious words deceived no man, and De Voss tried again. There were three points which it was beyond his power to concede. The Duke alone could repeal the *gabelle*, and the edicts anent confiscation, and the use of guild banners; for the rest, he was prepared to do all they wanted, but the burghers were adamant; they would never disarm, they averred, until they had obtained full satisfaction. At last, after much parleying, messengers were dispatched to the Duke, who by the advice of his Council conceded every point. The obnoxious taxes were repealed, the *Kalfvel* was torn up, and the officers appointed in 1407 were thrust out of the city. Thus after four years' servitude Bruges was once more free.

The causes of the enmity between John the Fearless and his cousin Philippe of Orléans are intricate and multiple and do not come within the scope of this book, nor would the tragedy in which it culminated be here alluded to were it not that some of the chief actors were either Bruges men, or intimately connected with Bruges, notably John Gerson, the famous theologian of the Council of Pisa, and perhaps the most brilliant scholar of his day. The following are the main outlines of the story. Towards the fall of the year 1407 the Duke of Burgundy set out for Paris, determined to rid himself forever of his powerful enemy and rival the Duke of Orléans. When, however, he reached the French capital, to the surprise of all men, for all men were well aware of his morose and sullen temper, he gave favourable ear to the words of King Charles, consented to a reconciliation, had an interview with Orléans at his house, the *Château de Beauté*, and on the following Sunday (November 20), by way of sealing their friendship, received Holy Communion with him at the Chapel of the Augustinian Friars.

Three days after, when Orléans was at the Queen's palace, a messenger arrived from the King to summon him to his presence. Attended by two esquires and four or five lackeys bearing torches, for the night was dark, he mounted his mule and set out for the royal abode.

Hardly had the little cavalcade left the palace gates when a band of armed men sprang out at them, crying, 'Death, death!' 'Hold,' shouted the prince, *'je suis le Duc d'Orléans.' 'C'est ce que nous voulons'*, was the reply, and they slashed him to death with their axes.

At that moment a tall man, with his face concealed by a red slouch hat turned down over his eyes, rushed out from Burgundy's house and cut off the dead Duke's hand, and with a club smashed in his skull.

The only one of his attendants who had made any show at resistance was a Flemish page called Jacques de Mene. This youth interposed his own body to receive the blows intended for his master until he fell dead by his side. The rest took flight.

When the Orléanists heard what had happened next morning, they were filled with consternation, and all kinds of rumours were abroad as to the identity of the murderer, but strangely enough no one suspected the Duke of Burgundy. He had attended the funeral, which took place in due course, attired in deep mourning, and had there exhibited every outward manifestation of grief, but it was afterwards remembered that during the ceremony he had laid his hand on the coffin, and that, as he did so, blood had spurted out from his victim's wounds.

Be this as it may, when, after the completion of the funeral ceremonies, the Provost of Paris entered the royal chamber and demanded permission to extend his inquiries 'even into the palaces of princes,' the Duke, who was present, turned pale, and drawing the Duke of Berri aside, avowed to him that he was the author of the crime. 'The devil,' he said, 'had beguiled him.'[34]

Berri for the moment held his tongue, but next day at the house of the Lord of Nesle, the Duke of Burgundy made public confession of his guilt. 'In order that no man may be wrongfully accused of the death of the Duke of Orléans, I avow that I myself and no other am the author of that which has taken place.' Immediately afterwards he fled the city, never halting until at half-past twelve in the afternoon he reached Bapaume. The number of his confederates must have been considerable, for relays of horses were awaiting him at successive stages, and the Admiral of France and a handful of knights, who almost immediately gave chase, found all the bridges over which he had passed entirely demolished.

In memory of the peril which John had so successfully evaded, he gave orders that henceforth the great town bell should be daily rung at half-past twelve, and for years afterwards the Duke's Angelus, as the citizens called it, kept alive the memory of his escape.

Presently John was at Ghent, endeavouring by the mouth of Chancellor Saulk to justify his conduct in the eyes of the communes, for he had convoked the estates of Flanders to meet him there. Presently he was at Amiens, guarded by three thousand men-at-arms, making conditions with the royal envoys whom Charles had sent to dissuade him from joining hands with England; closeted with Friar Petit, whom he had summoned from Paris 'to advise him anent certain secret matters greatly touching his honour'; doing anything and everything to safeguard his person and his interests, and to further his ambitious schemes. At last he deemed it safe to return to the French capital.

The sudden death of the Duke of Orléans had sown terror and confusion in the ranks of his supporters, whilst so mighty was the name of Burgundy that his friends among the roughs of Paris had feared not to insult the remains of his victim as they were being solemnly carried to the place of burial. True the King had promised the Duchess of Orléans vengeance, but it was a promise beyond his power to keep; the influence of Jean Sans Peur was increasing day by day, and when early in March he once more returned to the French capital, he was hailed as the saviour of the realm. The Duke of Berri made a banquet in his honour in the very house in which he had first avowed his guilt. 'Maître' Jean Petit, who was not only a *persona grata* at Court, but a divinity professor at the Sorbonne, whose opinions were not without weight in the world of the learned, did not hesitate to avow in the presence of the Dauphin and the royal princes that it was lawful to slay tyrants, and that those who did so deserved no punishment, but ought rather to receive reward.

In a solemn assembly, at which were present the King of Sicily, and the Dukes of Guienne, of Berri, of Lorraine and Bretagne, not a few counts and several bishops, John ratified all that Master Petit had said anent the laudable motives which had inspired his action, and soon his speech, reproduced by a host of scribes, was echoing all over France, 'like a triumphal pæan in the midst of the stupefied silence of the Orléanists,' and to crown all, the King himself published letters of approval. 'Seeing that our very dear and well-beloved cousin has explained that it was with a view to our own safety and the preservation of our line, for the utility and welfare of our realm, and to keep with us that faith and loyalty by which he is bound, that he has caused to be put out of the world our very dear and well-beloved brother the Duke of Orléans, whom God forgive, we make known, and will, that the aforesaid Duke of Burgundy is, and remains, in our singular love even as he was before.'

Thus ended the first scene of the tragedy, and twelve years passed by, replete with strife and turmoil, which concerns not these pages; then came the grand finale.

'Joab,' had thundered John Petit in his famous glorification of the Duke of Burgundy, '*Joab a répandu le sang de la guerre au milieu de la paix: sa viellesse ne descendra pas paisiblement dans la tombe*,' and in the light of after events the words of the notorious friar seem almost prophetic. On the 10th of September 1419, some twelve years after the murder of the Duke of Orléans, John the Fearless was himself slain on French soil. It happened thus. About a month previous to this date, John had requested an interview with the Dauphin, who was now chief of the Orléanist party, with a view to concluding peace. After some hesitation, the latter had consented, and on the 14th of August, on the bridge of Montereau-Faut-Yonne, the meeting took place. During the discussion which ensued, words ran high, and presently the spectators on either bank of the Seine observed that the men on the bridge were struggling. For a moment they suspected foul play, and a cry went up that the Dauphin had been slain, but it was not the Dauphin but John himself whom the crowd had seen hurled to the ground, and the figure bending over him, and perhaps essaying to staunch his wounds, was no other than that of Guillaume le Bouteille, once servant to Philippe d'Orléans. 'As thou didst serve my master,' muttered the old man, as he hacked off the dead Duke's hand, 'as thou didst serve my master even so do I now serve thee.' But the crowd on the banks heard not his words, and wist not what he was doing.

Was John the victim of his cousin's treachery, or had he at length been taken in his own net? In a word, was he slain by the Dauphin in self-defence? Such the latter averred to be the case, and there is this much in favour of his assertion—Juvenal des Ursins, the most reliable and impartial historian of his century, gives credence to it. So too Olivier of Dixmude, who relates the following anecdote:—

One night, towards the hour of matins, about a month after Philippe's murder, whilst the Duke of Burgundy was staying at Ypres, a strange and lurid light appeared in the air over the cloister of St. Martin, where he was lodged. Thither ran a host of citizens from all quarters of the town, thinking that the place was on fire, but they soon perceived the true cause thereof—a dragon hovering over the Duke's chamber, which suddenly turned his flaming dart on himself and so disappeared, and, Olivier adds, even thus did John the Fearless die—in a plot of his own hatching.

When in the year 1408 Duke John the Fearless, glorying in the crime he had committed, and vaunting it as an act of virtue, was heaping wealth and favours on the shameless friar who, as he cynically avowed, for gold and the hope of more gold had made himself his apologist, there was one man who ventured to lift up his voice in protest; this man was Jean de Gerson, erst chaplain to Philip the Hardy, and since 1394 Dean of the great Collegiate Church of St. Donatian's at Bruges.

Burning with indignation at the bloody deed and at the sophistry of the priest who had dared to defend it, he publicly proclaimed Petit's doctrine anent tyrannicide to be false, scandalous and heretical, and never rested until he had prevailed on the Bishop of Paris to condemn it as such. The Duke of Burgundy was furious, and gave orders for Gerson's arrest, but the Dean had received timely warning, and when the *pursuivants* came to seize him they found their quarry flown. He had eluded pursuit by concealing himself among the rafters between the vault and the roof of Notre Dame. Presently he succeeded in leaving Paris, and in due course, after many hairbreadth adventures, reached German soil. Whereupon John declared him legitimately dispossessed of his deanery (May 27, 1411), and appealed to Pope John XXIII., one of the three claimants to the Papal throne, who, after having appointed a commission to examine the case, quashed the Paris decision. But the intrepid Dean of Bruges would not suffer the matter to rest here; he, in his turn, appealed to the Council of Constance, and with such good effect that 'Master' Petit's theories were unanimously condemned, and though the Duke of Burgundy had sufficient credit with the assembled fathers to prevent the name of his favourite from appearing in the condemnation, all those who obstinately maintained his opinions were declared to be heretics, and ordered to be dealt with as such in accordance with Canon law.

As long as John lived, Gerson remained in Germany, but when at length his enemy was called to his account, he took up his abode at Lyons, where the chief delight of his declining years was to teach little children. He died in 1429, and the men of Lyons called him a saint. Be this as it may, he feared not to withstand, for justice sake, the fiercest tyrant in Christendom. It was chiefly owing to his efforts that the schism which for so many years had rent Christ's seamless garment was at length healed; he was a brilliant scholar, a kindly, gentle, God-fearing man, perhaps the author of *The Imitation*, and unquestionably the greatest divine of the age in which he lived. The life of John de Gerson was not then spent in vain, and Flemings may well be proud of the Frenchman whom Philip the Hardy set over the time-honoured church of Bruges.

CHAPTER XX

The Great Humiliation

THE great struggle with the communes of Flanders was continued by Philippe l'Asseuré, who ascended the throne upon the death of his father, John the Fearless, in 1419, but from this time forth, slowly but surely, the cities lost ground, and ere Philippe was gathered to his fathers, in 1467, the stubbornest of them had made their submission.

It was not until 1437 that serious trouble began at Bruges. Its ostensible cause was the old dispute anent her jurisdiction over Sluys, but in reality it was the outcome of the people's discontent at Philippe's centralizing policy, and at the ignoble means by which he pursued it; by stirring up strife betwixt class and class, and town and town, and man and man; by corrupting magistrates, in order that they might lend themselves to the falsification of money, and the increase of taxation; by undermining the authority of city officers by modifying the basis on which it reposed, and by exciting the lower classes against them.

The treaty of Arras, by which Philippe concluded, on July 1, 1435, a formal alliance with France, was profoundly unpopular with the Flemish burghers, and the war with England, in which it involved them, was still less to their liking. They knew very well that it was not to their interest to quarrel with their former ally, and if in those days there had been in England an Edward III., or an Artevelde in Flanders, they would have had no hesitation in joining hands with the English against the tyrant who was oppressing them, as they had done in the days of Louis of Maele. As it was, it needed all Philippe's tact and sophistry, and no inconsiderable expenditure of cash in bribes, to induce them to render him assistance, and perhaps even then there was some secret understanding with the enemy. The force which the burghers had given him only remained under arms some two months, from June 11 to August 26, (1436). When the Burgundian fleet under De Horne fled before the English admiral, a great cry went up from the Flemings encamped before Calais—'Go, go wy zyn all vermanden,' and they forthwith packed up their traps, staved in the casks of wine that they were unable to carry with them and returned to their homes.

In consequence of this defection Philippe was compelled to raise the siege of Calais, and soon the English were overrunning the greater part of West Flanders. Henry VI., as soon as he had learned what had happened, sent letters to all the towns which acknowledged his authority, bitterly complaining of 'the disloyal conduct of that most faithless Philippe, commonly called Duke of Burgundy,' who, having acknowledged his suzerainty from his (Henry's) youth upwards, had at length ventured to renounce it. In doing so, the letter continued, Philippe had rendered himself guilty of *lèse-majesté* and had thereby forfeited all claim to the county of Flanders, which, as its suzerain, Henry now awarded to his own uncle, Humphrey, Duke of Gloucester. This letter was dated August 30, 1436. Soon all the towns in the neighbourhood of Calais were in Gloucester's hands; at Poperinghe he was solemnly recognized as Count, and presently the English fleet was seen slowly coasting along towards the waters of the Zwyn where De Horne was anchored off Sluys, but dared not go out to engage it. Indeed the news of its approach filled him with such consternation that he fled to shore. His fate is not without significance. Wandering about amongst the sandhills, he presently fell in with a band of Karls, who recognizing in the woe-begone stranger the admiral of their Count's fleet, used him so ill that he died from the effects, at Ostend, a fortnight later.

About this time the burghers of Bruges sent an armed force to Sluys, demanding that the fleet and the town should be handed over to them, on the ground that from time immemorial Sluys had been subject to their jurisdiction. But Sluys was a hot-bed of Leliaerts, or Burgundians as they were now called, as it had been since the days of Louis of Maele, and though the Bruges men brought with them an order, signed by the Duchess of Burgundy, and had come ostensibly to defend the port against the English, the governor, Roland van Uutkerk, refused to permit more than forty of them on board ship, and the rest were forced to spend the night in the open, in torrents of rain, save some half-dozen, who perhaps had friends in the city, and somehow or other managed to find a lodging there. These men, however, next morning incurred an inconvenience greater than a wetting. When their comrades remonstrated on the treatment which they had received, the men who had lodged in the city were forthwith thrown out of window. Every other citizen of Bruges, who happened to be in Sluys, was ordered to at once quit the town under penalty of losing his head, and Van Uutkerk, declaring that the whole gang of them were traitors and mutineers, bade them go back to the place from whence they came.

What was the true cause of this extraordinary reception accorded by the Sluysers to men who were supposed to be their allies, and had come forth ostensibly to fight for the Duke? Was it simply the outcome of the national jealous temperament, or did the Sluysers suspect, or had they, perhaps, been secretly informed, that some great act of treachery was in contemplation by the men of Bruges, that if the fleet and the citadel had been given into their keeping, they would have handed them over to the

English? It is hard to say. 'The influence of the Dukes of Burgundy,' notes Kervyn, 'has so deeply penetrated the historical sources of this period that it is almost impossible to throw light on questions relative to the movements of the Flemish burghers.' Certain it is that Bruges was profoundly mortified and disappointed, and that a riot ensued, during which the Duke's representative, *Écoutète* Eustace Buch, fell a victim to the people's anger. But this was not all. The charter of 1323, which placed Sluys under the jurisdiction of Bruges, having been solemnly read from the Halles gallery, the city magistrates were called upon to explain why and how they had connived at its infraction, and their answers not appearing satisfactory, so great was the feeling of the people, that the houses of several of them were sacked. So terrified was the Duchess of Burgundy at the threatening attitude of the mob that in the midst of it all she set out for Ghent, where Philippe was at present stationed, and though no attempt was made to offer Isabelle violence, or to restrict her personal liberty of action, the burghers deemed it prudent to retain as hostages two of her women, the widow of Jean de Hornes, and the wife of his successor, Roland van Uutkerk, who were actually snatched from the ducal litter.

In all this we may see the handiwork of the guildsmen, and likewise in the events which followed. The city of Bruges was not left to fight her battle alone. The Franc gave her assistance—a circumstance not a little remarkable, as the men of the Franc and the men of the city had already begun to grow jealous of one another—and, more remarkable still, all the neighbouring communes, including Ghent, rallied round her. Philippe, unable to resist the united pressure thus brought to bear on him, acknowledged the rights of Bruges over Sluys, consented to the banishment of Roland van Uutkerk for a hundred years and a day, and intimated that he would shortly come to Damme with a view to redressing grievances.

Thus far fortune had favoured the men of Bruges, but she was not destined to show herself their friend much longer. When Philippe reached Damme, on the 4th of October, he at once made it known that before anything else could be done, the burghers must lay down their arms; but that, if within three days a general disarmament were effected, he would at once re-establish and confirm all the ancient rights and privileges of the city. The guildsmen seem to have been satisfied of Philippe's good faith, for by the 9th of October the disarmament was completed, but when four days had gone by, and Philippe made no sign of fulfilling his part of the contract, they began to grow suspicious; and when presently information was brought them that the Duke had only named Damme as the place of conference in order to obtain possession of that important vantage post, and that since his arrival there he had been secretly reinforced by troops from Lille and from Holland, they knew that they had been duped, and at once made ready for battle. Soon the market-place was again filled with armed guildsmen, and auxiliaries from sixty-two neighbouring communes to boot.

OLD HOUSES AT DAMME

Far from precipitating hostilities, these war-like preparations had the effect of deferring them. Philippe had not sufficient soldiers to risk an engagement, and when three days later the foreign merchants resident in Bruges volunteered their good offices, he consented to resume negotiations. By the end of the month terms were agreed upon. The burghers once more disarmed, Philippe confirmed their rights and privileges, and when he had done this, they in their turn sent deputies to Damme to make humble apology for the disturbances which had recently taken place in their city. But so little confidence did they place in the Duke's good faith that they detained his ambassadors at Bruges until their own had returned from Damme.

Thus was peace for the moment established. Neither party was satisfied at the issue of the negotiations, but neither party was at present strong enough to re-open the contest, and the winter passed on amid much grumbling and no little display of sulkiness on each side.

Meanwhile, Philippe was watching the course of events. Early in the spring (February 11, 1437), with a view to weakening the three *bonnes villes*, he granted a charter to the Franc, by which he recognized that corporation as fourth member of the Estates of Flanders, and forbade any freeholder submitted to its jurisdiction to become a burgher of the city. Whereat riot ensued, and blood again flowed in the streets. Burgomaster Maurice van Varsenare who endeavoured to quell the tumult, was slain for his pains in front of the Belfry, and beside him too fell his brother Jacob, who essayed to defend him. Presently the storm ceased, and the burghers began to tremble for the consequences of their hot-headedness. They sent an embassy to Philippe with excuses and explanations, and Philippe gave them a curt reply. Business in Holland demanded his attention, but on his way there he would pass through Bruges. Three months later, on May 22, he reached *St. Michel*, a stone's throw from the city. With him was a numerous retinue of knights, and four thousand Picard footmen—men hated of Flemings—but in order to disarm public opinion, he had sent word to Burgomaster van de Walle that he alone would enter Bruges with a handful of attendants, and that the soldiers should camp at Maele.

Great then was the astonishment of that magistrate when next morning he went out to welcome the Duke, and found all his Picards with him, and recrimination and confabulation ensued, which lasted two hours, during which time, unperceived by the angry burgomaster, the soldiers were preparing to march.

At length, turning to his men-at-arms, and at the same time pointing to the city, Philippe dropped the mask. 'That,' he cried, 'is the Holland that we have come to conquer,' and, without waiting for further parley, made for the city. Some of the foremost knights had already reached the market-place ere the tocsin gave the alarm, but hardly had it sounded than armed burghers seemed to spring up from the pavement; they were swarming through the crooked streets and narrow lanes like angry ants whose home had been disturbed, and so threatening was their attitude that Philippe, when he reached the Church of St. Sauveur, bade his men withdraw by the way they had entered. Covering their retreat with arrows, they made for the Bouverie gate, but only to find it shut; and thus Philippe, cut off from the bulk of his army, was at length in the power of the guildsmen, who, raging about him like rabid hounds, had already struck down not a few of his bodyguard. In another instant the Duke himself would have been slain and Flanders saved from long years of misery. If it had not been for the tenderness of heart and misplaced loyalty of Burgomaster van de

THE CHURCH OF ST. SAUVEUR

Walle, the whole course of European history would have been altered, less blood and fewer tears would have been shed, and perhaps to this day Bruges would have remained a great and flourishing city. This intrepid old man, when he found that all his efforts to calm the mob were unavailing, somehow or other procured a smith, and at the risk of his life stood over him whilst he broke open the lock of the Bouverie gate. Philippe rushed out, and with a handful of knights escaped to Courtrai.

As for his Picards, they fled in dismay. Twenty of them were taken prisoners, and they paid the penalty of their would-be depredation with their heads. A hundred and sixty of the Duke's own retainers likewise fell into the hands of the guildsmen, but at the intercession of the clergy and the foreign merchants their lives were spared, and they even received honourable treatment.

Then followed nine months of dire warfare, and at each successive step the men of Bruges suffered themselves to be hoodwinked. At the very outset, as we have seen, they had lost a grand opportunity by allowing Philippe to slip through their fingers. Then came the raising of the siege of Sluys, almost in the hour of victory (one of the town gates had been actually demolished) at the instigation of the Ghenters, who averred that the Duke was prepared to treat for peace, a matter of the highest moment, as foreign merchants were on all sides fleeing the country.

The accomplishment of the task in hand was a matter of life and death to Bruges, for with Sluys in the hands of the Burgundians, the way of the Zwyn was barred, and Bruges cut off from the sea, and yet the burghers had not sufficient backbone to withstand the entreaties of their so-called friends, and presently they regretted their pusillanimity. No sooner was the siege raised than the Burgundians poured out of Sluys, and harried all the country round, and a band of a hundred and thirty of them ventured even to the very walls of Bruges, and were on the point of driving off a large herd of cattle intended for the provisionment of the city when a thousand guildsmen swooped down on the marauders, took not a few of them prisoners, and put the rest to flight.

The final catastrophe was brought about by the open defection of Ghent. For some time past she had been halting between two opinions, but the success which the men of Bruges had obtained over the marauding knights, at the gates of their city, had emboldened her to make a definite engagement to fight shoulder to shoulder with Bruges until peace were established in Flanders, and even to despatch to her assistance a small band of fighting men; but presently one of her leaders, Rasse Onredene, a man who passed for an ardent patriot, but was in reality in Philippe's pay, pointed out that it would be more to the advantage of Ghent to act the part of peacemaker, with a view to arranging honourable terms than to openly side with either of the belligerents; and when a deputation of Bruges men went out, as they thought, to confer with their allies at Eecloo, they found them posing as neutral mediators. Soon they discovered that they were not even neutral, but open supporters of the Duke, and that they would compel them even by threats to absolute submission. Bruges refused the terms offered with disdain, Ghent retaliated by declaring her an enemy of the state, and if it had not been for the inclemency of the season—it was now December—she would have forthwith commenced a campaign against her rival.

Bruges was thus left alone to brave Philippe's fury, and in what plight! Cold, starving, plague-stricken, eaten up with leprosy. The absence of supplies from foreign ports—she had long been cut off from the sea—and the devastation of the surrounding country had produced famine; then came that other handmaid of war, Pestilence, and on her heels, Winter, before his time. Added to this, the prevailing misery had favoured the spread of a disease always lurking in the insanitary cities of the period, and the weird cry of the lazar and the clang of his doleful bell were now heard in every street.

The Lepers' Hospital, Marché au Fil

'From the wretched hovel of the working man writhing in the clutches of famine, from the burning couch of the plague-stricken, and from the barred cell of the leper, there rose up one cry, poignant as the necessity which dictated it: Peace, peace.' Thus Kervyn, in his usual high-flown way.[35]

In face of evils such as these, and with the entire population clamouring for peace at any price, what could a handful of burghers do, however brave and resolute? There was but one course open to them, and early in February (1438) Bruges threw herself on the Duke's mercy; but Philippe was deaf to the prayers of her representatives, prostrate and trembling before him, nor was it until Isabelle of Portugal had thrown herself at his feet that he at length vouchsafed to hear them, and even then the declaration which he made on March 4, 1438, breathed a spirit of cynicism, in which generosity had no part. He was mighty enough, he said, to destroy the town of Bruges *et le mettre à toute misère et povreté*, but, at the same time, it did not suit his convenience to utterly crush the chief purveyor of food stuffs in his domains.

For the rest, the conditions which Philippe exacted were sufficiently burthensome. Bare-headed and bare-footed the burgomaster, sheriffs and other officials must meet him a league from the city upon the next occasion he should come there, and after having sued on their knees for mercy, and made him an offering of their persons and their goods, present to him the keys of the city, which he should be free to keep or return according to his good pleasure.

All this, though sufficiently galling to the burghers, inflicted on them no real or, at all events, no material injury, but the remaining conditions threatened alike their pride, their persons and their pockets—a fine of two hundred thousand golden Philippes (afterwards reduced to thirty thousand), the re-establishment of the hated *Kalfvel* of 1407, and forty-two noble citizens, whom Philippe mentioned by name, excluded from the general amnesty which, if these terms were accepted, he professed himself ready to accord. Needless to say that Bruges acquiesced, and soon the headsman was plying his bloody trade in the market-place.

Note amongst those who were condemned to death the chivalrous burgomaster, Louis van de Walle, who had saved the Duke's life at the risk of his own, during the riot of 1437, and likewise his wife and his son. Philippe showed his gratitude by commuting the death sentences of the two former to one of life-long imprisonment in Winendael Castle. But the son was executed before his parents' eyes, and Louis himself, ere he was reprieved, was put to torture. Did he wish that he had let the guildsmen have their way on that memorable occasion before the Bouverie gate?

The standard-bearer of Oostcamp was another of Philippe's victims. His bloody head, adorned with that wreath of roses which Bruges had awarded to his commune for having been the first to come to her assistance when Philippe was plotting against her in 1436, was impaled on an iron spike, and set up on the parapets of the Halles.

To the Franc, too, was meted out punishment—twenty-two of her freemen excluded from amnesty, and a fine so heavy—twenty thousand golden Philippes—that many of her most opulent landowners were reduced to want.

This was not the kind of peace which Bruges in her misery had prayed for. All kinds of rumours were afloat, a general spirit of disquietude was abroad, men on all sides were expecting some fresh and terrible act of vengeance. Not a few resolved to emigrate, and in order to hide their purpose from the Duke alleged that they were going on pilgrimages to our Lady of Walsingham, to the three Kings of Cologne, to St. Martin of Tours—to any popular shrine that was not within reach of his long fingers. But Philippe got wind of their real design, succeeded in arresting not a few of them ere they had crossed the frontier, and all who fell into his clutches he put to death. Whereupon the foreign merchants waxed wroth. How could trade flourish in face of the *espionage*, the persecution, the bloodshed with which Philippe had been so long harassing Flanders? and then, too, there was the war with England, which in itself was fatal to their interests. Unless peace were forthwith made, commercial intercourse with that country re-established, and Flanders tranquillised, they would in a body quit the realm, and indeed not a few of them packed up their chattels and went. Thereupon Philippe took fright, set bounds to his evil humour, opened negotiations with England, concluded a truce for three years, prolonged it next year to five, and thus little by little confidence was restored and peace once more established, and when two years later Philippe triumphantly entered Bruges amid flaming torches, and clashing bells, and the blare of silver trumpets, the people received the tyrant who had crushed them with enthusiastic ovations and every outward manifestation of goodwill.

Not content with performing the stipulated humiliation, the burghers did more than Philippe had prescribed. They erected triumphal arches, adorned their houses and their public buildings with rich drapery, and strewed flowers along his path; nor was this all—at intervals they set up allegorical groups, typical of repentance and submission. Thus, hard by the *Porte de Ste. Croix* stood St. John the Baptist, bearing in his hands a scroll on which was written: *Ego vox clamantis in deserto: parate viam Domini.* Further on stood four prophets, each with his parchment scroll, after the manner of the figures in the painted windows of the period. On the first was inscribed—'Thy people shall rejoice in thee'; on the second—'The prince of God is in the midst of us'; on the third—'Come let us return to the Lord,' and on the fourth—'Let us do all that the Lord saith to us.' Thus did these worthy merchants cringe—an edifying sight—before the blood-stained tyrant who twelve months before had tortured and slain their noblest fellows. For them he had become as the Saviour of the Gospel, aye and as the God of Abraham, for they chose the sacrifice of Isaac to typify the absolute obedience which they owed to him. And who shall blame them? The craven cur who licks the hand which has struck him is after all a more sagacious beast that the mettlesome hound who resents an unjust blow by springing at his master's throat. The former is sometimes received back into favour, the latter is not unfrequently hanged. In the present case, as we shall see, the burghers had their reward.

Till the close of Philippe's reign Bruges was at peace.

During ten years a great calm reigned throughout Flanders. 'Remember Bruges,' Philippe had said to the citizens of Ypres, who for a moment showed signs of being restive, and the warning was enough. But the men of Ghent were made of sterner fibre, and when in 1450 Philippe would have taxed their salt, they broke out in open rebellion. For three years the burghers did battle for liberty with heroism and fortitude, but with so redoubtable an opponent there could be but one issue to the conflict, and in 1453, the year of the fall of Constantinople, the saddest year of the fifteenth century, Kervyn calls it, Ghent too was conquered.

All this time the prosperity of Bruges was seemingly increasing by leaps and bounds, but it was but the glow of the sunset which presaged eternal night, though the pomp and splendour of the Ducal Court—the most splendid Court of the richest sovereign in Europe—made the sunset a golden one.

Magnificent *fêtes* and gorgeous tournaments were following one another in rapid succession, sumptuous palaces were springing up on all sides, sanctuaries were being everywhere enlarged and adorned with a countless array of art treasures. But there was another side to the picture. In spite of lotteries and the sale of annuities, in spite of direct taxation—a means of producing revenue hitherto unknown in Bruges—there was now a constantly recurring and constantly increasing deficit in the annual city budget, and the list of persons constrained to accept public relief, including as it now did not only obscure names, but alongside of them the names of clergymen, of merchants, and of men of honourable and ancient lineage, was each year growing longer and longer. Intrigue, and riot, and suppression, and the silting up of the Zwyn were driving trade from Bruges. A host of merchants had left for Antwerp, a city less subject to internal commotions; not a few, as we have seen, had emigrated to England, to Germany, to the South of France, whilst the shipping, which could no longer find its way into the harbours of Sluys and Damme, now sought shelter in other ports.

This was the state of affairs at Bruges during the time which elapsed between her humiliation in 1440 and the death of Philippe l'Asseuré in 1467—a time of peace and quietude after the long years of strife; a time of *fêtes* and royal pageants; a time of much intellectual activity; a time of music, and poetry and art; but a time also of gradual commercial wane, and in the midst of it the stupendous intellect of the man who had accomplished all this became clouded, like the city which he had beautified and destroyed, by premature decay. The astute tyrant, who had been able to tame the burghers of Flanders, and, in spite of bloody deeds, to make himself beloved; the cultured patron of art who had known how to appreciate the works of the Van Eycks, and of Roger Van der Weyden; the clear-headed man of business who had received a heritage encumbered with debt, and, before his decease, was the richest prince in Europe, now passed all his time in a little workshop dyeing old fragments of cloth, fitting together pieces of broken glass, and sharpening needles.

Early in 1466 he was struck down with apoplexy; though he rallied from the attack, his physicians knew that his days were numbered, and on Monday, the 15th of June, 1467, the end came. They buried him at Bruges in the Church of St. Donatian, and so great was the throng at the funeral, and the heat engendered by thousands of candles, that they shattered the gorgeous stained windows to let in the air.

CHAPTER XXI

The Terrible Duke and his Gentle Daughter

DURING the short reign of that sombre and fantastical hero Charles the Terrible, or, as he is generally called, Charles the Bold, things went on at Bruges in something of the same fashion as they had done in the days of his predecessor. There was much surface glory, a vast amount of rottenness within, and, added to this, a very general feeling of disquietude and a continuous undercurrent of grumbling, which, as time progressed, grew louder and louder, at the hazardous policy of the Duke, whose dream it was to restore the old Burgundian kingdom, or, at least, to free himself from the vassalage of France, and who used to ask with indignation whether it was a seemly thing for a lineal descendant of Charlemagne to acknowledge the suzerainty of Hugh Capet's heirs.

There were gorgeous jousts and tournaments, when amid shouts of Noël, on Palm Sunday 1468, Charles made his solemn entry into Bruges, swore to maintain her rights and privileges, and held his first Chapter of the Golden Fleece in the Church of Notre Dame, where, by the way, the escutcheons of his knights are still hanging, and amongst them that of Edward IV. There was much feasting and merriment, too, when three months later he brought home his third bride, Edward's sister, Margaret of York; but it was presently turned into tears and ashes by a sudden and virulent outbreak of plague, made more terrible by wild rumours that the nurses, impatient to grow rich on the spoils of their patients, had infected the wells and even the holy water stoops in the churches in order to spread the disease. There was much real distress when Warwick the King-maker, angered with Charles, because he had urged the citizens of London to oppose the restoration of Henry VI., surprised some Flemish vessels charged with wine from Saintonge, and blockaded the port of Sluys; great rejoicings when, two months later, the Lord of Ter-Vere encountered Warwick's fleet and, after a terrible conflict, dispersed it, but which, in its turn, gave place to dismay at the fact, made manifest by the recent naval battles, that the Zwyn was shallower than ever.

Whereupon the estates of Flanders conferred as to remedial measures, and after much confabulation, and strenuous opposition on the ground of expense on the part of Ypres and Ghent, manufacturing towns, whose interests were not at stake, and the men of the Franc, pastoral folk, whom the matter in no way concerned, thanks to the support of Charles, a plan was at length adopted which its advocates averred would restore the harbour of Sluys to its former depth—to wit, the cutting of a dyke which closed an ancient channel by which the sea formerly ran into the port of Sluys, and towards the close of July 1470 it was put into execution.

Many there were who believed this scheme would be inefficacious, and after events justified them. Eighteen years later the *Echevins* of Bruges decided to re-make the dyke, seeing that the 'Haven of Zwyn was closing up yet faster than of yore.'

Meanwhile Charles's schemes of conquest were pressing harder and harder on his unfortunate subjects. In 1474 the Carthusian nuns of the Convent of St. Anne were forced to part with a portion of their property in order to pay their taxes, and the burghers grumbled louder than ever. The obstinate canons of St. Donatian went a step further; they absolutely refused payment, and were, in consequence, dragged to prison. In 1476 Charles made fresh demands, and the deputies of the estates of Flanders waited on him at Bruges to remonstrate, but after much haggling and many bitter words, granted a subsidy—a hundred thousand *ridders* and the pay of four thousand sergeants. Presently fresh defeat constrained him to ask for more, and this time the communes refused. The people, they said, were overwhelmed with taxes, no further succour of men or money would they afford him for any of his foreign wars, but if he should haply find himself in peril from either Swiss or Germans, they would risk their lives and goods to bring him back safely to Flanders. Traitors and rebels! thundered Charles, they should soon learn how terrible was his vengeance. Vain threat; on the 5th of January 1477 the defeat of Nancy put an end to all his dreams of conquest. In the first shock of battle the Burgundians were dashed to pieces, and in the dismay and confusion which followed the Duke had disappeared. No one knew what had become of him. Some said they had seen him streaming with blood, but still defending himself like a man. Others averred that at the moment of defeat he had turned tail and fled. Three days later they discovered in a frozen pond the remains of a naked human body, scarred with wounds and half-devoured by beasts of prey. On one finger was a ring which a humble member of the Duke's household— the woman who washed his linen—fancied she recognized as having once been the property of her master. On this testimony the shattered fragments were said to be the body of Charles, and as such they were honourably buried in the Church of St. George at Nancy. They were not, however, suffered to rest there. More than fifty years later the Emperor Charles V. caused them to be brought to Bruges, and laid them up in the Church of St. Donatian. Five years afterwards his son, Philip II., translated them to a marvellous shrine in the Church of Notre Dame. Here they remained in peace till the close of the last century, when the iconoclasts of the Revolution scattered them, on the ground that they were the bones of a tyrant. May be they were, but it is equally likely that they were the relics of some humble toiler.

But to return to the epoch of Charles's death, or, at all events, of his disappearance. 'The people, the masses'—we are quoting from Kervyn—'who had lately been astounded at the pomp and wealth of the great Burgundian Duke, and who had so long been accustomed to bend to his iron will, utterly failed to understand how so great a prince, the sovereign of so many realms, a man so redoubtable throughout all the West, could have been suddenly swallowed up with all his glory in a pit which his own foolhardiness had digged for him. At the siege, too, of a petty town in Lorraine, by a troop of Rhenish boors and a handful of Swiss shepherds. It altogether passed their comprehension, and they persuaded themselves that he had escaped, and would one day come back again, as his great ancestor Baldwin of Constantinople had done two centuries before.

Some of the vanquished had succeeded in crossing the Meurthe, and were known to have escaped by concealing themselves in woods and so forth; perhaps he was among this number. As late as January 15 Margaret of York still cherished this hope. 'From news which we have received from divers quarters,' she wrote at this date, 'we expect and hope that by God's mercy the Duke is still alive and well,' and on the 23rd his daughter Mary wrote that she was not yet sure that her father was dead. Five years later a report was set abroad that he was leading the life of a hermit at Bruchsal in Suabia—*genus vitæ super humanum morem horridum atque asperum*. An old servant who had fought beside him at Nancy, and had there been made prisoner by the Swiss, went to see, but he failed to recognize his master. The figure, voice, beard, hands, scars of the recluse were not those of Charles the Terrible. But others there were who believed in the marvellous stories of the hermit of Bruchsal, and loaded him with presents, thinking to receive them back tenfold when he returned to his estates. Others swore they had seen Charles at Rome, at Jerusalem, at Lisbon, at London. Others again whispered that he had been spirited away by the machinations of Louis XI.[36]

Upon the mysterious disappearance of Charles the Terrible after the defeat of Nancy, his dominions devolved on his only daughter, a girl of nineteen years of age, without army, without treasure, without any rock of defence save those Flemish communes which her ancestors throughout seven generations had never ceased to persecute. They did not refuse to help her, but they demanded that their grievances should first be redressed. Flanders, they urged, was not a fertile land, its prosperity depended wholly on commerce. Commerce could only flourish where freedom was respected, and hence it was of paramount importance that the time-honoured rights and liberties and privileges of the Flemish people should be once more restored to them.

Nor did the new Sovereign turn a deaf ear to their reclamations. The whole land was seething with misery and discontent bred of a hundred years' oppression, and her ministers were wise enough and patriotic enough to see that only one policy was possible—a policy of general appeasement. On February 11, 1476, she signed a charter, by which was established a representative council for the government of all her states, and note the concluding clause, which is not a little significant—the Duchess declares that if any of the enactments herein contained be at any time violated, either wholly or in part, her subjects and vassals shall be thereby absolved from their allegiance until such time as they have obtained redress.

Nor was this all; to each of the cities and towns of Flanders a special charter of liberties was granted. Bruges, by the mouth of Louis of Gruthuise, had demanded the revocation of the edict by which Philippe l'Asseuré, thirty years before, had taken away her independence, and by the 7th of April the Lord of Gruthuise was able to ascend the balcony over the great door of the Hôtel de Ville and declare, amid the cheers of the assembled multitude, that Marie had granted their request. Next day the list of the privileges of the town was solemnly read in the market-place, as well as a new and more liberal charter than any hitherto granted, which gave back to the city of Bruges all her communal liberties and commercial monopolies, as well as her lordship over the Franc and over the town of Sluys.

If the communes of Flanders had been at one with themselves, and if their burghers had been agreed together, the timely concessions of their new Sovereign would perhaps have enabled the Flemish people to withstand the machinations of the feeble tyrant whom we shall presently see compassing their destruction. But the feuds which had so long hampered them in their conflicts with former rulers had not one whit abated; the little men still envied the big men, the petty towns the *bonnes villes*, the Franc Bruges, Bruges Ghent, and, added to this, there was a fresh source of disunion, a burning thirst for vengeance which could only be slaked by blood. The men who, under Philippe and Charles, had bartered liberty for pelf must pay on the scaffold the penalty of their offences, aye and if need be (for according to the law of Flanders no citizen could be put to death unless he had previously acknowledged the justice of the sentence which doomed him), if need be torture must wring from them the avowal of their guilt. The pleading of the greatest lady in the land was powerless to save them. Pale with anguish, alone and on foot, attired in deep mourning and with no headgear but a simple veil, Marie had made her way to the *Hooghuis* and from a window there had addressed the vast throng of angry guildsmen assembled in the Marché au Vendredi. 'O men of Ghent,' she had besought them, 'remember that I forgave you, and for my sake forgive your enemies.' But the burghers refused to listen. It was the first duty of a Sovereign to administer justice with an even hand, and it should never be said that in Flanders there was one law for the rich and another for the poor. Whereupon, says Philippe de Commines, '*retourna cette pauvre demoiselle, bien dolente et descomfortée.*'

In other towns besides Ghent the burghers were as firmly resolved to have their pound of flesh, and in exacting it they incurred the enmity of men no less cruel than themselves, as later on they learned to their cost.

At Bruges the burning question for the moment was the question of the Franc. Would the bond after all be dishonoured, and would the *Franchosts* submit? And when, on the 5th of April, Marie was receiving the homage of the burghers in the Church of St. Donatian, the mob burst into the cathedral with cries of 'What of the Franc?' In vain the Duchess once more proclaimed the overlordship of the city, in vain Louis of Gruthuise assured them that their apprehensions were unfounded; the guildsmen refused to disarm, nor was it until the 13th of April, when the men of the Franc sent in their submission, that peace was once more restored.

OLD ROOFS BELOW THE BELFRY

Three days afterwards, on April 16, 1477, ambassadors arrived at Bruges from the Emperor Frederick III. to demand for his son Maximilian the hand of the girl Duchess. Louis of Gruthuise and Philip of Hornes received them solemnly with lighted torches and led them to the Princenhof. 'I understand,' was Marie's reply, 'that my father approved this match, and as for me I desire no other.' The proposed marriage was no less pleasing to the Flemish people, for though Maximilian was so short of funds that Flanders was obliged to defray his travelling expenses, 'he brought to the communes menaced by France the august support of imperial blood and the contested traditions of the suzerainty of the Germanic Cæsars.'[37]

Three days later the Duke of Bavaria solemnly plighted his troth to the Duchess Marie in the name of Maximilian.

The reader will call to mind how one summer's morning, at daybreak, Longfellow from the summit of the Belfry witnessed this quaint betrothal, along with many other scenes in the history of Bruges.

'I beheld proud Maximilian
Kneeling humbly on the ground;
I beheld the gentle Marie
Hunting with her hawk and hound;
And her lighted bridal chamber
Where a duke slept with the queen,
And the armed guard around them
And the sword unsheathed between.'

The poet's account of the proceedings is not quite accurate. There was no question of sleeping. The Duchess of Burgundy and the Duke of Bavaria placed themselves on the nuptial couch for an instant only, and, moreover, Marie was never a queen. She died before her husband was elected King of the Romans.

Four months after the betrothal, at eleven o'clock on the night of August 18 (1477), the youthful bridegroom—he was only eighteen years of age—reached Ghent, and at once waited on Marie at the Hôtel de Ten Walle, where a sumptuous banquet had been prepared for him. When he met his *fiancée*, note the Flemish chroniclers of the day, both she and he bowed down to the ground, and they each turned deathly pale. Sign of their cordial love said some, presage of coming woe croaked others.

Next day the marriage was celebrated very quietly (August 19, 1477) in the chapel of the Hôtel de Ten Walle, at six o'clock in the morning, in the presence of Louis of Gruthuise and Jean of Dadizeele, of whom later on. The same day Maximilian swore to respect the liberties of Ghent, and shortly afterwards he took a similar oath at Bruges, where the burghers had adorned their streets in his honour with bunting and greenery and flowers, and had everywhere traced this one device, significant alike of present misery and the expectation of brighter days: *Gloriosissime Princeps defende nos ne pereamus.* Alas! their hopes were doomed to disappointment. It could hardly have been otherwise. With such a feeble pilot at the helm a prosperous voyage was out of the question.

Maximilian's faculties had developed so slowly that at the age of twelve years he had not yet learned to articulate, and it seemed probable that he would remain all his life with the intellect of a child. It was doubtless owing to the hopelessness of the task that up to this time no attempt was made to instruct him, and indeed, if his poor feeble brain had been early pestered with facts and figures, it is not unlikely that it would have altogether broken down under the strain. That he was able, however, later on not only to entirely overcome the difficulty which he had in speaking, but also to acquire an accurate knowledge of Latin, French and Italian, shows that there was no radical brain malady, though he remained, till the day of his death, unusually lacking in will power, morbid, vacillating, vain, and so given to day-dreaming that his waking visions sometimes almost amounted to hallucination. It would seem, then, that his good qualities—his kindliness of heart, his generosity, the ease with which he forgave injuries—were but the outcome of inclination, and that his shortcomings—his overweening ambition, his transparency, even whilst essaying to be most secret, his utter inability to keep his word, even when sanctioned by the most solemn oaths—were, after all, rather mental than moral defects.

Such was the man into whose keeping the honour and the freedom of Flanders were now entrusted, nor were the burghers long in discovering that the stalwart champion from whom they had hoped such great things was after all but a broken reed, and soon their enthusiastic loyalty was turned to bitter resentment.

As the war with France dragged on, and Maximilian, by his hesitancy and vacillation, continued to frustrate the plans of his generals, and render his own undoubted courage of no avail, his unpopularity increased from day to day. His lavish prodigality too was no small cause of annoyance to the thrifty burghers. Notwithstanding the hard times, they had contributed generously and without complaint to the cost of the war, and it was bad enough that the feebleness of their Sovereign should render their sacrifices unavailing, but not to be borne that he should lavish on foreign favourites those funds which they of their penury had contributed for the defence of the fatherland.

But this was not all: Maximilian was rapidly exhausting his wife's treasure. In 1479 he had already sold to the great house of Medici no small portion of the famous Burgundian plate. Jewels of incalculable value had found their way into the hands of Foulques Portinari, who was now threatening to put them into the smelting pot if the cash for which they had been pledged were not immediately forthcoming. He had borrowed large sums from Spanish merchants at usurious rates of interest, paying sometimes as much as thirty or even forty per cent., whilst a syndicate of Bruges merchants, amongst whom was Hendrieck Nieulandt, of whom we shall again hear later on, had advanced him no less than four thousand *livres de gros*, and, worst of all, by the end of 1481, the famous library of the Dukes of Burgundy, 'the richest and noblest library in the world,' had been in great measure dispersed. No wonder that discontent was rampant in the land, and that Maximilian, or rather the men on whose advice he acted, was daily more and more hated. Presently the deputies of the communes met to consider the situation. On one point they had made up their minds: in these hard times, with trade paralysed, industry at a standstill, and the country ravaged by war, no more of their money should find its way into the pockets of foreign favourites.

It was the beginning of the great struggle which ended, so far as Bruges was concerned, in the cancelling of all her liberties, the total destruction of her commerce, and the utter and irreparable loss of her influence and her prestige.

There was one man who, had he lived, might perhaps have rescued Flanders—John of Dadizeele, the leader of the popular party. Himself the scion of an old and noble house, after making his studies at Arras and at Lille, he had entered the service of Simon de Lalainy, when that warrior was defending Audenarde against the men of Ghent, and had remained with him till his death in 1465. About this time he married Catherine Breidel, a descendant of the great patriot, and returned to his ancestral home, where it was his delight to give hospitality to the numerous pilgrims who came to offer their vows at the famous shrine of our Lady of Dadizeele, amongst them Philippe l'Asseuré, Charles the Terrible, the English Earl of Scales (Edward IV.'s brother-in-law), Marie of Burgundy, and Maximilian himself.

From this moment two varied occupations divided his time—the trade of war and the paternal administration of his estate. At one time we find him establishing a fair in the little town subject to his sway; at another, busying himself with the erection of new and more commodious dwellings for the poor; often leading his vassals to battle, as was the case at the great triumph of Guinegate, the yeomen mounted on horses which had lately drawn the plough, and the farm labourers armed with pitchforks. He had shown himself a loyal and a devoted friend to Charles the Terrible, and when that prince disappeared after the defeat of Nancy he became the counsellor and defender of Marie of Burgundy. He had received Maximilian on the Flemish frontier, and along with Louis of Gruthuise, as we have seen, was present at the marriage which took place next day. Later on, called by his victories to the supreme command of the Flemish host, on more than one occasion he succeeded in foiling the projects of Louis XI.; presently created Grand Bailiff of Ghent, and anon High Steward of Flanders, again and again by his moderate counsel he was able to quell the rising tide of sedition amongst the craftsmen of Bruges and of Ghent. Respected alike by the Court and the communes, he was the one man capable of defending the fatherland, threatened as she was by intrigue and conquest abroad, and by anarchy and treason at home.

It was destined to be otherwise. In the dusk of the evening of October 7, 1481, as John of Dadizeele was passing along an unfrequented lane in Antwerp, he was attacked by a band of armed ruffians, and so grievously wounded that he died three days afterwards.

The authors of this dastardly crime were never discovered, and perhaps there was no wish to discover them; but rumour pointed to the Lord of Montigny and the bastard of Gaesbeke, the first the father-in-law, and the second an illegitimate son of Philip of Hornes, a man known to be one of the chief foes of the victim and high in the favour of Maximilian. Had John of Dadizeele lived, he might perhaps have moderated the passions of his friends, and protected even those who hated him. 'His death was the bursting of the last *digue* which opposed itself to the flood of civil discord which had so long been threatening the country. It was fatal alike to the men who had compassed it and to the burghers, who celebrated his funeral in a manner befitting a prince; it was the mourning of all Flanders, condemned as she now was to see the extinction alike of her domestic peace and of the last faint ebullitions of her power and liberty.'

Hardly had poor Dadizeele's mangled body been put under the sod than the first clap of thunder rolled in the lowering heavens and the first flash of lightning glittered across the sky. It happened thus. Maximilian, as usual without cash and at his wit's end to know how to replenish his empty treasury, ventured on a course of action which, had Dadizeele been still alive, he would never have attempted. Under various flimsy pretexts he caused to be put under arrest five of the principal magistrates of Bruges, men of standing and unblemished character, universally respected in the town and, to their cost, well known to be the possessors of great wealth— one of them, Martin Lem, had from his own purse lavished thousands on the war with France—hence the prosecution. Maximilian hungered for their gold, and presently for a consideration of two hundred thousand *louis d'or*, paid by way of a fine, he consented to release them.

Though the *Echevins* of Bruges were so terrified at the arrest of their colleagues that they not only made no protest, but in order to propitiate Maximilian granted him a very considerable subsidy, the *Echevins* of Ghent retaliated by pronouncing a sentence of exile for fifty years against Philip of

Hornes, who immediately after Dadizeele's murder had fled to Marie's Court at Bruges, where, under shelter of her popularity, he knew that no man would dare lay hands on him, for the sweet and comely daughter of the Terrible Duke of Burgundy was very dear to the Flemish people. As Philippe de Commines quaintly has it, '*Elle estoit très honneste dame et bien aimée de ses sujets, et lui portoient plus de révérence et de crainte qu'à son mary.*' Keeping herself entirely apart from the intrigues and machinations of her husband, and leaving the reins of government entirely in his hands, her delight was to mix with her people like the wife of some plain citizen. When before the victory of Guinegate all the women of Bruges walked through the streets in procession barefoot and with candles in their hands to implore God's blessing on the Flemish hosts, Marie was among the rest. When in winter time the Minne Water was frozen and the lads and lasses of the city disported themselves on skates, many a happy burgher was as pleased and as proud at the skill and the grace of his beautiful girl-sovereign as if she had been his own daughter. So too was it when Marie, along with her ladies, went out to hunt. As she rode down the *rue des Pierre*, across the *Grande Place*, and along the *rue aux Laines* towards the *Porte de Gand* on her way to the marshes of Oostcamp or to the woods of Maele the people cheered her to the echo.

One morning early in the spring of 1482, about

THE BELFRY FROM THE QUAI VERT

six months after Dadizeele's death, Marie went out by the *Porte des Maréchaux* to hunt in the forest of Winendael, preceded by bands of music, joyous, radiant, in festive attire. In the evening they carried her home on a litter, pale, insensible, half dead. Her steed had suddenly reared, overbalanced himself, and rolled on her. Marie was expecting the hour of her delivery. From the first there was no hope of saving her life. She lingered on for three weeks, and on the 27th of March, 1482, passed quietly away.

Though the greater part of the stately Princenhof has been pulled down, and the fragment which still remains has been irreparably disfigured and spoiled, at least so far as the exterior is concerned, by stucco and plaster, and the addition of three new storeys, the room in which Marie died is still standing, and has been little changed, so it is said, since the days when that hapless princess occupied it. It is an oblong-shaped, comfortable-looking apartment of not very large dimensions, with a beautiful panelled ceiling moulded all over with flowers and foliage, and it gives on a pleasant garden.

The fair young Duchess was laid to rest in the Church of Notre Dame, and if her wraith is not among the many ghosts who wander about that mysterious fane, the memory of her beauty and her gentleness still lingers there, kept green by the cunning workmanship of Pierre de Becker, erst artist, sculptor, setter of gems, and skilled craftsman in metal work at Brussels. This man conceived, and with his own hands carried out, patiently toiling at it for seven years, from 1495 to 1502, and thereby expending health, strength, fortune, and receiving in return no adequate reward, a masterpiece the like of which is rarely seen. An altar tomb of black marble, enriched with statues of saints and angels of the most delicate workmanship, and with creeping plants and scrolls and heraldic shields in bronze and gold and enamel, which now stands in a side chapel off the southern ambulatory of Notre Dame. On it reposes the form of a beautiful girl with her crowned head resting on a cushion and at her feet two hounds. A quaint epitaph in old French proclaims her name and rank, and begs also those who read it not to forget her soul.

Sepulcre de très Illustre princesse dame Marie de Bourgoigne.... Laquelle dame trèspassa de ce siecle. En l'age de vintcinq ans le 28ᶜ jour de mars, l'an 1482.... Regrettee plainte et ploree fut de ses subjets et de tous autres qui la cognoissoient. Autant que fut onques princesse. Priez Dieu pour son ame. Amen.

But what of her once beautiful body? All that remains of it lies in a vault beneath the choir, and here too are the bones of the Terrible Duke and the dried-up heart of the son who erected to the memory of his mother the glorious monument described above. They are all scattered about pell-mell amongst the débris of the casket and the coffins which once contained them. Thus: until the spring of 1796, the monument of Marie of Burgundy, as well as the monument of her father, stood side by side in the chancel of Notre Dame just over the vault which still contains their ashes. At this time the French Revolutionists were playing havoc with the churches of Bruges, and in order to preserve these treasures from their fury, Peter de Zitter, who was then parish beadle, with the assistance of Stephen of Sierzac, a stone mason, dismounted them and secretly carried away the fragments to a house hard by the church. The Republicans, thus baulked of a rich booty, vented their spleen on the ducal sepulchre, broke it open, wrenched off the lids of the coffins, carried away all the iron and lead they could lay hands on, and scattered the bones of Charles and of Marie on the bare stone pavement.

Ten years after, in 1806, the monuments were brought forth from their hiding-place and erected in the chapel where they now stand.

CHAPTER XXII

The Final Catastrophe

UPON the death of Marie of Burgundy the storm for a moment lulled. Philip of Hornes had fled the country; the Estates-General had assembled at Bruges to provide for the administration of the realm during the minority of the legal heir to all Marie's domains, her son Philip, now an infant of three years of age; and Maximilian, who knew very well that, in accordance with the marriage treaty of 1479, his authority over the Netherlands should now come to an end, and who hoped, nevertheless, to prevail on the communes to appoint him Regent of Flanders and guardian of his infant son, was showing himself as conciliatory as possible. He consented to the perpetual banishment of his favourite Philip of Hornes, suffered the burghers to open negotiations with Louis XI., with a view to the instant termination of the war with France, and did not hesitate to confirm a treaty of peace, which they concluded at Arras on December 23, 1482, and that, notwithstanding that the King of France was thereby acknowledged suzerain of Flanders, and that as such Louis XI. had confirmed and renewed all the rights and privileges granted by Marie at the commencement of her reign.

Meanwhile little Philip had sworn to respect the liberties of Flanders, and the deputies of the Estates-General had quietly appointed a council of regency to act in his name, viz., Adolphe of Clèves,[38] Lord of Ravestein, a kinsman of Maximilian's, erst his competitor for Marie's hand, and the most popular man in Flanders; Philip of Beveren;[38a] Adrien of Rasseghem; and Louis of Bruges, Lord of Oostcamp and Lord of Gruthuise, knight of the Golden Fleece, peer of Flanders, France and England—Edward IV. had created him Earl of Winchester in gratitude for the kindness which he had shown him in the days of his exile at Bruges—and, what he prized most of all, a burgher of his native town. The patron and friend of Caxton and of Colard Mansion, he was a marvellous lover of books, and had gathered together in the fascinating palace which he built for himself on the banks of the Roya—not his least glory, and which still bears witness to his love of the beautiful, and to the distinction and refinement of his taste—so rich a collection of choice manuscripts that the Gruthuise Library was said to equal, if not to surpass, the world-renowned library of the Dukes of Burgundy. In a word, he was a worthy scion of the house of Erembald, a patriot true to the core, the richest and the mightiest and the most beloved of the burgher-nobles of Bruges.

As for Maximilian, he was as meek as a lamb. A rebellion had broken out in Holland, and perhaps he was unusually short of cash. Certain it is that on the eve of his departure for that country, on June 5, 1483, he confirmed at Hoogstraeten, for an annual pension of twenty-four thousand *écus*, the authority of the council of regency appointed by the Estates-General. Before the end of the year, however, the conjunction of events had changed the Duke's dispositions. The man he most feared, the royal burgher of Ghent, that most incomprehensible of devotees, who stopped before no crime, and never undertook any matter of moment without first commending it to God, King Louis XI. of France, had at length set out on that inevitable journey which all his life long he had looked forward to with apprehension and dismay.

For years past the old man had been ailing. Some said that he was a leper; he had certainly had a paralytic stroke in the spring of 1480, and the sands of his life were fast running out when the Flemish ambassadors waited on him at the Château du Plessis, at the beginning of the year 1483, to obtain his ratification of the Treaty of Arras. It was evening when they reached the palace. They found the old King huddled up in the corner of a room purposely ill-lighted so as to hide the disfigurement which disease had wrought in his countenance, and so weak that he was unable to rise to receive them. His right hand was completely paralysed, and when they brought the Book of the Gospels, on which he was to swear to observe peace, he just managed to raise his arm sufficiently to touch it with his elbow.

Louis knew that his end was near. He had summoned François the thaumaturgus of Paula from the depths of Calabria to beseech him on bended knees for a few days' respite, and the saint had given him no hope. 'Set thy house in order,' he had said, 'for thou wilt die and not live.' Presently, towards the close of the year, it became clear to the King's physicians that there was no hope of further prolonging his life. Louis had strictly forbidden that any one should pronounce in his presence *le cruel mot de la mort*, his approaching end must be euphoniously announced to him by the sentence, *'Parlez peu;'* but Olivier le Dain, erst barber of Thielt, now Count of Meulan, who had for thirty years past been in the King's service—ever since the days when Louis was in exile at Bruges—with brutal levity hurled these words at his dying benefactor: *'C'est fait de vous pensez à votre conscience,'* and a few hours afterwards the old King passed quietly away.

The news of Louis's death found Maximilian elated by an easy and unexpected triumph over his Dutch rebels. Men wiser and more wicked than he had little difficulty in persuading the weak and vacillating prince that fortune herself had cancelled the bond of Hoogstraeten, and he lost no time in revoking the powers therein granted anent the government of

Flanders. Nor were the Regents slow to reply. On the 15th of October they sent in a long memorial: in virtue of the marriage treaty of 1477, the right of *mainbournie* did not appertain to the Duke of Austria, his assumption of the arms of the county of Flanders was altogether illegal, he had overwhelmed the land with taxes, pledged the Sovereign's domain, sold the crown jewels and given ear to the perfidious counsel of strangers—let France, the suzerain, judge betwixt them. To all of which Maximilian replied with reproaches and insult: he in no way recognized the right of the Regents to speak in the name of the country—men of little weight, headstrong, proud, who desired more their own profit than the welfare of the realm. Gruthuise and his comrades responded no less warmly: Adrien Villain, William Rym and the rest were men of as great weight as by far the larger number of the Duke's friends, some of whom, alike Germans and Burgundians, were in a very small way before they came to Flanders; for the rest, they had in no wise usurped the government of the county, no prince had ever been acknowledged in Flanders save by the consent of the 'three members,' and in the absence of the Sovereign, or during his minority, it was for the Estates to provide for the government of the county, and after all, justice was better administered in Flanders than in Brabant, where Maximilian still retained about his person the murderers of Myn Heer van Dadizeele. Further declaration from Maximilian: whilst he in no way recognized the right of tradesmen to put themselves on a par with the gentlemen of his Court, he begged leave to observe that the treaty of 1477 was invalid; the Duchess of Burgundy had affixed her signature to a document the contents of which she did not understand; and he ended up by summoning the Lords of Gruthuise, and Ravestein, and Borsselle, and Beveren, who were knights of the Golden Fleece, to Brussels, on the feast of St. Andrew, November 30, there to submit their conduct to the judgment of their fellow knights.

No further correspondence between Maximilian and the council was carried on for the moment. The States sent a mission to Charles VIII. to appeal for his arbitration; as suzerain, they said, and affianced spouse of the heiress-apparent, he was doubly interested in the matter, they would abide by his decision; and Maximilian, on his side, prepared to make war on his subjects, hoping to prevent by his victories the mediation of the French King. With this object in view he advanced on Bruges with the army which had lately been victorious in Holland,—this was in the beginning of February 1484—with much trumpeting drew up his men in order of battle in front of the Bouverie gate, and sent a herald to the city fathers demanding that it should be opened. But Sheriff Van Bassevelde, who was their mouthpiece, would have none of it. 'Go tell your master,' he said, 'that if he desires to speak with the magistrates of Bruges they are ready to give him audience in the council chamber of the *Hôtel de Ville*, where they are now assembled, provided his escort do not exceed ten or at most twelve persons.'

Maximilian had reckoned on a rising in his favour. A plot to assist him there certainly had been, but his friends, who were numerous, made no sign, and he retired to Oudenburg in dudgeon, thereby leaving them at the mercy of their foes. Active inquiries were at once set on foot as to the number of conspirators, and not a few leading citizens were found to be compromised. Note amongst them ex-burgomaster John Breidel, a descendant of the great patriot; this man, along with many others, was put to death, and Peter Lanchals, of whom we shall hear again, condemned to banishment.

For sixteen weary months the war dragged on. Backed, as they were, by a large French army, under the command of Crévcœur, the greatest captain of the fourteen hundreds, it seemed at first almost certain that the Flemings would presently succeed in driving Maximilian back again to Germany; but Crévcœur was not a *persona grata* to the burghers, they could never forget that he had fought against them in the days of Louis XI., and when the palm of victory was almost within their grasp, it was snatched from them by the frenzied hand of suspicion.

In the month of June 1485, Crévcœur encamped at Ghent—here too was little Philip—nor were quarrels slow to arise between the burghers and the men who had come to defend them—matter for no great wonderment; the hosts were Flemish merchants, and the guests French soldiers.

One morning Crévcœur set Philip on horseback, and made him ride through the city, in order to show him to the people. Forthwith a report was spread abroad that the French were going to carry the young prince off to Paris, and so threatening was the attitude of the mob that Crévcœur deemed it prudent to quit Flanders and take up his headquarters at Tournai. This was on June 11, 1485.

Meanwhile Maximilian, profiting by these quarrels, for it was not only at Ghent, but throughout Flanders, that opinion was divided, had been scattering gold broadcast amongst those burghers who were known to be wavering in their allegiance to France, and by this means had succeeded in raising up a party in his favour at Ghent and at Bruges. On June 1, when the people of the latter city were making solemn procession round the *Place du bourg*, with relics, and incense, and torches, to implore the protection of Heaven for the armies of Flanders, news came that the town gates had been treacherously opened to Maximilian's mercenaries, and immediately afterwards a great troop of knights and German horsemen galloped into the market.

So sudden and so unexpected was the calamity which had befallen them that the burghers, who seem to have lost their heads, made no show at resistance, and when John of Houthem, the German commander, made them a speech, and asked the vast throng assembled before him whether they wished for peace or war, a great cry went up: Peace! Peace! 'Then will you accept the Archduke for regent,' demanded Houthem, 'and acknowledge his right to the guardianship of his son?' and, with one mouth, the people answered, 'We will.'

So too was it at Ghent. The funds expended in corruption there proved an equally satisfactory investment. Hardly had the burghers hounded their French friends out of the city than, just chastisement, Maximilian's Germans took possession of it.

Presently the Archduke of Austria himself arrived at Bruges, and, before the end of the month, a treaty of peace was signed, in virtue of which he obtained the regency he had so long coveted, and the guardianship of his son. He in return granted an amnesty to all who had taken arms against him, save only certain of the ringleaders. Amongst them note Jan van Keyt, erst Burgomaster of Bruges, and Franz van Bassevelde, famous for the boldness with which he had opposed Maximilian's threats two years before. These men suffered death in the market-place, and their heads were set up on the turrets of the Halles. Note also among the excluded, Louis of Gruthuise, and that, notwithstanding that he had claims on Maximilian's gratitude, for no man had done more than he to strengthen the tottering throne of Marie of Burgundy. As a knight of the Golden Fleece, Louis of Gruthuise had the right to be tried by the brethren of his order, but he refused to exercise it. He was a burgher, he said, of the city of Bruges, and desired no other judges than the magistrates of his native town. Maximilian, however, did not dare go to extremities, Gruthuise was too popular and too powerful; he sent him prisoner to the Château of Vilvorde, and made him pay a fine of three hundred thousand *écus*.

By the end of the year 1485 the Archduke of Austria had not only re-established his authority in Flanders, but also throughout the whole of his son's domains.

Maximilian was one of those men whose appetites grow larger with eating. Conciliation increased his exigencies. Yield to him but an inch, and he asked for an ell, and when he got his ell he wanted a furlong. Fortune was singularly kind to him for a time; she gave him so much rope that he did not know what to do with it, and presently essayed to hang himself.

The first use which he made of his re-established authority was to break the oath which he had solemnly sworn at Bruges, and carry his son Philip out of the county; the second to further irritate the three *bonnes villes* by appointing the Franc fourth member of Flanders. The charter by which he committed this piece of folly was signed at Frankfort on February 16, 1486, immediately after he had been elected King of the Romans. The acquisition of this new and pompous title seems to have completely turned his head, and he gave himself over to the wildest dreams of ambition, fatuously believing that his would be the glorious destiny which the crowd of soothsayers and astrologers who frequented his Court had predicted for him. The kingdom of Hungary, the duchy of Milan were already his by right of conquest, and by the same right also the crown of Naples, and at the sword's point he had demanded, and led back from France, his daughter Marguerite, whom the Treaty of Arras had made the bride of Charles VIII., that direst foe who had stirred up trouble for him at Liège, equipped fourteen great ships in support of his rebellious Dutch subjects, and, worst of all, by promises and deeds had aided and abetted the hated burghers of Flanders, and would, but for their suspicions, have brought their affairs to a successful issue.

Presently the time arrived when Maximilian believed that he was going to realize this vision. On the 14th of August 1486, at the head of a great army, he set out for France. At Bruges the day before he had listened to an harangue by Hermolao Barbaro, the Venetian ambassador, who told him that all his successes had been his own handiwork, and his reverses the work of destiny. Puffed up by this flattery, he started fully convinced that he would soon be reckoned amongst the greatest conquerors the world had ever seen, and so sure was he of his approaching success that he dated his letters from Lens, '*première ville de notre conqueste.*'

Never was man doomed to be more bitterly disappointed. Disaster followed disaster; the treasure which he had squandered in corruption brought in no return; the princes whose support he had purchased failed him in the hour of need; his mercenaries threw down their arms for lack of pay, and presently he was constrained, with his cap in his hand, to humbly ask the help of the men he most despised, and withal to endure the shame of a curt refusal. The burghers of Flanders, the three *bonnes villes* made answer, in no way approved of the war with France, and were perfectly content with the Treaty of Arras; and when Maximilian threatened to collect taxes himself, they not only laughed at his threats but clamoured for redress of grievances. Whereupon Maximilian, in desperation, led the remnant of his army against his own subjects; but his efforts in Flanders were no more successful than they had been in France, and he was constrained to fall back on Bruges, the one town which had not yet openly broken with him.

Great was the consternation of the burghers when on December 16, 1487, Maximilian entered their city. His German mercenaries, it was well known, had for months past received no pay, and were now living on plunder. This in itself was no small cause of alarm. Moreover, the burghers profoundly distrusted him. His shameless disavowal of the Treaty of Arras had shattered their dearest hopes and overwhelmed them, to boot, with taxes, and it was now more than suspected that the real object of his visit was to wring from them fresh supplies—nay, that the city was to be deprived of its franchise and handed over to plunder. There were some garrulous old men still living who remembered the horrors of fifty years ago under Philippe l'Asseuré, and a new exodus to Antwerp was the outcome of their harrowing stories. Whereat Maximilian sought to re-establish confidence with fair speech:—he desired nothing better than peace with France, had, in fact, demanded and received a safe conduct from the French King, with a view to a meeting anent this very object.

Meanwhile the Ghenters had taken Courtrai, and the Duke, in consequence, had sent an embassy to them to treat for peace, but the victors proudly refused to deal with any but Flemish, and Maximilian, at his wit's end, besought the good offices of Bruges.

The burghers did not refuse, but they made their conditions:—the dismissal of the German guards, whose insolence and insubordination were intolerable in a commercial community, and until this was accomplished they would themselves take charge of the city gates.

After some hesitation the Duke deemed it prudent to yield: Philip of Hornes would soon be at Bruges with reinforcements and then he would be in a position to reassert his authority.

Presently (January 24, 1488) the deputies returned from Ghent with news that they had failed in the object of their mission. Maximilian, who received them in the hall of his palace, was bitterly disappointed, and though at his urgent request the burghers promised to try again, from that moment he again resumed his machinations against them, and mistrust and suspicion and evil foreboding were once more rife in the city. That very night his conduct at a banquet given in his honour at the *Hôtel de Richebourg* by the widow of Martin Lem (burgomaster in the time of Charles the Terrible) was not a little disquieting. He had suddenly left the table to make a tour of the ramparts, carefully examining the number of guards at the gates, distributing money amongst them, and so forth. On January 27 he left the city, ostensibly for the purpose of hawking, but no one believed that sport alone was his object. So too on the 28th, and on the 31st he received two pieces of news:—Philip of Hornes was close to Bruges, and the second deputation to Ghent had been as unsuccessful as the first.

The die was cast. Maximilian drew up his German guard in the courtyard of the palace and sent messengers to Hornes to enter the town at once by the *Porte des Maréchaux*. The same evening, accompanied by Burgomaster Van Nieuwenhove, one of his creatures, and a small band of attendants, to this gate he came, and demanded that it should be opened; but the gatekeepers, who suspected foul play, flatly refused. No power on earth, they said, should make them open their gates. There was no time to waste in parleying, the main object being to quietly admit Hornes and his reinforcements; but the burghers were aware of what was doing, and the Regent hastened with like result to the *Porte de Gand* and the *Porte Ste. Croix*. More fortunate at the *Porte Ste. Catherine*, by this exit he went forth—may be its guardians believed he was bent on some further excursion—dispatched messengers to Hornes to bid him enter at this spot and not to attempt to do so by the *Porte des Maréchaux*, once more returned to the city and endeavoured by force to keep the way open for him. But the guardians, crying 'Treason, treason,' had meanwhile aroused the neighbours, and before Hornes could effect an entry they had lowered the portcullis. Whereupon Maximilian fled to the Princenhof and

PORTE DES BAUDETS

summoning *Écoutète* Peter Lanchals bade him take measures to obtain possession of the city gates. It was too late. What had occurred at the *Porte Ste. Catherine* was now known throughout Bruges, and all the gates were strongly guarded by armed guildsmen. Almost in despair, the Regent gave orders to fire the town, hoping that in the confusion Hornes would somehow or other be able to effect an entrance—vain hope; the fires were no sooner kindled than extinguished. Maximilian, however, was not yet at the end of his tether. The *Porte de Gand* had been entrusted to Mathew Denys, Dean of Carpenters, who was said to be favourably disposed towards him. Again he sallied forth with a handful of faithful Germans, and again he was disappointed. With rude speech and violent gestures Mathew disdained his addresses. 'Deliver your dean into my hands,' cried Maximilian, furious at his refusal, 'and I will load you with benefits.' This, to the soldiers under Mathew's command. 'While there is a drop of blood in our veins,' was the reply, 'we will never abandon him.' 'Then at least let me leave the town,' cried Maximilian, but neither would they grant this request; they felt sure he would be off to Damme to summon the little garrison there to join the army of Hornes.

Whereupon council of war, and assembly in the *Place du bourg* of all the Duke's forces, strenuous exertions on the part of Peter Lanchals to rouse the burghers of his party to rally round Maximilian, much reluctance on their part to do so, great curiosity on the part of the multitude to learn what was going on, and no little anxiety on the part of the Germans to maintain order. *Stact! Stact!* they shouted, making a hedge with their halberds as the crowd pressed them closer and closer, which, in plain English, means 'keep back,' but in the excitement and turmoil of the moment, the people thought the soldiers cried *slact, slact*, that is 'strike, strike,' and fled helter-skelter, cry-out as they went that the Germans were going to slay them. Whereat panic unspeakable, and whilst the tocsin shrieks over the city, a host of armed guildsmen file into the market-place, bringing with them forty-nine cannons and fifty-two standards; and a crowd of trembling priests secrete in the crypt of St. Donatian's, in the secret chambers in the thickness of the walls, in the vast *grenier* above the vaults, in holes and crannies, wherever they can, their relics and their art treasures, and frantically call on clerk and sacrist to save them from the Germans; messengers are sent off in hot haste to summon help from Ypres and Ghent; Maximilian, trembling for his life, withdraws to his palace, but not by way of the market-place; the whole town thrills with excitement and a burning desire for vengeance, increased tenfold when news comes of the arrest of the incendiaries, two Moors in the service of Count van Zollern. Not a burgher but was convinced that Bruges had escaped disaster by the skin of her teeth.

Meanwhile Lanchals's house had been searched; it was found to be full of weapons, but Lanchals himself was not there—fresh proof of his nefarious designs—and in the market-place a reward of fifty *livres de gros* was publicly offered for his arrest.

Though the patriots Van Keyt and Van Bassevelde had been dead three years, their skulls were still impaled above the Halles—one on each of the turrets which flank its façade. To suffer them to remain there, now that the city was in their power, were an insult to the dead, and the burghers determined to remove them, were actually engaged in doing so, when suddenly the Regent's ministers appeared on the scene, conciliatory, quaking. He was ready, they said, to pardon the people's sedition. 'Pardon us!' roared a thousand throats, and a thousand fingers pointed to the ghastly relics of Maximilian's vengeance. 'Pardon us! The miscreant who offers us pardon is ten times more guilty than we.'

'What then would you have?' faltered Paul de Baenst. 'A new burgomaster and a new *écoutète*,' replied the guildsmen, 'instead of Peter Lanchals and Jan van Nieuwenhove, who merit death.' So terrified was Maximilian that he dared not refuse the demand, and Josse de Decker was named burgomaster, and Peter Metteneye *écoutète*.

For two days Maximilian remained shut up in his palace; on the 4th of February he ventured out, and from the balcony of the Halles endeavoured to explain, but the people refused to hear him. 'Wait,' they shouted, 'wait until the deputies of Ypres and Ghent come'; nor was this all. He was forced to listen in silence to a long letter from the sheriffs of Ghent, which must have been gall and wormwood to him, a letter promising help, announcing the defeat and death at Courtrai of his favourite Hornes, and offering congratulations that Bruges was now out of danger. Nor until he had heard the command given to make diligent search for his counsellors, in order to bring them to justice, was he at length suffered to return to his palace.

On the morrow fresh news came from Ghent. Adrien of Rasseghem had just torn up the *kalfvel* of 1485. 'For God's sake do not disarm. Be not deceived by Maximilian's specious promises, but keep good watch over him until the meeting of the Estates-General, and make sure of the persons of his counsellors.'

Great was the enthusiasm of the burghers, and they set about pitching tents in the *Grande Place*, for the weather was bitterly cold, and they were determined to remain under arms until all danger was past. In the midst came news that Maximilian had fled, news which turned out to be false, but in order to calm the people the burghers invited him to show himself among them, and presently he appeared in the market-place, gorgeously arrayed in cloth of gold and seated on a magnificent charger. Nor did he meet with a lukewarm reception; the people cheered him to the echo. Their hatred was for the moment transferred to the members of his council. Whereat Maximilian, no doubt relieved, made them a speech: he had no thought of leaving Bruges; if they doubted his word, let them set a watch at the palace. The burghers, who were practical men, replied that they would consider his proposal, and at the end of half an hour informed him that the deputies of the three *bonnes villes* were just about to meet, and that while they were discussing matters it would be well for him to take up his abode in the Craenenburg.

The Craenenburg was at this time the property of Hendrieck Nieulandt, a merchant of great wealth, to whom Maximilian was heavily indebted. It was situated at the corner of the *rue St. Amand*, and was the most magnificent private residence in the market-place. From its balcony the Counts of Flanders were wont to witness the public games and festivities which so frequently delighted the citizens of Bruges, and there Maximilian had himself been diverted, some three weeks before, by the squeaks and grunts and ungainly bounds of a herd of frantic swine, and the no less uncouth shouts and falls of the blind sportsmen who were pursuing them. Not a very edifying spectacle, one would think, for a prince who longed for and afterwards grasped an imperial diadem, and who would, if he could, have put on his finger the ring of the fisherman. But, other times other manners, and let us never forget, as a recent writer aptly and pithily has it, 'Notre ancêtre du moyen âge est un grand enfant, il s'amuse aux choses extraordinaires pullulant aux pays lointains, et par dessous tout ... il est grossièrement joyeux.' He was all that certainly in Bruges at the close of the fourteen hundreds, and perhaps his descendants in the same city are all that to-day.

The King of the Romans, attended by a numerous suite, took up his abode in Nieulandt's palace on the evening of the 4th February 1488. Shortly afterwards, perhaps the next day, the deputies from Ghent and Ypres arrived, the Ghenters bringing with them two thousand armed men. All the trades guilds of Bruges were assembled in the *Grande Place* to welcome them, and their advent was greeted with cheers and the thunder of cannon. After solemnly attending Mass in St. Donatian's the general assembly of the three *bonnes villes* was declared open, and presently business commenced. There were some who were sanguine enough to believe that peace would be the outcome, but for the burghers to come to an understanding with Maximilian was in reality a task almost impossible of accomplishment. The Prince was so shifty and the people were so exacting. The chief point at issue was the guardianship of young Philip. Maximilian had shown himself in forty several ways, the men of Ghent alleged, unworthy to exercise the rights of a father, and he must never again be permitted to do so. Had he not sworn to educate his son in Flanders, and then taken him out of the county? Before any terms of peace were arranged they must have some solid guarantee that Philip would be brought back again. Then there was the question of the Treaty of Arras, and the alleged plot to ruin Bruges, a matter which called for instant investigation, and if their suspicions—they were more than suspicions—should prove correct, justice must be meted out to the men who had instigated it, and there were a hundred other grievances to be redressed before any lasting peace could be established.

Meanwhile Charles VIII. was doing all in his power to help the Flemish people. Divesting, as suzerain, of their legal authority all those officers who continued to act for and in the name of Maximilian, 'who,' he averred, 'had usurped the regency, violated sworn treaties and minted base coin in his own name,' authorizing the burghers to themselves appoint magistrates who should 'act in the name of the child Philip, now held prisoner by the King's enemies,' and to coin their own cash, signing charters innumerable, confirming ancient privileges, conferring new rights, granting full liberty to the merchants of Flanders to travel without let or hindrance throughout the kingdom of France—in a word, showing himself generally the friend and staunch supporter of democracy, the last barrier, as it seemed to him, to the Germanisation of the Netherlands.

On the 13th February all these charters were solemnly read in the market-place at Bruges, as well as the text of the Treaty of Arras, and a long report on the attempted destruction of the city, whereat the guildsmen wax furious, break into Maximilian's palace—the Princenhof—find there four hundred barrels of gunpowder, scaling ladders innumerable, and something more ominous still, coils upon coils of stout rope. What was this for? Not a man of them but believed that the Duke had meant to hang him. Next day, in consequence, arrest of fourteen privy councillors, Flemings, Burgundians, Germans, four of them in Maximilian's own chamber. All of these men had fancied themselves safe because they were attached to the royal person.

The same evening a deputation of burghers pay Maximilian a visit of condolence, bid him take heart, and assure him that they bear *him* no enmity; that his person is perfectly safe in their hands, and that they are ready to do anything in their power to make him comfortable. Maximilian, nevertheless, unconvinced and exceedingly depressed. February 16, commencement of trial of Jan van Nieuwenhove and sundry others arrested the day before. Great deliberation on the part of the judges who, sitting with closed doors, have already spun out the proceedings for two days, when the mob outside, losing all patience and frantically shouting that the judges have gone

to sleep and it is time to awaken them, break into the Court House, drag the accused forth into the market-place, and presently bring hither the rack.

On the evening of February 17, Carnival. Hell let loose:—a weird farrago of gibbering masks, and wailing ghosts, and gorgeous dresses; a veritable pandemonium of obscene songs and lecherous yells and hysterical laughter; a drunken whirlwind of mad furies shrieking vengeance, whilst, to the strains of delirious music, they wildly dance around the headsman's block and bloody axe, and, a still ghastlier thing, a rack of new and improved fashion, which has never yet been used, but soon will be, set out in grim array before the Halles. Suddenly the air grows thick with smoke, the Belfry gleams out roseate against the black sky, and great tongues of flame dart up to heaven. Somehow or other the venders of fruit and fried fish and cheap finery have managed to fire their booths, and thus, during the small hours of Ash-Wednesday morning, the fierce orgies are fittingly brought to a close with a fiercer conflagration.

The tumult of Monday night seems to have had the desired effect. When the Court re-assembled on Ash-Wednesday morning the judges were wide awake, and one after another in rapid succession the accused were found guilty and condemned to death. Before, however, the sentences which had been passed were carried out, it was deemed prudent to change the place of Maximilian's imprisonment. On more than one occasion he had almost effected his escape, and the Craenenburg was not thought to be sufficiently secure. Moreover, it was not roomy enough to accommodate the numerous retinue of gaolers with which, under the guise of attendants, it was deemed necessary to surround him. Perhaps too the burghers wished to spare Maximilian the pain of seeing his friends die. During the whole period of his captivity they seem to have treated him with the utmost consideration, regarding him not so much as a criminal as an amiable but dangerous lunatic, whom, indeed, for the sake of the public weal, they were bound to put under restraint, but whom, at the same time, they were no less bound to make as comfortable as possible. When he passed through the *Grande Place* on his way to his new prison and in trembling accents besought the people to see that no harm befell him, 'have no fear,' they cried, 'we bear you no grudge, your counsellors alone are to blame,' and the palace to which they led him, in the *rue St. Jacques*—it had recently been occupied by Jean Gros, Chancellor of the Golden Fleece—was in all probability hardly less spacious and no less luxuriously furnished than the Princenhof itself.

KITCHEN IN GRUTHUISE

Some idea may be gathered of the stately homes of the burgher-nobles of Bruges during this period from the recently-restored habitation of the Lords of Gruthuise, the most perfect and the best preserved of the few mediæval palaces still left to the city; and be it noted that the *Hôtel Gruthuise*[39] of to-day is only a fragment of the original building; there was another great wing on the further bank of the river connected with it by a bridge, nor is it likely that the mansion of the Chancellor of the Golden Fleece was in any way less magnificent. Here, then, we may picture to ourselves the same beautiful pavements of glistening white tiles relieved by delicately-designed patterns in red and blue and green and gold; the same wealth of carved oak in door and shutter and ceiling; the same huge chimney-pieces of carved stone, brilliant with colour, jutting out over hearths not deeply set in the thickness of the wall, as in England, but shallow and broad and high and all lined with fair ceramic tiles of russet and sage green, and glowing now, for it is winter-time, in the light of flaming timber placed on dogs richly wrought in brass or iron. We know that costly tapestry was hung on the walls and that curtains of silk and velvet draped the windows; of their delicate texture and marvellous design a visit to the museum beneath the Belfry will show something, and here, too, are treasured up not a few specimens of the beautiful carved oak furniture, as well as of the glassware and pottery, which was used at Bruges when Maximilian was a prisoner there; whilst the pictures of the Van Eycks of Memlinc and of other artists of the period bear witness to the glorious colouring of the woven fabrics and the embroidery of those days.

Nor was the King of the Romans without companions or means of distraction. Twelve members of his household were permitted to share his prison. *Tir à l'oiseau* was inaugurated in the courtyard. From time to time the trade guilds with flaunting banners marched past his windows, 'in order to occupy his leisure and to drive away his melancholy.' His table too was sumptuously served. The burghers had even got his plate out of pawn for him, and every evening some of the most stately of them were wont to pay him visits, in order, as they said, to cheer him with conversation friendly and loving—*vriendelic end mimusamelic*.

CHIMNEY-PIECE IN THE GRUTHUISE PALACE

Nor was this all. *Écoutète* Peter Metteneye was in constant attendance, as he was in duty bound to be, and at his beck and call were thirty-six servants, who, like their chief, never left the house. But Maximilian knew very well that all this solicitude on the part of Myn Heer Peter was not the outcome of a keen desire to exactly fulfil the obligations of his office, but was rather prompted by fear lest his victim should escape; that his thirty-six servants were in reality thirty-six turnkeys, and that the *Écoutète* himself was gaoler-in-chief. What wonder that when Antoine de Fontaine came to visit Maximilian in Master Jean Gros's mansion he found him '*fort amaigry et pâle.*'[40]

In consenting to quit the Craenenburg Maximilian had removed the last obstacle which might perhaps have prevented or at all events retarded the execution of those of his friends who were prisoners like himself. The day after he left a great scaffold draped in black was erected in the *Grande Place*. Gilbert du Homme, a Norman, erst Burgomaster of the Franc, died first, then came Jan van Nieuwenhove; so battered and weak was he with the torture which he had undergone that they had to give him an armchair in which to await his turn for death. Perhaps the sight of his misery had unnerved the executioner; he struck three times before he succeeded in severing the head from the body.

Another man who had been Burgomaster of Bruges perished the same day, Jacob van Dudzeele, Lord of Ghistelle. He had been arrested in the Craenenburg under the very eyes of Maximilian, and to the last he protested his innocence. 'For fifty years,' he said, 'I have served the princes who have succeeded one another in the government of this county, and I have never played the traitor. If any man affirm the contrary, I am ready to do battle with him, no matter who he may be, and to do all that behoveth a good and loyal knight, a nobleman, and a burgher of this town.'

Note that Ghistelle here esteems his citizenship no less highly than his knighthood or his nobility. Such was the wont of the burgher-nobles of Bruges. In vain the lady of Ghistelle besought the guildsmen to spare her lord. In vain his children, the Provost of St. Donatian's, the Dean of Notre Dame and the foreign merchants, joined their supplication to hers. Jacob's head rolled on the scaffold.

On the 15th March Peter Lanchals, long sought for, was at last found, betrayed by one of his friends for a hundred *livres de gros* and to save his own head, for death had been decreed against any man who should shelter him. He was arrested the same day by Burgomaster Jan van Haman, who conducted him to the Steen, and the howls of contempt and hatred which greeted his passage through the city were kept up around his prison all night. The men of Bruges were beside themselves with a delirium of fierce gladness. Volleys of cannon were fired off, bands of music paraded the town, and they danced and drank in the streets till morning, for had not this man been Maximilian's head and heart and right hand in all his infernal machinations? Had he not intended to deliver Bruges over to be pillaged by the Germans? Had not the whole devilish plot been of his hatching? That cruel instrument of torture which he had invented, more cruel than any known hitherto in Flanders, should persuade him to own it. And it did, whatever we may think of an assertion made under such circumstances. By a strange irony of fate Lanchals was the first to test the efficacy of his own invention. Tortured as he had been, and in pitiable plight, Peter still clung to dear life. 'Put me in some black hole and there let me eat out my heart,' he vainly pleaded, 'but for God's sake let me live!' When at length he saw that the people had no pity, he suffered the executioner to strip him of his clothes. One of the guild deans touched the gold chain which he wore round his neck. 'Sir Dean,' said the dying man, 'you know well that no burgher of Bruges can be condemned to forfeit his life and his goods,' and he handed the chain to his confessor and begged him to give it to his wife; then he besought the people that his body might receive honourable burial, and having commended his soul to God, he bade the executioner do his duty. In addition to his tomb and the chantry erected by his widow in the Church of Notre Dame—the same chantry in which now stand the tombs of Charles the Terrible and Marie of Burgundy—there is yet another souvenir at Bruges, and a more pleasing one, of poor Peter Lanchals:—the graceful, long-necked birds which disport themselves in great flocks, sometimes as many as thirty or forty of them together, on the canals and streams of the city. These birds belong to the corporation, and they are the descendants, tradition says, of the swans which Maximilian, when he regained his liberty, bade Bruges maintain for ever as a perpetual memorial of his favourite's death. Lanchals, it should be noted, signifies in Flemish, long neck, and the swan is a prominent figure in the Lanchals family arms.

The news of these executions and of others, which, like them, were the outcome, it was said, of 'the justice of the people,' made Maximilian tremble in his prison. Perhaps he had cause to do so. The men of Venice had written to the men of Bruges to urge them to cut off his head: *Homo mortuus non fecit guerram*. And there were others who trembled for him—his father, the Emperor Frederick III., who wrote to the magistrates of Bruges warning them that he should hold them personally responsible for any evil which might befall the King of the Romans; the Pope, who threatened interdict; several German princes, who were making ready, it was said, for invasion; and his son Philip, who summoned the estates of Hainault and of Brabant with a view to obtaining their good offices. They invited the communes of Ghent and Bruges to meet them in conference at Malines. Louis of Gruthuise, now set at liberty, threw in his weight on the side of conciliation, and early in the spring of 1488 the Estates-General of all the provinces of the Netherlands met in solemn conclave at Ghent. Two great measures were the outcome of their deliberations—a treaty of confederation by which the various provinces mutually bound themselves to defend their rights and privileges, and a treaty of peace with Maximilian of which the conditions are sufficiently curious. The communes on their part promised to set their prince at liberty without further delay, on condition that he should undertake to dismiss his foreign *gens de guerre* within four days. In order to facilitate their departure the three *bonnes villes* undertook to pay Maximilian within a month twenty-five thousand *livres* Flemish upon the understanding 'that if the aforesaid *gens de guerre*' had not departed within the stipulated period, the money should be expended in the payment of '*autres gens de guerre* who by force should expulse them.'

For the rest, it was agreed that Maximilian should at once bring back his son to Flanders, and that during his minority the county should be administered by the three Estates in Philip's name, that Maximilian should strictly adhere to the Treaty of Arras, cease to quarter the arms of Flanders on his escutcheon and promise to protect Flemish merchants all the world over, and that the communes should pay him by way of *solatium* an annual pension of a thousand *livres*.

There was some difficulty at first as to sureties. Maximilian had named the Duke of Saxony and the Marquis of Baden, but these princes hesitated to guarantee his good faith; it were an undertaking, they averred, too risky. The knot was at length cut by Philip of Cleves, who, on learning of the difficulty, wrote to Maximilian offering to do anything in his power to help him. Philip was the son of the Lord of Ravestein, one of the four regents whom Maximilian had accepted at the commencement of his son's reign. He was a man deservedly popular amongst the burghers, his influence with them had contributed in great measure to the successful issue of the negotiations, and in due course his name appeared at the head of the list of guarantors.

The communes, however, were not yet satisfied, and that, though Maximilian, in order to further reassure them, had renounced Philip's homage so that he might be free to take up arms against him in the event of his breaking his troth, and Philip, at his request, had bound himself by oath to do so. The treaty of peace, they said, must be ratified by the Pope, the Emperor and the imperial Electors, and before Maximilian was set free he must undertake to obtain such ratification. He seems to have had no hesitation in doing so, for the same day he left Jean Gros's palace and, preceded by priests with relics, and guildsmen with banners and torches, betook himself to the market-place, where, on the very spot on which the scaffold had lately stood, a magnificent throne had been erected, surmounted by a richly-embroidered canopy. Hard-by there stood an altar, and on it was set a Book of the Gospels and amid flaming torches the Host. Before these sacred objects Maximilian presently knelt down and 'with much seeming fear and reverence took the appointed oath. "Of our free will we promise," he said, in a voice so sweet'—we are quoting the words of one who heard him—'that it would have melted a heart of stone, "of our free will we promise and swear in good faith on the Sacred Host here present, on the cross, on the Book of the Gospels, on the precious body of St. Donatian and on the Canon of the Mass to carry out wholly and entirely the treaty of peace and alliance which we have concluded with our well-beloved Estates ... and on our princely and royal word, on our honour, and on our faith we hereby promise never to do anything to violate it." ' Maximilian having thus pledged himself, the Bishop of Tournai solemnly blessed all those who should keep inviolate, and afterwards solemnly cursed all those who should presume to infringe, the treaty agreed to that day (May 16, 1488). Then followed a sumptuous banquet, then, at St. Donatian's a *Te Deum*, after which Philip of Cleves, who had only just reached Bruges, took oath 'to aid them of Flanders against all infractors of the said peace, union and alliance.' At length, after an imprisonment of eleven weeks, Maximilian was once more free. Towards sundown he set out for his château at Maele, the deputies of the Estates of Flanders accompanied him part of the way, and before he bade them farewell he again confirmed his promises. 'Monseigneur,' Philip had said, 'you are now a free man, tell me frankly your intentions.' 'Fair cousin of Cleves,' replied Maximilian, 'believe me I shall keep my word,' and thus they parted.

Great was the joy of the city of Bruges, and the people determined to make a night of it in the *Grande Place*, as is still their wont upon festive occasions, with malt liquor and music and dancing, without which accompaniments no Flemish festival ever has been, or probably ever will be, complete. Suddenly the band of musicians who had stationed themselves on the summit of the Belfry ceased playing. They had descried a hundred tongues of flame rising up from the woods of Maele. Maximilian's foreign *gens de guerre* were celebrating their master's return by firing the peasants' homesteads, and though next day Maximilian sent word to Bruges that the incendiaries had not acted under his instructions, and perhaps he spoke the truth, what had happened was far from reassuring, and men began to doubt whether the peace which had just been signed would after all be one of long duration; nor were their fears ill founded. From the first the King of the Romans had been playing a double part. Even whilst the negotiations with his burghers were pending he was secretly pressing the imperial Electors to send their armies against them; four days after the peace of May 16 had been publicly proclaimed in the cities of Flanders he felt himself strong enough to drop the mask.

Maximilian had now taken up his abode in the impregnable fortress of Hulse, and from thence he issued a proclamation to all the communes of Flanders informing them that he did not intend to observe the treaty he had sworn to. An oath, he said, taken under obligation had no binding force.

It was enough. Maximilian had once more shown the cloven hoof, the Flemings had once more been deceived, and soon in every city and in every hamlet in Flanders the tocsin was shrieking war.

In an age when treason and suspicion of treason were rampant throughout the realm, when on all sides men were plotting against their neighbours and at the same time were surely convinced that their neighbours were plotting against them, Philip of Cleves affords us a bright and shining example of loyalty and good faith. An honest, straightforward, generous man, conscious of the cleanness of his own heart and his own hands, he found it difficult to convince himself that even those whom he felt it his duty to oppose were inspired in any sort by motives less conscientious than his own. As soon as he had learned of Maximilian's treachery he thus wrote to him:—

'PRINCE MONSEIGNEUR,—In fulfilment of my oath, and for fear of offending God our Creator, I have promised to aid and assist the three members of Flanders. This with very great regret of heart I now signify to you, for, inasmuch as it toucheth your noble person, as your very humble kinsman I would fain do you all service and honour, but inasmuch as it toucheth the observance of my oath I am bound to God, the Sovereign King of Kings.'

They made him captain of the Flemish army, and all that was noblest and all that was best in Flanders rallied to the side of the communes; men like Louis of Gruthuise and Philip of Burgundy, and even the Lord of Chantraine, who from the walls of Sluys had threatened the frantic guildsmen during the reign of terror at Bruges. Nor under Philip's leadership do we find the burghers guilty of the excesses—the bloodshed, the violence, the illegal confiscations—which had rendered their government so evilly notorious at the time of Maximilian's captivity. Their chief object for the moment was to quell the German mercenaries who were scouring the whole country, pitiless in face of submission, craven when their victims showed fight. Thus, on the night of the 8th of June these marauders had surprised Deynze; before morning it had gone up in flames, and of its people but a handful were left to tell the tale; so too Courtrai, where the citizens and their wives and their children perished along with the churches in which they had sought refuge; but when they appeared before the walls of Ypres and found there the burghers of Bruges under Louis of Gruthuise standing beside their cannons, they halted and cried out for a truce. 'What God can your master invoke to witness his oaths?' were the scornful words hurled back to them.

It does not lie within the scope of this handbook to give any detailed account of the incidents of the campaign which followed. Save the abortive attempt to take Sluys, and Maximilian's equally futile endeavour to obtain possession of Damme, they only concern indirectly the city of Bruges. Suffice it to say that though during the first few weeks of the struggle the Communes held their own, after twelve months' hard fighting they were compelled to submit.

Under the circumstances no other issue was to be expected. Maximilian had behind him the strength and resources of the empire, and he was actively supported by Henry of England, who for political reasons had now become his staunch friend, whilst the Flemish mistrusted their only ally the French, and by their jealousy and suspicion foiled all their efforts to save them.

On October 30, 1489, a treaty of peace was signed. By it the communes undertook to acknowledge Maximilian as Regent of Flanders, to pay him a fine of five hundred thousand livres, of which two-thirds was to be forthcoming before Christmas, and to send deputies to beg his pardon and perform in their name the usual childish humiliations; whilst the King of the Romans agreed to dismiss his German garrison, to grant a full and complete amnesty, to confirm all the administrative acts of Philip of Cleves and his council, and to swear to observe all the rights and privileges of the county of Flanders.

When first the treaty was signed the joy at Bruges was unbounded, but when it became a question of the first instalment of the indemnity, and of assessing the amount for which each commune was liable, trouble again broke out. The three *bonnes villes* complained that they had been assessed unfairly and appealed to Philip of Cleves, who, foreseeing at the time that the treaty was signed that the trouble was not yet in reality over, had retired to the great fortress at Sluys, and from that vantage post was watching events.

About this time Adrien van Rasseghem, a citizen of Ghent, who had hitherto been taken for an honest man and a staunch patriot, having been corrupted by Maximilian, turned traitor and opened the city gates to the Germans. Some four nights afterwards, as he was returning home, he was attacked by a band of armed men and slain, and next day Philip of Cleves publicly avowed that he was responsible for what had happened; whereupon the Count of Nassau, Maximilian's lieutenant in Flanders, threatened Bruges with fire and sword unless she should instantly submit and break her alliance with Philip. The burghers refused. The city and the whole country round was seething with misery. The land, long untilled, and almost bereft of inhabitants, was so infested by wolves that the peasants dared not lead out their flocks to pasture. The dikes, altogether neglected, because no man in these troublous times had leisure to repair them, had at last given way, and great part of the country-side was flooded. But this was not all. The peasants had to contend with a foe more to be dreaded than wolves and fiercer than rushing waters: English and Spanish and German adventurers were ravishing and slaying and burning everywhere. The historic castle of Maele, save the basement and one great tower, which is still standing, had been reduced to ashes, and every night the watchers on the Belfry saw the sky grow suddenly red with some new fire. In the town matters were worse. So great was the expense of the war, that from August 1 to October 27 (1490) it had cost the burghers ten thousand six hundred *livres de gros*, and the city treasury was empty. Trade was altogether at a standstill, for months past no vessel had entered the harbour, the foreign merchants had migrated to Antwerp, the land supplies were all intercepted by the Count of Nassau, and even rich men were starving. So real and so great was the distress, that among the crowd of famished wretches who daily waited outside the bakers' shops to obtain a meagre pittance of bread, not a few dropped dead in the streets. Yet, notwithstanding all this, Bruges was resolute. In the hour of his necessity she would not break with the man who had risked his all to save her. Nor did Philip of Cleves show himself less generous. As soon as he knew that he alone was the obstacle to the re-establishment of peace, he wrote to the *Echevins* of Bruges, begging them to make the best terms they could, leaving his interests out of the question. At last, after several abortive negotiations, a treaty was signed at Damme on November 29, 1490. Bruges agreed to pay eighty thousand *couronnes d'or* as her share of the fine fixed by the Treaty of Tours, to make humble apology to the Count of Nassau, and to hand over to him sixty persons to be dealt with according to his pleasure; but for all that she did not escape pillage. A house-to-house visitation was made, and all the gold and silver and precious objects that they could discover the Germans laid hands on. Nassau reserved no small part of the booty for himself. It is said that the famous Hôtel de Nassau at Brussels was built with the funds thus raised, and a hundred years later, during the troubles under Philip II., his descendant William of Orange was reproached with it: *le Comte Inghelbert vouloit que l'on vous hachât tous en pièces, et la maison du Comte Henri de Nassau fust faicte des amends de ceux de Bruges.*

Thus disappeared amid riot and terror the last remnant of that prosperity which had so long made Bruges glorious.

As for Philip of Cleves, he held his ground manfully at Sluys for two years longer. At length, owing to an accidental explosion by which he lost all his ammunition, he was compelled to surrender to Maximilian's English allies under Sir Edward Poynings. Nevertheless, such was the esteem in which he was held, even by his enemies, that he obtained an honourable peace. True he swore fidelity to Maximilian and resigned to him the town of Sluys with the small fortress. But he was permitted to hold the great castle until such time as Maximilian should pay him a sum of forty thousand florins, for which he was in his debt. Further, he was assured an annual pension of six thousand florins, and all his property, which had previously been confiscated, was assured to him.

Later on we find him fighting under the banner of the Cross, and presently, when he visited Rome, Pope Alexander VI. averred that to him, along with Gonzalves, was due the honour of having kept the Infidel out of Italy.

V.—Genealogical Table of the Counts of Flanders from Philippe le Hardi to Philippe le Beau.

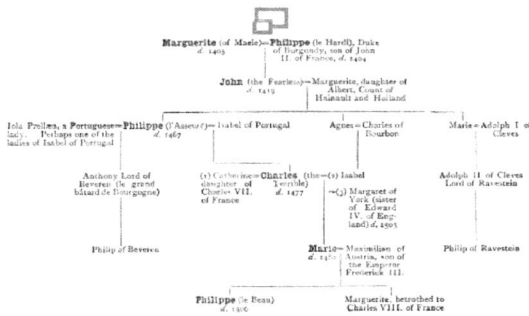

Philip ended his days in the forest of Winendael, hard-by Bruges, clad in a hair shirt and leading a life of no little austerity, perhaps by way of penance for the murder of Adrien van Rasseghem, the one blot on his character.

CHAPTER XXIII

The Architects and Architecture of Bruges in the Fifteenth Century

FROM the commencement of the fourteen hundreds until the dawn of the struggle with Maximilian, which ended in the final catastrophe of 1490, the city of Bruges was growing almost daily more picturesque and more beautiful. Most of her public and private buildings date from this period, and those of them which were erected earlier were now enlarged and adorned with sculpture and painting. We have seen poor Louis of Maele laying the foundation stone of the *Hôtel de Ville* at the close of the previous century, but it was certainly not completed until the opening years of the fourteen hundreds. The documents are still in existence which prove a fact not generally known that at this time no less an artist than John van Eyck was gilding and colouring the façade. The stately octagonal lantern, the crowning glory of the Belfry, was erected some sixty years later, in 1482, when the signing of the Treaty of Arras had re-kindled hope; the same year the chevet of the Cathedral was commenced and the Church of St. Jacques completed, whilst the southern aisle of Notre Dame and the beautiful Paradise porch at the foot of the tower date from the middle of the century. About this time too the present aisles and transepts and choir were added to the Church of St. Gilles, the Jerusalem Church was finished, the Church of

the Beguins and the Hospital Church of St. John rebuilt, and a host of convent chapels and chantries and shrines were springing up all over the city.

In 1477 the beautiful building in the *Place des Biscayens*, which is now the Municipal Library, was erected for a Custom House; the architectural gem which adjoins it, the guild-hall of the porters, dates from seven years earlier, and all over the town the great city companies—there were no less than forty-seven of them—were building for themselves chapels and courts, a few of which exist to the present day, notably the Shoemakers' Hall in the *rue des Pierres* and in the same street the hall of the great guild of masons; the beautiful shrine which the painters erected in the *rue d'Argent* (it is now the Chapel of the Josephite nuns) and dedicated to their patron St. Luke; and the Smiths' Chapel in the *rue des Maréchaux*, in front of which every year, on the feast of St. Eligius, the horses of Bruges were blessed. Strangely enough the building in question now serves as a stable. The foreign merchants, too, were vying with one another in the erection of sumptuous palaces, where the traders of each nationality dwelt together in almost monastic seclusion.

Note amongst those still standing the Black House, as it is called, a grim, weird-looking building behind the theatre. It is erroneously said to have been used later on as the Court House of the Inquisition, and of course is in consequence haunted. A most interesting habitation this, with mullioned windows in which much of the beautiful old green glass is still remaining, protected on the outside by wrought-iron grills. It contains a spacious hall with a timber roof, vast chambers with low ceilings moulded all over with fruit and flowers and foliage, and a suite of apartments panelled in cedar, the whole fast falling to decay. Then there is the Paris Hall, where French merchants formerly congregated, now degraded into a pot-house called *Charles le Bon*. The façade has been spoiled with whitewash and plaster, but the old gables at the back are still brown and beautiful, and have endured nothing worse than the caresses of time. At the corner of the *rue des Pelletiers* at its junction with the *rue Flamande*, stands an old mansion of beautiful grey stone, embellished with sculpture and Gothic windows rich in geometrical tracery. Unspoiled and unrestored, it is still a fair and stately building. It was once the hall of the merchants of Genoa.

Looking on to the canal at the end of the *rue Espagnole* stands a spacious habitation which has evidently seen better days. Here dwelt the merchants of Spain. A little further down on the banks of the same canal was the loveliest palace of all, the *Maison des Orientaux*, the home of the great traders of the Hanseatic League (1480). The builders were already at work at it in the month of August 1478,[41] and when it was completed three years later, it was one of the most beautiful edifices in brick in the city of Bruges. Zegher van Maele, who lived early enough to behold it in all its glory, affirms of the tower that in his day there was not its equal in all Flanders, and Guiccaiardini, who wrote in the early sixteen hundreds, informs us that all the iron work in the interior was gilded. Mark Gheeraert's plan of Bruges, published in 1562, furnishes an illustration of this wondrous mansion. It was a large, oblong-shaped, crenelated building, four storeys high, with slender turrets at each corner corbelled out from the walls at the second storey, and terminating in iron finials surmounted with metal flags. The façade giving on the *Place des Orientaux* was divided into five vertical panels or bays with round-headed arches. In these the windows were placed, and the spaces between each storey were filled with flamboyant tracery. Adjoining the main building, but slightly in the rear, there was a turreted annex of smaller dimensions, though conceived in the same style. This, perhaps, was the refectory, for all the inhabitants dined at a common board. In front of this building was a spacious courtyard, two sides of which were formed by the façade of the refectory and the eastern façade of the main building, and the other two by beautiful crenelated walls with a slender and very graceful turret at their angle. The tower and spire which called forth the admiration of Van Maele sprang from the side of the main building, which gave on the courtyard, and for the rest, towers, turrets, chimneys were everywhere adorned with graceful panelling or dainty Gothic tracery in moulded brick. All this splendour is among the things which have been. Only a fragment of the old palace now remains: the main building, shorn of its tower, its pinnacles, and its upper storeys, and there is now nothing left to indicate its glory of former days. This piece of vandalism was committed about a hundred years ago, when the prosperity of the city of Bruges was at its lowest ebb. The proprietor at that time was without the means of keeping so extensive and costly a mansion in repair, and the city fathers either could not or would not come to his assistance.

It was not only, however, by these public or semi-public buildings that Bruges was enriched during the period we are now considering. At this time, and more especially during the long peace of over thirty years which followed the great humiliation of 1437, there appears to have been a veritable mania for construction. From Duke Philip himself to the meanest householder in Bruges, every man seems to have been afflicted with it.

Those of the great burgher-nobles who already possessed palaces enlarged and embellished them; the new men who had recently amassed fortunes vied with the old aristocracy in the magnificence and luxury of the mansions which they now built; plain, well-to-do merchants were everywhere constructing those roomy, comfortable abodes, which, with their high stepped gables and their façades enriched with stately panelling and Gothic tracery, still render the streets and squares and waterways of Bruges the most picturesque in Europe. Even working men, humble members of the great guilds of smiths, or masons, or carpenters, were making their homes beautiful with the fruit of their handicraft; constructing canopied niches at street corners, or over the doorways of the hovels in which they lived, and placing in them graven images of Our Lady or of some favourite saint; hammering out exquisite lanterns, which it was their delight to hang before them, from brackets of no less dainty fashion; fabricating, of wrought-iron, those quaintly beautiful trade signs by which it was their wont to call attention to their avocations; making door, and lintel, and chimney, and rafter comely with fruit and foliage, fascinating with heraldic devices, and grotesque and leering heads, and the images of devils and of saints.

Much of this work has of course disappeared, but some of it still remains to bear witness to the skill and the energy and the devotion of these poor toilers.

Amongst the nobles who about this time enlarged their palaces note Louis of Gruthuise, whose grandfather John had erected, probably during the closing years of the previous century, that portion of the *Hôtel de Gruthuise* which skirts the left bank of the river. The stupendous kitchen, of which we give a sketch, dates from this period. Not content with this magnificent pile, Louis added thereto, in 1464 or thereabouts, the great wing at right angles to it, and thus made the home of his ancestors the most magnificent mansion in the city. Here it was that he stored his famous library, and here he entertained, in 1471, King Edward IV. and Richard

Crookback. Even the upper chambers in this sumptuous abode are paved with encaustic tiles, and it is no less than three storeys high, and when it was restored some few years since, it was found that the spaces between the timber ceilings and the flooring in the rooms above were in each case filled with earth. Thus all noise is effectually confined to the floor in which it is produced. The palace is connected by a covered way with the Church of Notre Dame, and here Louis erected, in 1474, a very beautiful tribune of sculptured stone and carved oak. It is an exquisite piece of workmanship, in the flamboyant style of the period, adorned with rich tabernacle-work and fruit and flowers, and with Louis's initials and his family arms, and his proud device, *Plus est en nous*, which last appears over and over again throughout the whole palace. It is in a wonderful state of preservation, and, strangely enough, seems to have entirely escaped alike the hand of the iconoclast and the restorer. Indeed, the Gruthuise tribune in the Church of Notre Dame has probably been little changed since the days when its founder and his family worshipped there more than four hundred years ago.

There are two other points of interest about this fascinating mansion. During the process of restoration there was recently discovered a secret chamber in the great kitchen chimney, and in it the skeleton of a man. Behind the same chimney there was also discovered a secret staircase leading to two underground passages branching off in opposite directions. Neither has yet been explored, but it is supposed, and probably rightly, that one of them communicates with the vaults beneath Notre Dame. As for the other, the *concierge* avers that it leads to the Château of Maele some four miles out of the town, a most unlikely conjecture. True there is a tradition that an underground passage exists between the Chapel of St. Basil and the château in question, and this is sufficiently conceivable. Subterranean ways and subterranean chambers are not unknown in Bruges, and they have sometimes been discovered in strange places. Only recently, when a heavily-laden waggon was entering the *rue Flamande* from the *Grande Place*, the ground sank beneath its weight, and one of the wheels was embedded in a deep hole. Some bricks in the vault of an unsuspected cavern had suddenly given way, and the vast chamber thus disclosed was afterwards found to extend for a considerable distance along the street and beneath several houses on each side of it. Moreover, St. Basil's was originally the Court Chapel, and Maele, as we have seen, had from time immemorial been a favourite residence of the Sovereigns of Flanders. But why should the Lords of Gruthuise have secretly connected their town house with one of the ducal castles? It is much more likely that the passage in question communicated with their own manor at Oostcamp.

Chief among the *parvenus* who at this time laid out vast sums in bricks and mortar note Peter Bladelin, son of Peter de Leestmaker, by trade himself dyer of buckram, and who, in his youth entering the service of Philippe l'Asseuré, presently rose to the important position of Controller-General of Finance. Not content with erecting a palace at Bruges and a *château fort* in the open country beyond Maele, around the walls of his castle he built a whole town (1444), which he endowed with a church (1460) in honour of St. Peter, and surrounded with fortifications. This place he called Middelburg, and though it has now dwindled down to a mere village, it was at one time a centre of no small importance. Here, after the sack and burning of Dinant by Charles the Terrible in 1466, a colony of brassworkers found refuge. Bladelin obtained for them from Edward IV. the same privileges and exemption from English custom dues as they had enjoyed in their native city, and to this day a street in Middelburg is called *La rue des Dinantais*.

In the great quarrel with Maximilian, Middelburg took the side of that shifty prince, and the men of Bruges repaid them in 1488 by razing their fortifications and destroying their castle.

We first get a glimpse of the founder of Middelburg in the spring of the year 1452, when we find him, in company with Louis of Gruthuise, shutting the gates of Bruges in the face of a deputation of Ghenters who had come to beg that city to give them her support in their struggle with Philippe l'Asseuré, and afterwards, along with Gruthuise, going out to parley with them and trickily making them believe that they had attained the object of their mission. 'He was a man,' says the Flemish chronicler Chastelain, 'of much wealth and of much sense, and the most trustworthy person in the county of Flanders, although his honesty was not to the taste of all, and many, alike gentle and simple, grieved thereat.... He was, moreover, controller of the Duke's household, one of the four treasurers of the order of the Golden Fleece and but a plain citizen of Bruges. One excellent quality he had—he managed the Duke's affairs marvellously well; there, where there was rent or wound, he always found means to heal or mend, and he paid cash for all goods delivered at the palace. All this the Duke was well aware of, and on this account and for other reasons he gave him the high position he held. For in sooth he was a wise man, and one to be relied on, comely alike in person and in morals, and none more industrious and diligent than he could well be found.'

THE HÔTEL BLADELIN

In the *rue des Aiguilles* at Bruges there still stands a fragment of this worthy's town house. It is a spacious, picturesque gabled construction of tawny brick, with a bold octagonal tower of the same material crowned with a balustrade of sculptured stone and a beautiful crocheted steeple. Beneath a canopy of delicately-carved tabernacle work, which, in its turn, is sheltered by a more substantial canopy of lead and wrought-iron and oak, note, over the doorway, a statue of the Madonna and Child, with Bladelin himself kneeling in adoration, and, in a carved niche below, a shield displaying the arms which Philippe l'Asseuré granted him. This is a restoration of some five or six years since. The original work, save some fragments of the stone canopy, had totally disappeared, but drawings fortunately existed from which it was possible to construct a facsimile.

Sir Peter Bladelin was treasurer of the Golden Fleece, and the emblems of this order appear over and over again carved on the great oak beams in the interior of his mansion.

All that is most interesting in Bruges is, somehow or other, associated with the Church of Notre Dame, and here, though his palace was in the parish of St. Jacques, Bladelin founded a chantry, which he dedicated to St. Margaret, the patron saint of his wife. It is the second chapel off the northern ambulatory, but is now completely shut off from the rest of the church and converted into a chamber for the *marguilliers*. Together with some interesting old pictures, and a few quaint pieces of furniture, it contains the only ancient stained-glass window in the Church of Notre Dame. This relic, however, is in no way connected with the Lord of Middelburg, and dates only from the year 1520.

Peter Bladelin died on the 6th of April 1462, and was buried in the parish church of the town which he had founded.

There is still in existence in the museum at Berlin a portrait of the worthy Peter. It was painted by Roger van der Weyden, or, as he is sometimes called, Roger of Bruges, the most famous of the pupils of John van Eyck (1400-1464) and is one of the master's last and most perfect works. It is in the form of a triptych, and was undoubtedly painted for the church at Middelburg, where it most probably remained until the opening years of the sixteen hundreds, for a copy on canvas of about this date is still in possession of the church. It was discovered in 1854 by Canon Andries, at that time parish priest, behind a panel in the wall of the presbytery kitchen. He had it restored and placed it in the chancel over Bladelin's tomb. The subject is the Nativity of Our Lord, and the artist's method of treating it is a curious and unusual one. *Lumen ad revelationem gentium: et gloriam plebis tuæ Israël*; this must have been the text which inspired him. In the central panel the Divine Infant is lying on the ground, adored by His Blessed Mother, St. Joseph and angels. On the left the Cumæan Sibyl is showing the Emperor Augustus, through the open lattice window of a typical Flemish apartment, an apparition of the 'Light to enlighten the Gentiles.' The Emperor, arrayed in the richly-embroidered garments of the fourteen hundreds, is in a kneeling posture, and holds his cap in one hand, whilst with the other he offers incense from a Gothic thurible. On the right-hand panel are the Magi presenting their gifts, and along with them Bladelin himself kneeling in adoration, whilst, in the background, is a view of the town of Middelburg.

The mansion called De Zeven Torens (the Seven Towers) in the *rue Haute* (Nos. 6 and 8) was also erected during this period. Who was its builder is uncertain, nor has its early history come down to us, but we know that Charles II. of England dwelt there two hundred years later, from June 1656 to February 1658, and when Mark Gheeraerts made his famous plan of Bruges in 1594 it was still a magnificent building, with four graceful towers springing from the façade which gives on the *rue Haute*, and three on the opposite side of the house. These have long since disappeared. The whole building was remodelled, probably during the course of the eighteenth century, and it is now, alas! no longer beautiful.

The Ghistelhof, in the *rue des Aiguilles*, so called from its having been at one time the home of the powerful lords of Ghistelle, has fared better. Erected in the year 1460, with its mullioned windows and high pitched roofs, and far above them its beautiful brown cylindrical tower crowned with a steeple of red tiles, it still forms a most picturesque group, though there can be no doubt that, in the heydey of its glory, it was a much more spacious and magnificent building than it is at present.

Then there is the Hôtel d'Adornes,[42] of which the Jerusalem Church was at one time the private chapel. These buildings were erected by two brothers, Anselm and John Adornes, the former in the year 1428, and the latter in 1465. The courtyard of the ancient palace, with its gables and Gothic windows, and beautiful wrought-iron, is a quaint and comely corner, and the little old-world sanctuary, though it has suffered much from the ravages of time, and more from the devastations of man, is no less pleasing. The plan is sufficiently uncommon, perhaps unique: a nave without aisles, and, at the east end, a huge tower of which an upper storey forms the sanctuary. This is approached from the nave by two

THE GHISTELHOF

staircases with balustrades of wrought-iron, and separated from it by a sculptured rood screen. The general effect is very curious, the high altar being thus

COURTYARD OF THE HÔTEL ADORNES.

raised some ten or twelve feet above the rest of the church. The building is lighted by eight windows, six of which are filled with ancient stained glass (1482-1560), with portraits of the founders and other members of the family, along with their wives and their patron saints. In the centre of the nave is an altar-tomb on which repose the effigies, carved in stone, of Anselm Adornes, the son of one of the founders, who died in Scotland in 1483, and his wife, Margaret van der Banck.

Beneath the choir, and slightly below the level of the nave, is a dark and gloomy crypt, the atrium to the Holy Sepulchre. This is approached by a passage so low that it can only be traversed by going on hands and knees, and so narrow that but one person can enter at a time. The sepulchre itself, which is behind an iron grill, is said to be a facsimile of the Holy Tomb in the garden of Joseph of Arimathæa. One of the founders of the Jerusalem Church is known to have visited Palestine. When Philippe l'Asseuré was contemplating a new crusade, he applied to this man for information as to the holy places, and there is still in existence an account of the pilgrimage which his son Anselm made to Jerusalem. Within the sepulchre, covered with a veil of richly-worked point lace, lies the effigy of the dead Christ, so realistically modelled that, in the dim light of the single taper which illumines the vault, it is difficult not to believe that one is in the presence of a corpse.

Note yet another glorious mansion—a stately pile of red brick at the end of the *rue du Vieux Bourg*. It is still a building of vast proportions, and in former times it was considerably larger. When Mark Gheeraerts made his map it was adorned with a beautiful steeple, and to this day it possesses a stupendous Gothic doorway through which there would be no difficulty in driving a coach and four. A house with marked features this, and a face full of expression—a house which one instinctively feels must have a story. Perhaps Peter Lanchals dwelt here; certainly in later and calmer days it was the home of Mark Laurin, Lord of Watevliet and Canon of St. Donatian's, and a staunch supporter of the New Learning, who numbered among his guests and intimate friends Erasmus, and perhaps too Sir Thomas More and Cuthbert Tunstall. Presently tenants of another sort inhabited its hospitable walls. Here for three weeks dwelt the Merry Monarch before he went to the *Zeven Toren*.

TOMB OF ANSELM ADORNES

For the rest, the Craenenburg in the Grande Place, of which we have already spoken; the great brown brick house with a tower and a grey stone gable by the *Pont St. Jean Nepomucene*, and where later on Perez Malvenda hid the relic of the Precious Blood; and, most famous of all the palaces of Bruges, the Princenhof of Philippe l'Asseuré; these too were erected during the period we are now considering, and there are others no less magnificent, all trace of which has long since disappeared; amongst them the mansion of Jean de Gros, where Maximilian was imprisoned. But if this sumptuous residence has been swept away, Bruges still possesses a sample, sadly mutilated indeed and shorn of all its splendour, of its founder's handiwork—the aisle which he built in 1472 off the southern side of the choir of St. Jacques.

And what of the architects who designed, and the masons and carpenters and other craftsmen who together produced all these glorious buildings? The names of some of them have come down to us—Nicholas Willemszuene, for example, who was Master Mason of the city of Bruges from 1414 to 1436, and Dean of the Guild of Masons from 1426 to 1432; he constructed the southern turrets of the Hôtel de Ville, and probably also the beautiful house of the Florentine Consuls (1429); George Weylaert, Dean of Masons in 1468 and 1473 and 1482; he was the architect and builder of the Church of St. Jacques, all his work is perfectly executed, and the brick moulding of the windows is especially excellent; Vincent de Roode, Master Mason of the Hospital of St. John, and probably the author of the beautiful chapel, now sadly defaced, erected in 1475; and, greatest of them all, Jan van de Poele, member of the Guild of Masons from 1472 to 1516. The most beautiful monuments erected in Bruges during this period are from his designs. He was not only an architect and a builder but a sculptor of no mean order. The stately octagonal tower of the Belfry is perhaps his work; the beautiful façade of the Palais du Franc, of which we shall have something to say later on, is certainly so, and it was he who designed the chevet of the Cathedral of St. Sauveur, with the ambulatory and the seven bays of the apse, and also the *Maison des Orientaux*, whilst we find him furnishing five statues for the adornment of the chantry of Peter Lanchals. Van de Poele's work in the Cathedral is not only in itself exceedingly beautiful, but it bears witness also to his skill as an engineer. He conceived and successfully carried out the daring scheme of converting the seven huge windows of the apse into arcades, whilst at the same time retaining the ancient triforium and clerestory above them. Thus the Cathedral of Bruges affords a perhaps unique example of a structure of the thirteenth century supported by piers and arches of the fifteenth. Van de Poele did not live to complete the chevet; he died in 1520, and the work was carried on and at last completed in 1527 by Ambrose Roelandts and John Beyts, each of them Master Masons and perhaps his pupils.

Until the end of the thirteen hundreds the houses of Bruges were all constructed of wood, and the designs of the buildings of brick which at this time began to take their place, with their lofty gabled façades, adorned, as they generally were, with a vast Gothic arch, were perhaps inspired by the reminiscence of the wooden edifices which preceded them. This is the opinion of the learned architect and archæologist Verschelde, who, for years, had made the ancient buildings of his native town his especial study, and Mr. Weale and Canon Duclos are of like opinion; but the most casual observer cannot fail to be struck with the resemblance which these great arches bear to the huge windows so common in the gables of churches of the thirteen and fourteen hundreds, and it may well be that it was from these that the architects of the brick dwellings of the period we are considering and of the similarly adorned timber façades of the century which preceded it alike drew their inspirations.

So too the series of panels or bays which presently superseded the single arch. These formed a frame for the windows of the various stages, and terminated at the summit, sometimes in pointed, more frequently in round-headed arches, which were at first filled with geometrical tracery. So like are they to the long, narrow windows usual in the public buildings of the period that a mansion thus adorned might easily be mistaken for some old Gothic church or hall with its windows bricked up converted into a dwelling-house.

Later on, towards the close of the century, the geometrical tracery above the highest storey became flamboyant, and the spaces in the panels between the various stages were similarly enriched. Jan van de Poele was probably the first to introduce this innovation, witness the *Hôtel des Orientaux*. One of the most beautiful specimens of this kind of ornament is to be found in the façade of an old red brick mansion, now divided into three houses, Nos. 38, 36 and 34 in the *rue de Jerusalem*, which dates from the opening years of the fifteen hundreds. In the *rue Pré aux Moulins* there is a smaller but yet more beautiful example of the same date; in the *rue Queue de Vache*, a whole series of houses on either side of the way, and, most beautiful of all, the charming bay window which Herman van Oudvelde, in his day Dean of Goldsmiths, added to his house at the foot of the *Pont Flamand* in 1514. This system of ornamentation, which gradually grew more and more elaborate as time progressed, continued to be employed until the middle of the sixteen hundreds, or perhaps even later. There is hardly a street in the city which does not contain one or more, often a long, unbroken series of façades thus adorned.

VAN OUDVELDE'S WINDOW BY THE PONT FLAMAND

The tower, too, was a very ordinary feature, not

QUAI DU ROSAIRE

only in public buildings and palaces, but in the ordinary domestic architecture of mediæval Bruges. Indeed, at the opening of the fifteen hundreds, as Mark Gheeraert's map bears witness, Bruges was a city of steeples. They have, however, for the most part disappeared, and those that have come down to us can be almost counted on the fingers. The old mansion in the *rue aux laines*, to which we have just called attention, possesses, as we have seen, one. It is at the back of the house, and the summit alone is visible from the street. A stone's throw from it, on the further bank of the Roya, hard-by the *Quai du Rosaire*, there is another—a beautiful, red brick, dilapidated structure, crowned with a silvery steeple, the last tower erected in mediæval Bruges. Those in the *rue des Aiguilles* we have already noted. There is a fifth in the *Place Memlinc*, very tall and very slender, octagonal in shape and wholly devoid of ornament. When the Smyrna Consuls, who dwelt in the house to which it is an adjunct, first erected it, it was not so comely as it is to-day. The waxing and waning of four hundred summers and the rude embraces of wind and weather have marvellously beautified it, and the blushing brick of which it is constructed is now all shot with gold. Close by, in the *Place des Biscayens*, there is another and a more stately tower of grey stone. It stands alongside of the *Poorters Logie*, a sort of mediæval club-house where the burghers in days gone by were wont to hold convivial meetings. There is a seventh and very beautiful tower on the ramparts at the end of the *rue des Carmes*. It adorns the home of the great military guild of St. Sebastian. There is an eighth by the *École Normale*, a mere ruin, the last remnant of the habitation of a kindred society—the Crossbowmen of St. George and St. Denis. It is a great square tower of red brick, which originally was considerably higher than it is at present, and it contains a very curious stone staircase with a beautiful groined ceiling. This building is the property of the town, and the corporation intend to restore it and convert it into a clock-tower for the *École Normale* and furnish it with a *carillon*.

The list of ancient turreted mansions in Bruges is completed by the *Hôtel Gruthuise*. Here are two octagonal towers, one of them of considerable dimensions and no less curious than pleasing.

GUILD HALL OF THE ARCHERS OF
ST. SEBASTIAN

It will be interesting to note that the taste for towers has recently revived in the city of Bruges. At least five new buildings are provided with them, nor do they compare unfavourably with some of the work of the builders of former days. Notably the red brick tower of the *Académie* in the *rue Ste. Cathérine*, from the designs of Monsieur de Wolf, who at present occupies the position of city architect, and the station clock-tower, of which the steeple is a reproduction in miniature of the glorious steeple which once crowned the Belfry.

As for the material employed by the ancient architects of Bruges, it was chiefly brick, not the smooth, fine grained, sharp edged kiln brick beloved of the modern English builder, but beautiful, rough surfaced, clamp brick, for the most part small in dimensions, in hue sometimes red, sometimes what is technically called white, more often parti-coloured, always fair to look on, exceedingly durable, and in some cases carved like stone. No less pleasing were the tiles and slates with which they roofed their buildings, the former flat, oblong, ruddy, of slender dimensions, the latter of similar shape but not quite so small, and their colour! grey, purple, green, and, when the sun shines on them, silver shot with gold. Go up into the Belfry on some glad summer's morning, look down on the ancient roofs of Bruges, and thou shalt not regret it.

CHAPTER XXIV

The Painters and the Pictures of Bruges in the Fifteenth Century

FROM time immemorial the culture of the arts, and notably of the art of painting, has largely entered into the lives alike of the people of Flanders and of the kindred folk of the neighbouring provinces. Thanks to the influence and the fostering care of the great monastic houses, which were everywhere scattered about these lands, the races which inhabited them had at a very early period attained no little proficiency, not only in the science of construction, but in the art of adorning their buildings with sculpture and pictorial representations, and it may be justly said that the monks of Flanders—her first artists and her first artisans—made possible that glorious page in the history of Flemish painting which begins with the divine harmonies of Hubert van Eyck and ends with the colossal splendour of Rubens.

The chronicles which these cloistered toilers compiled, the books which they made beautiful with gold and colour and fantastic devices, the frescoes which of late years have been brought to light in all parts of the country, these things bear witness to it.

Adelard II., Abbot of St. Trond, who died in 1082, was renowned in his day as a painter. At Liège there were frescoes in the Church of St. Martin dating from the close of the nine hundreds, the Cathedral of St. Lambert in the same city was similarly adorned years before the fire which destroyed it at the end of the twelfth century, and at this epoch the artist-monks of the Abbeys of Lobbes and of Stavelot were famous throughout Europe.

The great Abbey of St. Bavon at Ghent as early as the eleventh century possessed a school of artists. Some of their illuminated manuscripts have actually come down to us, and are at present in the Ghent university library. At the little town of Maeseyck in Holland they still preserve an eighth-century manuscript adorned by Harlinde and Rilinde, two of the abbesses who ruled the convent which in those days flourished there. Among the seven hundred and thirty-four manuscripts in the municipal library at Bruges, and in the library of the Bruges diocesan seminary, there are some which date from the thirteenth century, a few from the twelfth. Many of them are of rare beauty. Notably, at the city library, a thirteenth-century missal embellished with exquisite miniatures (No. 314), and, at the seminary, a Cistercian missal and a Cistercian Breviary of the fourteen hundreds, and a splendid Valerius Maximus in four volumes, with paintings which are perhaps by John van Eyck. The greater number of these books were written and illustrated in the famous Cistercian Abbey which once stood on the Dunes at Coxyde, between Furnes and Ostend, or by the monks of the affiliated house, called Ter Doest (All Saints), which Hacket founded at Lisseweghe.

Bruges in the thirteen and in the fourteen hundreds was famed for her miniaturists and her illuminators. The *Bibliothèque royale* at Brussels contains a whole series of manuscripts which once formed part of the sumptuous libraries of the last Flemish Counts—of Robert of Bethune, of Louis of Maele, of Philip the Rash, and which one and all bear witness to the marvellous skill and untiring patience of the men who wrote and adorned them; these assuredly were not all monks, many of them, doubtless, were laymen, members of that great artist-guild of St. Luke, of which we shall have something to say later on. Some of them basked in the smiles of princes, like John van Eyck, whom Philippe l'Asseuré enriched and to whose son he stood godfather, and who enjoyed too the patronage of the Regent Bedford; or Simon Marmion, who received from Charles the Terrible a sum equal to no less than three hundred and sixty pounds for a single book of Hours; or Jean Fouquet, the friend and confidential adviser of Louis XI. Others there were content with the position of sleek upper servant in the household of some lesser Mæcenas, and others again, who longed to hold such a post, but were unable to obtain it; men like poor Jehan Gillemer, for example, who, on the tramp in search of a patron, was presently arrested as a spy by the agents of Louis XI. and handed over to the tender mercies of Tristam l'Hermite, a circumstance, notes M. Lecoy de la Marche,[43] not too deplorable, since to it we are indebted for the details of his life which have come down to us, and are thereby enabled to lift a corner of the veil which covers the manners and customs of one of the most interesting corporations of the middle ages.

A poor, weak-spirited credulous creature was this obscure miniature painter, but for all that he seems to have had the soul of an artist and no little skill in his calling. Sometimes, indeed, he worked for princes, but he by no means despised the custom of their menials, was not above mere penmanship, and did not think it beneath him to alter or complete, even for a humble client, the unfinished work of a *confrère*. He journeyed half over Europe to dispose of his productions, to obtain new orders, to have his works bound in the most artistic fashion, to seek inspiration from the best models and to perfect himself generally in his art; and he used to collect wherever he went and from whomsoever he came in contact—from churches, from monasteries, from the private libraries of the nobles whose houses he frequented, from the menials whose acquaintance he made in the servants' hall, from courtiers, from begging friars, from the chance companions whom he drank with at inns, sometimes, perhaps, new receipts for mixing his colours and for laying on and burnishing gold, more often strange forms of devotion and talismans warranted to cure every imaginable ill, from love-philtres and charms to soothe toothache and settle disputes, to astrological formulæ to drive away the devil, and, above all, to enable him to keep in order 'those five great hulking apprentices' at home who always would idle away their time, and whenever he ventured to say a word to them ill-used him.

Amongst the illuminators enrolled in the Guild of St. Luke were all sorts and conditions of men; from polished courtiers like John van Eyck to men doubtless of as questionable character as the obscure individual, half artist, half perhaps fortune teller, though, for the matter of that, he swore on the damnation of his soul he had had no dealings with familiar spirits, whose vagabond life the rack of Tristam has revealed to us. But whatever their social rank may have been, like the monks who worked alongside of them, the cloister was the rock from which they were hewn, and 'the exquisite work which some of them produced is sufficient to alone explain the origin of Flemish panel painting.'

Thus, Monsieur Fiérens-Gevaert recently,[44] and Lübke and Wauters and Jules Helbig, before him, though these experts tell us that sculpture and wall painting had likewise some measure of influence, and traces of frescoes almost as old as the buildings they once adorned have of late years been found all over Flanders.

At Bruges, for example, we have the frescoes which Mr. Weale discovered at Notre Dame in the Chapel of St. Victor at the entrance to the tower. Here the lower portion of the wall was diapered in crimson and gold, and above were depicted five angels playing on instruments of music. Mr. Weale describes these paintings as exceedingly beautiful and in a sufficiently good state of preservation; alas! they have been again covered with whitewash. Others were found behind the woodwork of the churchwarden's pew at the west end of the nave, and yet another in the southern ambulatory near the sacristy door—a beautiful figure of St. Louis, dating apparently from the middle of the fourteen hundreds, and there can be no doubt whatever that, if the whitewash were carefully removed, it would be found that the whole building is similarly adorned. So too the Cathedral of St. Sauveur and the Church of St. Jacques, and, just outside the city, the Churches of Notre Dame at Lisseweghe and at Damme, in all of which there are, or rather there were mural paintings. Indeed, those in the last church extended round the whole building. Unfortunately they were much damaged in removing the whitewash, and they have again been hidden from view. Other vestiges of wall painting have been found in various parts of the city, and we know from documentary evidence that in 1336 Jan van Jabbeke was commissioned to paint a series of frescoes in the Justice Chamber of the old Hôtel de Ville. Even the vaults and brick graves in the churchyards were thus adorned, though in ruder fashion. Several discovered at Varssenaere, in the cemetery of Notre Dame, and in the *Place St. Jean*, where an old church dedicated to that saint once stood, have been bodily removed and are now in the museum beneath the Belfry. They suffered very little injury in the process and are in a marvellous state of preservation.

But this was not all; even the very stonework at Bruges, and this was no doubt also the case in other Flemish cities, glowed with gold and colour; sculpture, statuary, tracery, the mouldings of doors and arches and windows were not unfrequently thus embellished; we have seen Van Eyck and other artists engaged in illuminating the niches and the carved figures on the façade of the Hôtel de Ville; there is an ancient picture of the interior of Notre Dame which represents the capitals of the nave radiant with gold and vermilion; vestiges of polychromy within and without, on woodwork, on plaster, on iron, on stone, have been discovered all over the city. It is no exaggeration to say that Bruges at the opening of the fourteen hundreds, the richest, the mightiest and the loveliest city of Northern Europe, was at this time steeped in harmonious tints. She had already entered upon the autumn of her existence, but, like Nature, she had arrayed herself in a vesture of gold wrought about with divers colours, and the cunning workers who had woven and embroidered it—the painters of frescoes and the stainers of glass, the illuminators of vellum and the illuminators of stone—were the precursors and fathers and founders of the most glorious school of painting which the world has yet produced. The Van Eycks, the Memlincs, the Van der Weydens, all the Flemish primitives, whose marvellous pictures still fill us with admiration, lived and moved and had their being in the beauty which these men created. The statues, the miniatures, the mural painting of these poor craftsmen were the models which inspired their first work, and there is reason to believe that the insatiate thirst for colour which their predecessors had experienced led indirectly to the famous discovery which rendered its execution possible.

In a country like the Netherlands, devoid of precious marbles, there was only one way of satisfying it—to find some artificial means of colouring the material at hand, and in that damp, changeable climate the pigment applied must needs be of a nature to withstand the vagaries of weather.

The monk Theophilus, a writer often quoted in the twelfth century, gives exact formulæ for mingling colour and oil, but the pigment thus obtained was far from being satisfactory; a second coat could not be applied until the first was completely dry, and the length of time which it took in drying rendered it practically useless, at all events for the painting of pictures.

For centuries artists all over Europe were vainly endeavouring to remedy this defect, and it was not until the opening of the fourteen hundreds that the problem was at last solved, but long before that period oil paint had been successfully employed for decorative purposes. We know that the sculptor Wuillaume du Gardin made use of it for his statues as early as 1341, and when Hubert van Eyck first came to Bruges at the close of the fourteenth or at the opening of the fifteenth century the practice seems to have been generally adopted. It has long been known that John van Eyck was an *enlumineur des statues*, and a document recently discovered in the archives of Ghent makes it quite certain that his elder brother Hubert followed the same calling; what more likely then, than that the idea should have struck him of painting his pictures with the same pigment with which he had been in the habit of decorating stone? But whatever may have led to his great discovery, certain it is, that the day on which he made it was the birthday of modern art.

The invention of oil painting has until recently been generally assigned to the year 1420 or thereabouts, but if Mr. Weale is right in his calculations, and be it borne in mind he has devoted a lifetime to the study of the Flemish primitives, and has done more to elucidate their history than any living man, Hubert van Eyck's great oil-painting, the only picture which can as yet be certainly assigned to him, 'The Adoration of the Lamb,' at Ghent, cannot have been commenced later than 1415, probably even earlier. It follows then that the new process must have been invented prior to that date.

HUBERT VAN EYCK

Hubert van Eyck, the first and the greatest of the Flemish masters, was born at the little market town of Maeseyck in Limbourg, somewhere about the year 1366. He seems to have been of an old painter family, as not only Hubert himself but his brothers John and Lambert and his sister Marguerite all followed this calling. Of his life's story we know little, of his early years hardly anything. An illuminator of missals and an illuminator of statues, as well as a painter of pictures, perhaps, as Mr. Weale has recently suggested, he made his first studies at Maestricht or at Cologne and afterwards travelled in Spain and in Italy. By the opening of the fifteenth century he must certainly have been an artist of some reputation, for in 1413 John de Visch, Lord of Axel and Capelle, bequeathed to his daughter Mary, who was later on Abbess of Bourbourg near Gravelines, a picture which Hubert had painted. What was its subject or what has become of it is not known.[45]

He seems to have passed his middle life at Bruges,[46] and there are still in existence two pictures attributed with reason to him, which must have been painted during his sojourn there. The first represents Our Lady, St. Anne and Herman Steenken, who was Vicar of the Chartreuse of St. Anne at Woestine near Bruges, from 1402 to 1404, and from 1406 till his death on April 23, 1428. This picture is at present in the possession of Baron Rothschild at Paris; the second is now in the Berlin Gallery; it depicts the same monk, but apparently some ten years older, Our Lady and St. Barbara.

The last years of Hubert's life were spent at Ghent. In the year 1424 we find him receiving from the aldermen of that city 6s. gr. for the sketches of two pictures which they had commissioned him to paint for them but were apparently never executed. Perhaps he had not leisure to do so. About this time Hubert must have been fully occupied. He had a triptych in hand which Robert Poortier had ordered for a chapel in honour of St. Anthony, which he had founded in the Church of St. Sauveur, at Ghent, and a statue of the same saint to gild and colour, also for Robert Poortier. For years he had been at work on 'The Adoration of the Lamb,' and we know that he had not completed it when death struck him down on the 18th of September 1426.

These facts, if they be facts, represent all, or very nearly all, that is known of the story of Hubert van Eyck. Perhaps we have his portrait. Amongst the crowd of figures displayed on his marvellous triptych at Ghent, note in the foreground of the outer left wing a citizen riding on a white horse. Tradition tells us that this man is no other than Hubert himself, and that the rider behind him on the brown horse is his younger brother John.

But if we know little or next to nothing of the home life and surroundings of Hubert van Eyck, his merits, says Lübke, as the founder of an entirely new mode of painting are established beyond doubt. 'Not only by reason of the improvement which he effected in the process of mingling colour with oil, and his successful adaptation of the new method to the painting of pictures, does he justly deserve the title of Father of Northern art.' He was the first to bring back the cultus of beauty, and the first to bend before Nature's shrine. He was set in the midst of a plain full of dry bones, and by the might of his genius he made them live, and whilst he gave largeness and depth and reality to the conventional art of the Middle Ages he lost not one whit of its old ideal grandeur. Utterly discarding the golden backgrounds of former days, he bathed his creations in the glow of Nature's aureole as he saw it in the green fields and fair woodlands of his native land, and whilst he set on them the impress of his own epoch and his own race, he at the same time invested his sacred figures with sublime grandeur and dignity and a certain ineffable sweetness which is altogether peculiar to himself. In this respect his painting has been rarely equalled and never yet surpassed.

No vestige of Hubert's work remains in the city on the Roya, but hard by in the old Cathedral of St. Bavon at Ghent is his masterpiece, 'The Adoration of the Lamb'—a picture, indeed, not painted at Bruges, but for all that instinct with the ethos of Bruges, which still preserves the memory of her magnificence, still keeps alive one quivering ray of her aureole, and is perhaps the most perfect reflection we have of the beauty which enshrined her at the epoch when she was fairest. Nay, it is something grander and nobler and holier than this. It is a sublime transcription in gold and colour of the poetry of the Mass, an inspiration incomparable and altogether unique. 'Like Dante's Divine Comedy and Bach's Passion Music it stands, in its sphere, alone.' Make a journey to Ghent and gaze upon this marvellous picture, and perchance its splendour shall enlighten thy soul, and then go down into the crypt and kneel before the tomb of the man who created it.

John van Eyck

We know something more of the life of John van Eyck than of the life of his master and elder brother Hubert. His junior by twenty years, like him he was born at Maeseyck, and though his pictures have little in common with the primitives of Maestricht or Cologne he seems to have made his first studies in his own neighbourhood, and later on to have accompanied Hubert to Bruges. A man of many parts and many achievements, painter of pictures, stainer of glass, illuminator of parchments, illuminator of stone—no uncommon circumstance at a time when every artist was an artisan, and every craftsman an artist—he added yet to his varied talents no little skill in diplomacy, was entrusted by his sovereign with sundry private and delicate missions, and travelled for him frequently and far, sometimes in order to paint pictures, sometimes on matters of state.

Whilst still a young man John van Eyck parted company for a time with his brother. In the autumn of 1422 he was appointed *peintre et varlet de chambre* to Duke John of Bavaria, the famous Jean sans Pitié, Prince-Bishop of Liège. When that militant prelate was gathered to his fathers some two years afterwards, Philippe l'Asseuré received his heritage, and upon the recommendation of '*plusieurs de ses gens*' he confirmed Van Eyck in his office and in all the customary honours and profits appertaining thereto,' granting to him, over and above, an annual stipend of a hundred *livres*, a sum equal in current coin to about one hundred and sixty pounds.

After a short sojourn at Bruges the young painter journeyed to Lille, probably to execute some work there for his new master, for during his entire stay in that city, nearly three years, Philippe paid his house rent. In the summer of 1428 he set out on *certains lointains voyages secrez* which the Duke had commanded him to make, *en certains lieux dont il ne voulut autre déclaration être faite*. Probably Spain was the place of his destination, and the object of his journey to find Philippe a wife. If so, his sojourn there must have been of short duration, for before the end of the year we find him in Portugal busy painting 'a most life-like portrait of the Infanta' Isabella, who shortly afterwards became Philippe's affianced bride. By 1433 he was again at Bruges, and in the course of the year he purchased a house in the *rue de la Main d'Or*, which he henceforth made his headquarters. Often from home, sometimes at Hesdin, sometimes at Lille to visit his friend and patron and to obtain from him instructions as to work which he wished him to execute, once at least, in 1435, *en certains voyages lointains et étranges marches*, no doubt anent matters of state, here it was that he seems to have painted most of his pictures which have come down to us, and there are a whole series of signed and dated panels for each year from 1432 to 1440, save only 1435, the year of his secret journey. He must have been residing in this house when he illuminated the statues, six of them, of the Hôtel de Ville, and received for his labour, as the town archives bear witness, 33 *livres* 12 *escalins de gros*, a sum representing in purchasing value to-day from fifty to sixty pounds.

Here he entertained the burgomaster and aldermen of Bruges, who, on July 17, 1432, repaired in a body to his studio to inspect a picture which he had just completed, and which no doubt they had commissioned, perhaps a Madonna and Child at present at Ince Bloundel Hall, near Liverpool, for this picture, one of the few that are dated, bears the following inscription: *Complendum anno Domini 1432, als ich kan.*

It will be interesting to note that upon this occasion John's two apprentices made merry, for the city fathers presented them with five *escalins* by way of *gratification*. Here was born his only child, or at all events the only child of whom there is any record; we know that Duke Philippe was the godfather, and it may well be that he was present at the christening feast.

Here too he painted for the Guild of St. Luke that portrait of his pale, sad-faced, patient wife, which at present hangs in the Academy at Bruges. Though she looks considerably older, the quaintly-worded legend on the

frame informs us that at this time she was only thirty-three years of age—
Conjunx meus Johannes me complevit anno 1439° 17° Junii, etas mea triginta annorum, als ich kan; and lastly, here, not much more than twelve months afterwards, on July 9, 1440, the great painter died. They laid him to rest in the cloister of St. Donatian's, and it would seem that his obsequies were celebrated with some circumstance, for the city archives inform us that three bells were tolled:—Donatian, Leonard and Bernard.

It is still the custom at Bruges to toll several bells at solemn funerals. They are rung one after the other at intervals of perhaps half a minute, beginning with the highest bell, and ending with the *bourdon.* The effect produced is very solemn and very striking and somewhat uncanny.

Some two years after John's death his bones were translated to the Baptistry Chapel in the interior of St Donatian's.

His widow continued to hold, and no doubt to inhabit the house in the *rue de la Main d'Or* until 1443. On June 4, in that year, she paid the ground rent for the last time.

In all that concerns *technique* John was the equal, perhaps the superior of his great brother. His *mise en scène* is perfect. He arranged his figures in symmetrical groups, clad them in glorious apparel, and set them in the midst of fair courts, or stately shrines, rich in sculpture and polished marble and costly hangings. He delighted in the *clair-obscur,* in the lustre of gold, in the shimmer of silk, in the scintillation of gems. In the wealth and variety of his palette and in the richness and depth and harmony of his mellow colouring he is unsurpassed. In spite of his realism and his love of detail his pictures are full of poetry, and if, as Mr. Weale says, he only saw with his eyes, he has somehow or other managed to make us see the souls of the figures he painted, but they lack the seriousness, the grandeur, the simple dignity of Hubert's sublime creations.

All this is exemplified in a marked degree in the St. Donatian's altar-piece in the academy at Bruges. The scene is laid in the apse of an old Byzantine church, glowing with gold and colour—perhaps St. Donatian's. The columns are of shining porphyry—red, purple, green; the pavement is of encaustic tiles of the colour of amber, the brown walls are of stone, in the background beyond the choir pale green light streams through arched windows set with little circular panes of bottle glass. Our Lady with her Divine Child on her knee forms the central figure of the picture. She is seated beneath a canopy on a sculptured throne, her outer garment is silken and of the colour called Indian red, her kirtle is dark blue, a mediæval carpet is spread beneath her feet. On her right hand stands St. Donatian, a noble figure, but with a face too stern for a saint's. In one hand he holds his pastoral cross and in the other his traditional wheel with five lighted tapers.

He is attired in a cope of indigo and gold brocade lined with crimson silk and edged with sable. On the left kneels the donor, George van der Pale, Canon of St. Donatian's—thick-necked, asthmatic, kindly, obese, a devout old Flemish gentleman. In one fat trembling hand he holds his half-open Breviary, in the other his reading glass; he is robed in a white surplice, his spectacle-case hangs at his side. The portrait is full of detail, very life-like and evidently unflattered. Behind him stands a youth in polished mail, who naïvely raises his helmet as, with his left hand on the canon's shoulder, he presents him to Our Lady—his patron, St. George; a very loyal, large-hearted, human, joyous saint, who, one feels quite sure, will regard with a lenient eye the shortcomings of his clients and do his best to help them, but for all that he seems to have the air of being not quite at ease, not quite sure perhaps whether the poor old canon is worthy of an introduction. May be this strangely fascinating figure is also a portrait.

As for the scheme of colour, it is simply glorious. Gold gleams everywhere. We see it in the blue brocade of the canopy and in the blue brocade of St. Donatian's cope; there are threads of it in the intricately-embroidered borders of Our Lady's robe; it glisters round her neck and on her fingers and in her hair. St. George's armour is all golden, and on the other side of the picture there stands St. Donatian arrayed in a vesture of gold wrought about with divers colours; even

PORTRAIT OF GEORGE VAN DER PALE
From the St. Donatian's Altar-piece of John van Eyck, in the Municipal Gallery, Bruges

the sculptured capitals of the columns are gilded, and wherever there is gold there are precious stones. Diamonds and carbuncles and pearls glisten in St. George's breastplate and in St. Donatian's crosier and in the orphreys of his cope, his gleaming mitre is all sewn with amethysts and pearls; there are pearls, too, round Our Lady's mantle and on her breast and in her yellow hair, and all this splendour is so delicately manipulated and so minutely and carefully portrayed that it bears looking at through a magnifying glass, and it is arranged with such exquisite taste, and the figures which it adorns are so calm, and about the whole scene there is an atmosphere of such profound peace, that the picture is in no way tawdry or garish or vulgar.

This is the largest panel which John van Eyck is known to have painted; the figures are about half life size. It was placed originally over the high altar in St. Donatian's, and we know from an inscription on the frame that it was completed in 1436.

At that time Bruges was straining every nerve to free herself from the tyranny of Philippe l'Asseuré. John, indeed, was on the winning side, but the battle had not yet been fought out to the bitter end, and in 1436 it was as likely as not that his patron would be worsted, and yet he went on quietly painting, and the calm saints of the St. Donatian's picture bear no trace of the storm amid which they were created.

GERARD DAVID

Half a century later, when Bruges was once more in the throes of rebellion, and the burghers, for the moment triumphant, had the weakling who would have enslaved them under lock and key and were exacting the uttermost farthing from the instigators and instruments of his crimes, a painter less famous than John van Eyck, but for all that well skilled in his art, and one whose hand, in spite of the turmoil around him, had not lost its cunning, was at work on two panels which now hang in the gallery at Bruges hard by Van Eyck's picture. Similar in colour, hardly less delicate in design, adorned like it with jewels and gold, these pictures form the very antithesis to the calm altar-piece of St. Donatian's. It is instinct with serene splendour, they are quick with gruesome motion; it is the portrayal of God's mercy, they depict man's vengeance. Van Eyck was inspired by the spirit of love, David by the frenzy of delirium.

It was but a passing phase. As in the days of the French Terror men who before had been peaceful citizens, carried away by the fury around them, committed all kinds of excesses, and when the blizzard had passed stepped quietly back into the old humdrum groove of former days as if nothing had happened, so David, under similar circumstances, defiled his brush by painting one loathsome picture, and presently, when the storm had spent itself, clothed and in his right mind, again resumed his old themes and his old methods: busied himself in adorning altars with fair virgins and sweet-faced angels, and by making breviaries beautiful with the legends of the saints.

From the little that is recorded of him he seems to have been a devout and charitable man, and the placid scenes he delighted to paint indicate that he was naturally of a humane and gentle disposition.

We know that in 1508 he joined the brotherhood of Our Lady of the Dry Tree, a famous religious guild affiliated to the Franciscan order. The following year he presented to the Carmelite nuns of Bruges one of his most exquisite pictures, an altar-piece representing Our Lady surrounded by virgin saints, at present in the gallery at Rouen; and later on, when the same nuns were in straitened circumstances, he advanced them a very considerable sum free of interest, only stipulating that the money should be returned when he asked for it. This he did during his last illness, several years afterwards, and it is pleasing to find that the nuns at once complied with his request. But to return to the days of his aberration. Shortly after the execution of Peter Lanchals and other members of the magistracy of Bruges, who like him had been accused of corruption and of conspiring with Maximilian to deprive the town of its liberty, the new magistrates whom the people had chosen to fill their place commissioned Gerard David to paint for the Court of Justice in the Hôtel de Ville two pictures which should remind the judges that if they should at any time fail in their duty punishment would assuredly follow.

Gerard was a native of Oudewater in Holland, who some four years previously had taken up his abode in Bruges. On the 14th of January 1484 he was enrolled among the members of the Guild of St. Luke. He was probably an ardent patriot, at all events was in touch with the popular leaders, for we know from documentary evidence that they employed him to paint the iron gratings which were placed before the windows of Jean de Gros's mansion when Maximilian was imprisoned there, and, as we have seen, it was he whom they commissioned to paint the panels for the Town Hall.

The theme selected for his pictures is a horrible one—the conviction and the flaying alive of Sisamnes, an Egyptian judge who had been accused of receiving bribes. The story is first told by Herodotus, but David had probably culled it from the pages of Valerius Maximus, and there can be no doubt that the subject was suggested to him by the tragedy which had just taken place beneath the shadow of the Belfry. He has represented himself in the first panel calmly surveying the arrest of Sisamnes, and it may well be that he actually witnessed the execution of Lanchals, perhaps expressly with a view to these paintings. In each case the scene is laid at Bruges, the figures, the faces, the attitudes, the costumes, are all essentially Flemish, and it is in the highest degree probable that he introduced other portraits besides his own.

Mark the expression of Sisamnes in the flaying scene. See how his features twitch, how he clenches his hands and his teeth, and draws back his lips in agony. Did Peter Lanchals look like that when he was being racked in the infernal machine which he himself had invented?

There are only seven other pictures which can at present be certainly attributed to Gerard David. They are all of a sacred character, and four of them were painted for churches in Bruges. Of these the most beautiful is the triptych presented to the Carmelite nuns in 1509, and which adorned the high altar of their chapel until the community was suppressed by Joseph II. in 1783. Two years later, when their property was sold at Brussels, David's picture was purchased by a dealer named Berthels for fifty-one florins. He sold it to a French collector, Monsieur Miliotti, in whose possession it remained until his estate was confiscated by the Revolutionary government some years later. Presently it was hung in the Municipal Gallery at Rouen, where it still remains. This is the most decorative, and perhaps the most charming of David's pictures. The subject is Our Lady surrounded by angels and virgin saints. The grouping is sufficiently symmetrical and altogether excellent, the scheme of colour is rich and harmonious, and though the sacred figures almost entirely cover the panel, owing to the lack of detail in the background, a mass of deep, sombre green, almost black, they appear in no way crowded. The faces are for the most part somewhat heavy, and decidedly Flemish, but there is an air of calm repose about them which is very restful, and the fair-haired, white-robed angels which stand on each side of Our Lady's throne are of another type. David must have drawn them from peasant models. This picture is all the more interesting from the fact that the artist has introduced his own portrait, and also that of his wife Cornelia,[47] the daughter of a Bruges goldsmith, one Jacob Cnoop, a native of Middelburg in Holland. Unless David flattered his wife, she must have been a woman of singularly prepossessing appearance, with bright eyes and an intelligent face. She stands with her hands clasped in prayer, the last figure but one on the left-hand side of Our Lady, beyond her stands St. Lucy, a child saint who suffered martyrdom at fourteen. She is here represented as a woman of forty, gorgeously arrayed in two shades of crimson, fat and not fair. David himself balances his wife on the opposite side of the picture. A sufficiently artistic face this, but upon the whole not a pleasing one. His eyes are too prominent, his lips are too thick, and he has a weak, receding chin.

Gerard David painted two pictures for the Church of St. Donatian:— an altar-piece representing the mystic marriage of St. Catherine, and two panels which formed the shutters of a triptych. These, together with the wings of several other triptychs, were sold by the Cathedral Chapter in 1787 at the request of the sacristan, a lazy, clumsy fellow who, objecting to the trouble of opening and closing them, averred that he invariably broke the altar candles in doing so. One of David's shutters has disappeared, the other, after passing through several hands, was purchased in 1859, for five hundred and twenty-five guineas, by Mr. Benoni White, who, at his death in 1878, bequeathed it to the National Gallery.

Here we have a portrait of the donor Bernardin Salviati, Canon of St. Donatian's and the son of a wealthy Florentine merchant who had married a Flemish lady and settled at Bruges. The kneeling canon is attired in a surplice of fine linen and is accompanied by three saints—St. Donatian resplendent in black brocade glistering with jewels and gold, St. Martin in a crimson velvet cope, with richly-embroidered orphreys, and his patron, the Franciscan saint, Bernardin, in the rough grey frock of the poor man of Assisi. The heads are very fine, full of expression and more Italian than Flemish in type, but the figures are not gracefully posed; there is too much landscape, and the picture is hardly decorative enough for an altar-piece.

The St. Donatian's 'Marriage of St. Catherine' is also at present in the National Gallery. It seems to have been taken to Paris when the old cathedral was destroyed. It eventually became the property of M. de Beurnoville; when his collection was sold in 1881, the late Mrs Lyne Stephens purchased it for 54,100 frs. (£2164), and it was bequeathed by her to the nation.

This panel is far superior to the Salviati picture. The colouring is very rich and mellow, the composition is perfect, the faces are admirably painted and, though somewhat heavy and Flemish in character, are on the whole pleasing; the background, with its vine-clad walls and lovely garden of roses, and lilies, and trees beyond, and picturesque buildings, is altogether beautiful and in no way obtrusive. The whole picture is admirably adapted to the purpose for which it was designed.

The only one of David's sacred pictures which remains in Bruges is the triptych known as 'The Baptism of Christ.'

The history of this picture is a strange one. It was painted early in the fifteen hundreds for John des Trompes, who at that time was city treasurer, probably for his private oratory; later on, in 1520, it was presented by his heirs to the Guild of Advocates, and placed over the altar of their chantry in the crypt of St. Basil in the Bourg. A coat of black distemper inscribed with the Ten Commandments saved it from the fury of the Calvinists in 1579. Carried off by the French in 1794, it remained in Paris until 1815, when it was at last sent back to Bruges and placed in the City Gallery, where it still remains. It hangs alongside of David's other pictures, is in striking contrast to them, and as a work of art their inferior. The grouping is not happy. Two of the three principal figures in the central panel are decidedly weak, and those in the distance are for the most part stumpy and graceless. On the other hand, the figure of the kneeling angel who holds our Lord's garments is singularly beautiful. His sweet, placid face might have been drawn by Memlinc and his glorious vesture by John van Eyck. The landscape setting is the most interesting portion of this panel, and in all probability it is not David's work. Mr. Weale thinks that Joachim Patenier may have painted it, and Jules Helbig is of the same opinion. 'Nothing,' says Mr. Weale, 'can well be finer than this portion of the picture; the trees, vigorously painted and finished with wonderful minuteness, have evidently been studied individually from nature.... Between their trunks we get glimpses of real distant landscape. The herbage, lilies, mallows, violets, and other flowers in the immediate front have never been more admirably reproduced by the art of the painter.... The transparency of the water, the reflection of surrounding objects and the shadows on its surface are faithfully rendered. The bedding of the rocks too is imitated with perfect truth. The colouring of all this portion is so remarkably bright and lovely that the faults of the composition are not at first noticed.'

All this is no exaggeration. Bearing in mind the age in which it was produced, this piece of landscape painting is in truth a marvellous achievement. Considered in itself it is worthy of the highest admiration. But instead of being a mere accessory, as was the case in the pictures of the Van Eycks, of Memlinc, of Van der Weyden, of all the earlier masters, the landscape here forms, so to speak, the dominant note of the picture. The beauty of these fair fields and woods and mountains is the first thing which attracts the spectator's attention. The sacred figures are overwhelmed and belittled and cast into the shade by the splendour of their setting, and, after all, the sacred figures should form the principal feature of a picture like this, intended for an altar-piece. On the whole we cannot help regretting that Gerard David called in the aid of Joachim Patenier. The left wing shows the donor and his little son Philip, and his patron, St. John the Evangelist; the right, the donor's first wife, her four daughters and her patroness, St. Elizabeth of Hungary. Each of these panels has a landscape background, no less beautiful and no less obtrusive than the landscape in the central panel. The triptych when

GERARD DAVID'S 'BAPTISM OF CHRIST'
Municipal Gallery, Bruges

shut displays five figures—Our Lady seated beneath a canopy, with the Divine Infant on her knee, and facing them the donor's second wife, her little daughter and her patroness, St. Mary Magdalene. Here there is an architectural background of open arcades, with a view beyond, perhaps of Bruges.

This is perhaps the least satisfactory of the nine pictures which, to quote the words of Mr. Weale, 'can at present with certainty be assigned to Gerard David.'

In the Museum of the Holy Blood there is a triptych representing the Deposition, which, according to documents preserved in the confraternity archives, was painted by David in 1520. The authenticity of this picture is, however, contested, and it is certainly far inferior to any of his known paintings.

Gerard David married probably during the year 1496. His wife, as we have seen, was Cornelia Cnoop. They had issue one daughter, who was christened Barbara, and was already married at the time of her father's death. During forty years he held a foremost place among the painters of Bruges. He was elected a councillor of the Guild of St. Luke in 1488, and again in 1495 and in 1498. He was gathered to his fathers on the 13th of August 1523. They buried him in Notre Dame, beneath the tower, but no stone marks the place of his sepulture. When the church was repaired at the beginning of the last century it disappeared. Many of the old Notre Dame tombstones have been put to ignoble purposes, serve as doorsteps for houses in the neighbourhood, or to pave kitchens, or are stowed away in cellars and back-yards. Perhaps David's monument is among the number. It was engraved with his arms, which are known, and those of his wife, and the memorial inscription has been preserved. Hence in all probability it would be easy of identification.

Great painter as he undoubtedly was, the fame of Gerard David hardly survived him, even in the city in which he had so long dwelt.

Van Mander, writing as early as 1604, was obliged to avow that he had no information concerning him, save only this, that Peter Pourbus, who died in 1584, considered him to be an excellent artist, and Van Mander had long inhabited Bruges.

By the close of the sixteen hundreds even those of his pictures which still adorned the city of his adoption were attributed to other painters, and for more than two hundred and fifty years his name was buried in oblivion.

Less than half a century ago Mr. Weale brought it back to men's memory. To his diligent research the world is indebted for all that is now known of the life and labours of this great artist. From his writings in the *Beffroi de Bruges*, the *Gazette des Beaux Arts*, and elsewhere, we have culled the notes here set down on the history of Gerard David and the histories of the pictures he painted.

To return for a moment to John van Eyck. There are two other pictures at Bruges which are possibly his. The first is a small panel in the municipal gallery representing the head of Christ. Mr. Weale refuses to acknowledge this as an authentic picture, and says that the only part which is well painted is the embroidered collar of the tunic. Lübke, on the other hand, speaks of it as a genuine Van Eyck, and ascribes the date to 1440, the year of John's death, but he adds, 'like the head of Christ in the Berlin Museum, painted two years previously, it exhibits a certain want of expression, seeming to intimate to us the limits of John's genius.'

M. de Copman, the curator of the Bruges Gallery, has no doubt that it is authentic, and describes it as such on the frame. One thing is certain. If this picture was indeed painted by John van Eyck it is not worthy of him.

The second picture, a finely-painted Mater Dolorosa, is in the Cathedral. From the fact that it is signed with the initials *J. E.* it was formerly attributed to John, but it is now generally acknowledged to be the work of some other artist.

Among the crowd of artists who in the course of the fourteen hundreds flocked to Bruges, and whose method of painting was inspired either directly or indirectly by the brothers Van Eyck, note Pieter Christus, a native of Baarle near Tilburg, who died at Bruges in 1473, the only pupil of John van Eyck whose name has come down to us; Gerhard van der Meire, Dierick Boudts, Roger van der Weyden, all of them perhaps pupils of Hubert's; Roger's pupil, Hans Memlinc, the greatest of all the Bruges painters after the brothers Van Eyck, and, towards the close of the century, Quentin Metsys, Albert Cornelis and Jerome Bosch.

Strangely enough, of these men only one, Albert Cornelis, was a native of Bruges, and though they all of them spent a considerable portion of their lives there, the sum of their united labours is at present represented in the city by hardly a score of pictures. Of the work of Pieter Christus nothing remains; Quentin Metsys, Hugo van der Goes and Roger van der Weyden are likewise unrepresented, though several of the masterpieces of the last two were in the Church of St. Jacques at the close of the seventeen hundreds. When they disappeared, or what has become of them, is unknown. One picture remains in Bruges which was perhaps painted by Gerhard van der Meire, four which are probably the work of Dierick Boudts; Jerome Bosch and Albert Cornelis are each represented by one picture, Gerard David, as we have seen, by three or perhaps four, and Hans Memlinc by six which are certainly his work, and by some half-dozen others which are attributed to him with more or less probability, whilst scattered about the town there are many pictures, some of them very beautiful, which were no doubt painted at Bruges during the period we are now considering, but by artists who have not as yet been identified.

Of the lives and surroundings of these great masters little has come down to us. All that is certainly known concerning most of them is the place of their birth and death, and the date of those events—even these meagre details are in the case of some of them lacking—and that of the multitude of pictures of the Flemish school of this period scattered throughout the churches and galleries of Europe, not a few can be positively traced to one or other of the Bruges masters.

ROGER VAN DER WEYDEN.

Roger van der Weyden, the greatest of the immediate disciples of John van Eyck, was born at Tournai early in the fourteen hundreds. In 1436 he was appointed painter to the city of Brussels, and it was probably during this time that he adorned with gold and colour the statuary of the tomb of Jeanne of Brabant, which Philippe l'Asseuré erected in the Carmelite Church there. In 1450 he made a pilgrimage to Rome for the great jubilee which was celebrated during that year. We know something of the details of this journey. *En route* he sojourned at Ferrara, at Milan and at Florence, and in all of these towns he received the most cordial welcome, not only from his brother artists, but from the ruling princes. At Ferrara he must have worked for Lionel d'Este, for on his return to Brussels we find him receiving from that prince the sum of twenty golden ducats in part payment for *certe depicture* executed in his palace at Ferrara. At Milan he painted for Francesco Sforza a Calvary, with the portraits of Francesco himself, his wife, Blanche Visconti, and their young son, Galéas. This splendid picture is now in the *Musée des Beaux Arts* at Brussels. At Florence he was employed by Cosmo de' Medici. The fruit of his labours in that city is at present in the Stadel Museum at Frankfort—a glorious triptych which represents the Madonna and Child, with St. Peter and St. John the Baptist, patrons of the city, on the right, and on the left the mighty Cosmo himself and one of his brothers, perhaps Lorenzo, in the guise of the patrons of the Medici family—Saints Cosmas and Damian. He does not seem to have practised his art in Rome. Perhaps his stay there was a short one, and that his time was fully occupied by sight-seeing and devotion. That he fully appreciated the art treasures of the Eternal City there can be no doubt, and we know that he was enraptured with the Lateran pictures of Gentile da Fabriano, whom he pronounced to be the first painter in Italy.

During the later part of his life Roger seems to have resided at Bruges, and here perhaps he painted the Middelburg triptych now in the Berlin Gallery, and the missing triptych which formerly adorned the Church of St. Jacques. This picture excited the admiration of Albert Dürer when he visited Bruges in 1521. Its theme was the life of St. John the Baptist. The same subject is portrayed in a painting attributed to Roger, at present in the Berlin Gallery. Have we here the Bruges picture?

The exact date of Roger's death is known—June 18, 1464; we also know the name of his wife, Elizabeth Goffart, and that he was the father of four children, Corneille, Margaret, Peter and John, of whom Peter followed his father's calling. He seems, like his master John van Eyck, to have been a man of many parts; we have already seen him colouring statues, he was also an illuminator of manuscripts. A miniature of exceptional beauty, attributed with reason to him, is in the possession of M. Gielen of Maeseyck (see *Rev. de l'Art Chrétien*, 1889, p. 380). A reproduction of it is published in the *Annales de l'Académie d'archéologie de Belgique*, vol. xxiv. Perhaps, too, he was a wood engraver. Waagen is of opinion (*see* Sotheby's *Principia Typographica*) that the woodcuts of the *Biblia Pauperum* were designed by him.

Roger van der Weyden was, in his way, even more of a realist than John van Eyck, and he possessed all John's love of elaborate detail; but whereas the latter was pleased with serene immobility Roger delighted in tragic action, and his tall, wan, emaciated figures are often convulsed with weeping. He could, however, depict tranquillity when he liked, and his portraits are as calm and collected as any of Van Eyck's. His heads are invariably finely painted and full of expression, but they are almost always ascetic looking, and very often sad. Take for example the portrait of Bladelin in the Middelburg picture. He seems, indeed, to have been unable to appreciate the beauty of health and gladness, and to corpulence he had a rooted objection. If that fat, flabby-faced old canon, George van der Pale, had commissioned Roger to paint his portrait, he would somehow or other have managed, without losing the likeness, to make him look fragile and refined.

Of the Flemish painters of the fourteen hundreds M. Fiérens-Gevaert remarks: '*La morbidesse que Bruges dissimule si richement, se prolonge dans leur art. Ils créent des figures minces, élancées, splendidement vêtues.*' The assertion is too sweeping, but it is certainly true in the case of Roger van der Weyden.

DIERICK BOUDTS.

Of Roger's contemporary Dierick Boudts we know little save that he was born at Harlem, towards the close of the thirteen hundreds, that he passed a portion of his life in Bruges, and that in 1462 he settled at Louvain, where he continued to reside until his death in 1475.

Two of his most famous works are still in the Church of St. Peter in that city—an altar panel representing the martyrdom of St. Erasmus, and the central panel of a polyptych, of which the subject is the Last Supper. This picture has been broken up, and the side shutters are now in the Berlin Gallery. There is a contemporary copy of the entire painting, perhaps a replica by Dierick himself, in the seminary at Bruges. The Church of St. Jacques in the same city contains another of his works, or rather a work attributed, probably correctly, to him, a retable in three compartments, wherein is depicted the legend of St. Lucy. The soft, mellow colouring of this picture is perfect, and all the details, the rich brocades and velvets, the embroidery and precious stones, the flowers and fruit in the foreground, are quite admirable, but the figures are stiff and ill-proportioned. In the background is a view of the city of Bruges with the Belfry as it appeared before the lantern was added, and the Church of Notre Dame. This picture is dated 1480.[48]

There is a triptych in Bruges Cathedral, in the first chapel on the northern side of the chevet, which is attributed to Memlinc. The painting on the left shutter is quite in his style and is in all probability his work. Here are shown portraits of the donors, Hippolytus de Berthoz and Elizabeth van Keverwick, his affianced bride. This panel has been much spoiled by restoration, and the removal of the *glacis* has chilled the tone of the colouring. The other panels are evidently the work of another painter, and there is little doubt that that painter was Dierick Boudts. The ill-proportioned figures, the finely-drawn heads, and the rich, mellow colouring are all his. The scene depicted on the central panel is the martyrdom of St. Hippolytus, who is being torn to pieces by four horses; in the further panel he confesses himself a Christian and is condemned to death.

There is a fourth picture in Bruges, which perhaps may have been painted by Dierick Boudts. It is in the Chapel of the Sœurs Noires in the *Place Memlinc*, and represents eight episodes in the legend of St. Ursula. It probably dates from an earlier period than the famous shrine of St. Ursula in the Hospital of St. John, and it is not unlikely that we have here the prototype of that marvellous production.

The picture attributed to Gerhard van der Meire hangs in the southern aisle of the Cathedral. Therein are depicted three Passion scenes—the Carrying of the Cross, the Crucifixion and the Deposition. The treatment is coarse and realistic in the extreme. The picture is not a pleasing one. Alike in colour, in sentiment, in design it is far inferior to any of Gerhard's authentic works.

In the Municipal Gallery there is an 'Adoration of the Magi' (No. 28), which formerly belonged to the monks of the great Cistercian Abbey of Our Lady on the Dunes at Coxyde. Much spoiled by restoration, somewhat quaint and naïve in design, it is still a beautiful picture. There is no extrinsic evidence to show who painted it, but the style is the style of Jerome Bosch.

In the Church of St. Jacques, about half-way up the southern aisle, hangs the picture of Albert Cornelis—the central panel of a triptych on which is portrayed the Coronation of Our Lady in the presence of the nine choirs of angels. This is in every respect a most remarkable and a most interesting picture. Painted in 1520, at a time when the artists of Bruges had already begun to adopt the methods of the Renaissance, it is instinct with the spirit which animated the old illuminators of the beginning of the previous century. Of a delicate, miniature-like style, beautiful alike in sentiment, in design, in colour and in execution, it is the only known work of the master-hand that produced it.

HANS MEMLINC.

Hans Memlinc, the greatest painter in Christendom, as a writer of his own day calls him, seems to have been born somewhere about the year 1430. He was in all probability a native of Mayence, or of some locality within the electorate. M. Wauters, in his *Sept Études pour servir à l'histoire de Hans Memlinc*, published at Brussels in 1893, inclines to Memlingen, a village about forty miles from the city. M. Jules Helbig suggests Aschaffenburg, near which place flows a stream called the Mumling.

Be this as it may, the Jesuit Father Henri Dursart's discovery in 1889 of Romboudt de Doppere's journal (1491 to 1498) at least puts an end to the dispute as to Memlinc's nationality. There can no longer be any doubt that the great Bruges painter was, at all events, of German extraction, and the same document informs us that he died at Bruges on August 11, 1494, and that he was buried in the Church of St. Gilles—*Die. XI. Augusti (1494), Brugis obiit Joannes Memmelinc, quem prædicabant peritissimum fuisse et excellentissimum pictorem totius tunc orbis Christiani oriundus erat Maguncia co, sepultus Brugis ad Ægidii.*

A note at the beginning of his journal informs us that Doppere was a priest, a notary of Bruges and registrar to the Chapter of St. Donatian, and he himself tells us that in 1491 he had been attached to the Church of St. Donatian for over forty-six years—*Ego Romboldus de Doppere, presbyter, versatus sum hic in ecclesia S. Donatiani ultra annos XLVI.* ... We find him acting as notary from 1483 to 1491, and in that capacity he witnessed, on October 21, 1489, the translation of the relics of St. Ursula to Memlinc's new shrine. Doppere was then personally acquainted with Memlinc, perhaps his friend. In the later years of his life he seems to have been a canon of Notre Dame. He died, according to Meyer, in 1501, and was buried in the church he had so long served.

As long ago as 1861 Mr. Weale proved by documentary evidence, published for the first time in the *Gazette des Beaux Arts*, that Memlinc had obtained the freedom of the city of Bruges in 1478, that two years later he was in the enjoyment of a considerable fortune, a portion of which was invested in house property, and that the dwelling which he himself inhabited was in the *rue St. George* on a site now occupied by the garden of the house No. 20, that his wife's Christian name was Anne, that she bore him three children, John, Corneile and Nicolas, and that she died in 1487. This is all that is at present certainly known concerning the story of Hans Memlinc.

According to a legend long current in the city, Memlinc was a poor soldier who, having escaped with his life from the battlefield of Nancy (January 4, 1477), somehow or other succeeded in making his way to Bruges, sought shelter in the Hospital of St. John, and was there healed of his wounds. Having no money wherewith to requite the brethren for the kindness they had shown him, he painted them a picture, or rather a whole series of pictures—the famous Shrine of St. Ursula.

There is no documentary evidence in support of this story. The first writer to mention it is the Abbé Jean Baptiste Descamps in his *Vie des peintres Flamands*, which appeared in 1733, some two hundred and forty years after Memlinc's death, and since Mr. Weale's discoveries in 1861 it has been generally and perhaps too lightly regarded as devoid of all foundation.

The documents which have of late years been brought to light do not, however, touch the main outlines of the hospital story, though they certainly prove that some of the incidents could not have taken place as the Abbé Descamps relates them.

Perhaps, as Mr. Weale suggests, Memlinc learned the first elements of his art at Cologne. There is a tradition that he was at one time the pupil of Van der Weyden. May be he first conceived his love of that delicate, miniature-like style which he afterwards brought to such perfection from 'Master Simon Marmion of Valenciennes, who,' Louis de la Fontaine tells us, 'had such skill in the noble science of painting that he surpassed not only all the other artists resident in the said town, but likewise those of all the neighbouring cities,' that 'prince of illuminators,' whom Jean Lemain, the poet-secretary of Marguerite of Austria, in his *Couronne Margaritique* enumerates among the most famous painters of his day.

'Et Marmion, prince d'enlumineure
Dont le nom croit comme paste en levain
Par les effets de son noble tournure.'

We know that a young Brussels painter, whose Christian name was Hans, was sojourning at Valenciennes from 1454 to 1458,[49] and this same Hans seems later on to have returned to Brussels and entered the service of Roger van der Weyden.

Of course Hans was a sufficiently ordinary name in Germany, but it was not a common one in the Netherlands, and there is another circumstance which makes it probable that the Hans in question was Hans Memlinc.

No picture of Marmion has come down to us which can be identified as certainly his, but there are several which may be his handiwork. Amongst them four panels on which is depicted the life of St. Bertin. They once formed the wings of the sculptured retable of silver gilt, adorned with enamel and precious stones, which for more than three hundred years glistered behind the high altar in the Abbey Church of St. Bertin at St. Omer, the last resting-place of so many of the early Counts of Flanders.

Exquisite alike in colour and design, in days when Gothic art was least esteemed these marvellous paintings excited universal admiration, and Rubens himself is said to have been so enamoured of their beauty that he offered to cover them with *Louis d'or* if only the monks would consent to sell.

Presently came the evil days of the French Revolution. The old church was pillaged and razed to the ground, and the triptych disappeared. Fortunately the shutters were saved. Somehow or other they came into the hands of a baker of St. Omer, who later on sold them to an art collector in the neighbourhood. In 1823 they were put up for sale at the Hôtel Bullion in Paris and purchased for 7500 francs (£300) by Monsieur Nieuwenhuys for William I., King of the Netherlands. Only the larger shutters, however, were placed in the King's collection. The smaller ones were re-sold to M. Beaucousin, and when he died in 1861 they were purchased along with his other pictures for the National Gallery.

In days gone by these exquisite pictures were unhesitatingly attributed to Memlinc. There was an unbroken tradition at St. Bertin's that he had painted them. 'Never,' says M. de Laplane in his *Abbés de St. Bertin* (1844), 'had there existed a doubt at the abbey as to their authorship.' The Abbé Descamps, who visited St. Omer in 1769, was quite sure that they were Memlinc's, and for over a hundred years historians, artists and archæologists alike were unanimous in adjudging them his. Even as recently as 1881 the well-known Dutch art critic Victor de Stuers expressed the same opinion.

It was probably the Comte de Laborde who first expressed doubt as to their authorship. Writing in 1851 of the larger panels he says, 'To whom must we attribute these two delicious pages—to Memlinc in a peculiar phase of his talent, painting in a different and in some respects a less precise style than he painted at Bruges? or have we here the work of a disciple or, may be, of a rival? If so the artist who produced them must be reckoned among the most eminent.... I shall have no peace until I have discovered the date, the price, and the author of these pictures.[50]

Crowe and Cavalcaselle are no less undecided:—if Memlinc painted the shutters in question, he must have been aided by his pupils. Others shared their uncertainty, others again unhesitatingly averred that the triptych could not be Memlinc's.

The Comte de Laborde was never able, perhaps he had never time, to solve the riddle he had propounded, but of late years a no less capable and patient investigator has, at least in part, succeeded in doing so.

Mgr. Dehaisnes, like the author of *Les Ducs de Bourgogne*, was unable to affirm that the paintings on the St. Bertin's triptych were the handiwork of Memlinc. If now and again an angel for example resembled his angels, there were other figures reminiscent of the style of Dierick Boudts or of Roger van der Weyden. The scheme of colour too recalled rather the rich, mellow, sunny tints of the 'Adoration of the Lamb' than the clearer tones of the shrine of St. Ursula, and in point of vigour and precision the unknown artist fell short of the great masters of the Bruges school and especially of the greatest of them all.

The long and careful investigation which Mgr. Dehaisnes undertook resulted in the identification of the donor of the precious triptych, viz., William Fillustre, Bishop of Toul, who ruled the Abbey of St. Bertin from 1450 to 1473; in the discovery of the price he paid for it, 1828 *livres* 26 *sous*, a sum equivalent in current coin to at least £1400, not including the value of the gold, silver and precious stones, all of which were furnished by the abbey treasury; and in the discovery of the approximate date of its completion, between 1455 and 1459, probably in the June of the latter year. And although Mgr. Dehaisnes has not been able to establish the identity of the author of the pictures, he has shown that it is in the highest degree probable than Simon Marmion painted them.

If what Mgr. Dehaisnes modestly calls his *'conjectures vraisemblables'* should prove to be correct, and if Memlinc was indeed Marmion's pupil, it may well be that he aided his master in painting the marvellous shutters, and in that case the St. Bertin's tradition that he was their author may perhaps be thus accounted for.

The pictures which Memlinc executed at Bruges represent the work of his middle life and of his declining years. In former days they were sufficiently numerous, but now there are only six or at most seven of his authentic pictures within the limits of the city, and they are all of them save one, at present in the old chapter house of the Hospital of St. John. Of these the first in order of date is the great triptych which formerly adorned the high altar of the hospital chapel, and was painted in 1479. The subject of the central panel is the 'Mystic Marriage of St. Catherine.' Here Our Lady is seated in a cloister, on a rich throne backed with cloth of gold; above her head two hovering angels hold a crown. On her knee is the Divine Infant who, leaning forward, places a ring on St. Catherine's finger. Behind His mystic bride stands an angel playing on an instrument of music, and beyond St. John the Baptist with his lamb beside him. On the other side of Our Lady a kneeling angel holds a book of which she appears to be turning one of the leaves; hard-by is St. Barbara reading, and in the background St. John the Divine. Beyond the cloister in the background is a fair landscape in which are depicted scenes from the life of the Baptist and from the life of the beloved disciple. The principal theme of the left-hand panel is the martyrdom of St. John the Baptist, that of the panel on the right the vision at Patmos of the other St. John.

Painted, most probably at the suggestion of John Floreins, who at that time was hospital treasurer, by an artist bearing the same Christian name, for a church dedicated to St. John the Baptist and St. John the

Divine, at the cost of devout men and women who divided their time between labour and prayer, this triptych is in the first place the glorification of the precursor and the beloved disciple, and in the second of St. Catherine and St. Barbara, who typify respectively in mediæval art the contemplative and the active life.

In this picture we have the portrait of John Memlinc over and over again, for it was his wont, at least so it is said, to make himself his own model when he painted St. John the Baptist. Here too John Floreins appears twice. Once in the habit of his order—a small black-robed figure in the left-hand corner of the central panel, and again in the background of the same panel, between a marble column and Our Lady's throne. This time he is represented in his secular capacity as public gauger of wine, near a huge crane in the *rue Flamande*, with the old Church of St. John, long since demolished, in the distance.

Such are the main outlines of the hospital triptych, the largest of Memlinc's uncontested works, and the most beautiful in colour, at all events of his pictures in Bruges.

Its prototype is in England—perhaps it was painted there—and is at present in the possession of the Duke of Devonshire. Executed for Sir John Donne, who

was slain at the Battle of Edgecote near Banbury on July 26, 1469, this picture must be among the earliest, perhaps indeed it is the most ancient of Memlinc's uncontested works. Most of the figures herein portrayed are identical, or almost identical, with the figures in the Bruges triptych. Not only are they manifestly the same individuals, but their faces have the same expression and they are dressed in the same costumes. The colouring of this triptych is less rich than the colouring of the hospital picture, and perhaps the execution is less sure, but the grouping is more simple and more symmetrical, and there is an atmosphere of repose about it which one does not find to the same extent in the Bruges picture. The attention of the spectator is not distracted by a multiplicity of scenes in the background. Here there are no fluttering angels above Our Lady's head, and the calm, dignified figure of the Evangelist on the left-hand shutter is decoratively far more effective than the ecstatic Evangelist in the corresponding wing of the Bruges triptych.

In the same year that Memlinc painted the 'Mystic Marriage of St. Catherine,' he painted also the picture which hangs opposite to it. This work is likewise a triptych, but of much smaller dimensions than the first. It probably adorned the private oratory of John Floreins, as an inscription in Flemish on the frame informs us that it was painted for him: *Dit werk dede maken Broeder Jan Floreins alias vander Rüst Broeder Proffes vanden hospitale van Sint Jans in Brygghe anno 1479 opus Johanis Memlinc.*

If there is any truth in the Abbé Descamps's legend it was probably this picture, and not the shrine of St. Ursula, that Memlinc painted as a thank-offering to John Floreins, who, if he was not superior of the hospital when Memlinc is said to have been a patient there, certainly occupied a responsible position and was doubtless able to dispense favours. To the right of the central panel there is the figure of a man wearing a yellow cap, a form of headgear used until recently by convalescents in the hospital. Tradition says that we have here the portrait of Memlinc, and if Memlinc, indeed, portrayed his own features when he painted St. John the Baptist, tradition speaks the truth. These heads bear a striking resemblance to the head of the man in the nightcap.

The central panel represents the Adoration of the Magi, that on the right the Nativity, and the other panel the Presentation.

The triptych when closed shows two figures, St. John the Baptist— this, according to Jacques van Oost is the veritable portrait of the painter— and St. Veronica. On the frame are representations of the Fall and the Expulsion from Paradise painted in *grisaille*. These are also undoubtedly Memlinc's handiwork. '*Ici*,' notes Canon Duclos, '*nous avons tout un poème: celui de la chute, de la rédemption et des manifestations du Rédempteur.*' The picture is certainly a glorious one, alike in design and in execution, and the scheme of colour is magnificent. It is esteemed by some to be Memlinc's masterpiece, and it is without doubt the best of his Bruges pictures.

The third picture is a portrait of exquisite delicacy and finish, representing Marie, the second daughter of Willem Moreel, a master grocer of considerable wealth and standing in the city, and one of Memlinc's chief patrons. An inscription on the frame, which in Mr. Weale's opinion is certainly authentic, informs us that this picture was painted in 1480. The same year another Bruges tradesman, Master Tanner Peter Bultencke, commissioned Memlinc to paint a triptych for Notre Dame with scenes from the life of

ST. JOHN THE BAPTIST
From Memlinc's 'Adoration of the Magi' in St. John's Hospital, Bruges

ST. VERONICA
From Memlinc's 'Adoration of the Magi' in St. John's Hospital, Bruges

Christ. Alas! it has long since left the city and is now in the gallery at Munich.

The fourth picture is a beautiful diptych painted in 1487 for Martin van Nieuwenhove, and presented by him to the Hospice of St. Julian, a half-secular, half-religious house of entertainment for poor pilgrims, of which he was one of the two patrons appointed by the town. The left panel shows Our Lady with her Divine Infant, to whom she is offering a golden apple; the right has a portrait of the donor with his hands clasped in prayer, and an open breviary before him. This is one of Memlinc's finest portraits.

The date of the paintings on the shrine of St. Ursula is not certainly known, but since the relic for which it was constructed was placed in the new shrine on October 24, 1489, it is probable that they were completed before that date.

In this dainty casket we have a striking example of the imperfections and excellencies of the age which produced it. It stands in the centre of the chapter house and is in the form of a Gothic chapel. Bristling with heavy and superfluous ornament, with even the flat surface of the roof painted so as to simulate relief, the pictorial representations which adorn it are exquisite alike in design, in colour and in execution. Each side is divided into three round-headed arcades of equal dimensions; within them Memlinc has painted the pictures which tell the story of St. Ursula as it was current in his day. These six panels contain the arrival of the saint and her companions at Cologne, their arrival at Basle and then at Rome, their homeward journey, in which they are accompanied by the Pope and his cardinals, their return to Cologne, and their martyrdom in the camp of the Huns. Of the six scenes the third is the most beautiful, both in colour and composition. At the gable ends of the shrine are two other pictures. One of them represents Our Lady with her Divine Son in her arms, and two of the hospital sisters kneeling at her feet; the other St. Ursula sheltering beneath her mantle ten of her companions. The high-pitched roof is adorned on each side with a large medallion set between two smaller ones; these contain angels playing on instruments of music, and Ursula receiving the crown of martyrdom, and the same saint surrounded by her companions in heaven. All these pictures are executed in a delicate, miniature-like style, and with great care and finish.

There is one other picture in the hospital museum attributed to Memlinc—a triptych of which the subject of the central panel is the Deposition. It is perhaps the rough design of a picture which was never carried out.

There is also a triptych by Memlinc in the Municipal Gallery. It once adorned the chantry of the Moreel family in the Church of St. Jacques, and was the gift of William Moreel, the father of Marie Moreel, whose portrait we have already seen in St. John's Hospital. This picture was painted in 1484 in honour of St. Christopher.

In the central panel the gigantic form of the saint is seen wading through a river with the infant Jesus on his shoulders, and leaning on the trunk of a young tree which he uses as a staff. He cannot understand how it is that so small a burthen should weigh so heavily, and, wondering, turns his head to behold the child, who, with a smile on his face, lifts one hand to bless him, whilst with the other he steadies himself by grasping a white linen bandage which is wound round the saint's head. On his right stands the Benedictine saint, Maurus, in his monk's habit. One of Moreel's daughters was a Benedictine nun, and it was doubtless on this account that Memlinc introduced his portrait. On the other side St. Gilles caressing the doe whose life he saved by receiving an arrow, which a huntsman had aimed at her, in his own arm. The figure of the saint is very fine, his face is the most beautiful in the whole composition. The reason why he is here introduced is not apparent. The left wing shows the donor with his five sons and his patron, St. William; the right, his wife, her patroness, St. Barbara, and their eleven daughters. The figures of St. George and St. John the Baptist are painted in grisaille on the outer side of the shutters. These last are probably not Memlinc's work. Mr. Weale thinks that they may have been added in 1504 by order of John and George Moreel, two of the sons of the donor.

This picture is one of the most beautiful of Memlinc's later works. Unfortunately it has suffered much from the ravages of time and restorers. The lower portion of the face of one of the donor's sons has been clumsily repainted, and the removal of the *glacis* has chilled, and to a certain extent spoiled, the harmony of the scheme of colour.

We have said that Hans Memlinc was the greatest of all the Flemish masters of the fourteenth century save only the brothers Van Eyck. Mr. Weale places him on a higher pinnacle. In his estimation Hubert alone surpassed him. John van Eyck, he says, saw with his eyes, Memlinc beheld with his soul, and he adds—we are quoting from memory—that Memlinc was the most poetical and the most musical of all the Bruges painters. If this be so we can only say that John was more apt to portray what he saw than Hans what he imagined, that if Memlinc idealised the Flemish type he at the same time denaturalised it, that if his figures are more refined they are also less human.

That Memlinc was inspired by the true spirit of poetry no one can deny, but his imagination sometimes runs away with him and his verses are not wholly devoid of false quantities. In other words, by reason of the multitude of scenes which he not unfrequently introduces in single panels, his pictures sometimes lack the beauty and the dignity of simplicity; and though he at first composed in symmetrical groups, after the manner of his predecessors, in his later work he sacrifices too much to his love of the picturesque.

Hans Memlinc was a man of lofty ideals, and his creations are sometimes sublime, but not always.

John van Eyck was cast in a different mould. He was content to portray Nature as he saw her.

Give me beautiful models, we can imagine him saying, and I will paint you beautiful pictures. Give me ill-favoured models, and your pictures shall be beautiful still. Yet do I scorn to flatter; I will be true to life. If I must needs paint Flemings, my portraits shall be the portraits of Flemings. I will neither make a fat man thin nor a coarse woman refined. I will portray every blemish and every wrinkle, but I will place my figures to the best advantage. Their surroundings shall be magnificent; I will set them in the midst of fair courts and lovely temples; I will array them in the most becoming garments; I will bathe them in an aureole of glorious tones. Your eye shall be enchanted by the symmetry of my grouping and the graceful flow of my drapery; I will shower jewels with a lavish hand, and I will harmonize everything with my magic gold. Thus will I compel you to fall down and adore the splendour of the True.

CHAPTER XXV

Modern Bruges

WE have said that Bruges never recovered from the blow which Maximilian had dealt her. She had no chance of doing so. Misfortune followed misfortune. Most of her foreign merchants had migrated to Antwerp, and once settled there they were loth to return. The discovery of America, and of a new route to the Indies, added to her discomfiture by forcing commerce to forsake its old paths and its old havens; the river, the source of her wealth, was rapidly filling with sand. As early as 1410 the navigation of the Zwyn, even as far as Sluys, had become exceedingly difficult; by the close of the century no great vessel could reach Damme, and before another fifty years had elapsed Bruges was altogether cut off from the sea. If a ship canal had been made, as Lancelot Blondeel suggested, from the city to Heyst, where there is deep water quite close to the shore, she might perchance have yet found salvation. But still poor, and weary from her conflict with Maximilian, she had neither the means nor the heart to carry out so vast a project.

Then, too, there were the troubles bred of the religious revolution and the tyranny of Spanish rule; the cruelty of Philip, and the cruelty of Alva, and the no less cruel retaliation of 'the Beggars of the Sea,' who on March 26, 1578, captured the city, and by the aid of Colonel Henry Balfour, a Scotch adventurer in the service of William of Orange, held it for six years.

During this period Catholic worship was strictly prohibited, many of the leading citizens were thrust into prison, amongst them the bishop, a large-minded and liberal man, who had done his utmost to stay Alva's hand, and most of the clergy were driven into exile. Some of them fared worse still—were tortured, scourged, burnt at the stake in front of the Cathedral. Nor was this all. Sanctuaries were pillaged, altars cast down, art treasures innumerable were wantonly destroyed, the Church of St. Anne was razed to the ground, and Notre Dame was turned into a stable.

Two years later Balfour received his reward. It happened thus. About this time the Spaniards were threatening the city, and the Scotch colonel led out his troops to oppose them. Wounded in the conflict which followed, but apparently not grievously, for he was still able to keep his saddle, he turned his horse's head towards Bruges. Presently his comrades saw him reel, and then, without a cry or any other sign, he fell back dead. They carried him home to the city, and buried him in the churchyard of St. Sauveur.

During these troublous times hundreds of the best and wealthiest families left the city, and when peace was at length restored in 1584, the population hardly numbered thirty thousand souls. If it had not been for the Church, Bruges would in all probability have gradually dwindled down to a mere village like Sluys or Damme, or even little Middelburg.

The action of Pope Pius IV., who, at the instance of Philip II. in 1560, had made Bruges an Episcopal See, saved her from this fate. Bitterly opposed as the measure had been by all classes of society—by the higher clergy, who feared that the presence of a bishop amongst them would lessen their prestige; by the monks, who knew that they would be shorn of revenue for the endowment of the new See; by the nobles, who regarded the great abbeys as the appanage of their younger sons; by the people, who believed that this step was the prelude to the installation of the Spanish Inquisition—it proved in the outcome the town's salvation. And Bruges owed something more to the Church:—towards the close of the fifteen hundreds and during the opening years of the succeeding century, a vast immigration of wealthy families, who brought with them gold, and, better still, treasures of literature and treasures of art.

Many of the religious houses in the outlying country had been destroyed by the Ghent Calvinists, not a few in the immediate neighbourhood of Bruges by the burghers themselves, who, when the Gueux were threatening them in 1578, had caused all buildings within a mile of their walls to be razed to the ground, in order that the enemy might find no place for shelter. For fifty years after the settlement of 1582, even when the religious troubles were over, Flanders was the scene of continual warfare. Amid the coming and going of troops there was no guarantee of security outside the walls of the towns, and, as might be expected, the monks and nuns of the country-side flocked into the episcopal city. Amongst them were representatives of almost all the great religious orders—Benedictines, Carthusians, Dominicans, Augustinians, Carmelites, Capuchins, Jesuits, and, most noteworthy of all, Cistercians from the famous Abbey of St. Mary on the Dunes at Coxyde, and from the affiliated house called Ter Doest, at Lisseweghe.

Of all the religious communities to which Bruges now offered an asylum, this was the mightiest and the most renowned. It was unsurpassed alike in wealth, in learning, in numbers, in dignity of life, in dignity of tradition, in spiritual and temporal achievements. St. Bernard was its founder. Some of the holiest and wisest men of the Middle Ages had been numbered among its members; the abbey at Coxyde was magnificent; its church was, perhaps, the most beautiful in the land; thanks to the patient toil of its monks, as one of their abbots used to boast, the barren dunes which surrounded it had become a fertile garden.

BRUGES FROM THE RIVER YPERLET

A whirlwind of fanaticism swept them away, and now their vast domain is what it was before the white-robed brethren settled there—a wilderness of shifting sand.

Bruges during the opening years of the sixteen hundreds was seething in misery. War had brought forth famine and pestilence, and the flight of commerce had left thousands of working men without any means of gaining their bread; but there was still gold in the city. The fortunes which had been made in trade, or at all events a certain proportion of them, remained after trade had departed, and the monastic immigrants, as we have seen, were not without resources, nor did the possessors of the mammon of unrighteousness suffer it to remain idle. They made to themselves friends with it. Churches and monasteries were restored; the monks and nuns from the country built for themselves new habitations; hospices and almshouses, *Godshuisen* (God's Houses), as they are at Bruges picturesquely termed, were founded all over the city. Thus was work provided for those who were able to do it, and a permanent provision made for the aged and the infirm.

The buildings now erected in no way resembled the sumptuous palaces and stately guild halls of bygone days, but some of them are sufficiently picturesque. Take, for instance, the Carthusian Convent in the *rue du Vieux Bourg*, with its seven gables, and mullioned windows, and beautiful Gothic doorway surmounted by three niches, with statues of saints in the style of the Renaissance—it has recently been restored, and is now the *local* of a workmen's club, the *Gilde van Ambachten*; or the Leper Hospital, at the end of the *Marché au fil*; or the Pest House on the Grand Canal adjoining the thirteenth-century Hospice of *Notre Dame de la Poterie* and there are a host of others equally interesting, and above all and everywhere the little *Godshuisen* with their quaint gables, and blinking windows, and picturesque doorways, often with a niche above them and the image of a saint. They are not the least beautiful feature in the architecture of this beautiful city, and the number of them is legion. Some are large enough to afford accommodation for thirty or forty inmates. These are generally built round a courtyard laid out as a garden. In others again there is only room for six or seven persons. Some are for women only, some for men, some for married couples; each *Godshuis* has its little oratory; all of them are comfortable and clean, and all are picturesque.

The inmates are left very much to themselves, the oldest inhabitant generally acting as superior. Each inmate or married couple, as the case may be, in addition to his or their apartment, receives a monthly pension varying in amount from house to house, but in no case very large. Many of the inhabitants, however, are able to do a little work, others, perhaps, have children who are in a position to contribute to their support. Your true Fleming is rarely lacking in filial piety—it is one of the most pleasing characteristics of the race—and thus these old people are able to rub along, not perhaps in affluence, but for all that with a good roof over their heads, without enduring the pangs of hunger, and, no small boon, in the enjoyment of their liberty.

Thus was Bruges transformed in the seventeenth century, thus did she become what she still is—a vast conglomeration of religious houses and charitable institutions, a city of nuns and friars. The *évêché* had taken the place of the Court, the monk of the merchant; commerce had fled, and charity was doing what she could to supply its place.

Thus, thanks in great measure to the initiative of the Church, the evil days were tided over. When, later on, in the following century, the wars and rumours of wars had passed away, and the 'pastoral folk' of the Franc were enabled to obtain some profit from their former avocations, Bruges to a certain extent participated in their prosperity; but though she on more than one occasion essayed to revive her commerce—notably in 1722 by the canalization of the river Yperlet, with a view to putting herself in communication with Ostend—her efforts in each case proved abortive. Flanders had become, to quote the words of a seventeenth-century historian, *famosum antiquitatis sepulchrum*, and her capital was constrained to live on the reputation of its former glory.

Let us not, however, shed too many tears over the commercial decay of Bruges. If her prosperity had continued she would hardly have remained what she still is—the fairest city in Northern Europe.

We know indeed that her private palaces were suffered to fall into decay because their owners were too poor to maintain them, but if they had been never so rich the old buildings would have disappeared just the same. The art of the Middle Ages was abhorrent to the eighteenth century, and the Gothic palaces of Bruges would surely have given place to rococo mansions. Moreover, that same poverty which destroyed so much of her splendour not only endowed her, as we have seen, with a multitude of picturesque buildings, but has preserved for us what remains of her ancient domestic architecture.

On the 2nd of October 1670 the members of the Confraternity of the Blessed Sacrament established in the Church of St. Sauveur—now the Cathedral—decreed that the three fifteenth-century stained-glass windows in their chantry—the central chapel of the ambulatory, immediately behind the high altar—should be forthwith destroyed, in order that the public might the better appreciate the new altar they had erected, which 'was such an admirable imitation of marble.'

In 1739 a like act of vandalism, but on a larger scale, was perpetrated in the same church. The ancient stained-glass windows were at this time removed from the clerestory of the choir and replaced by white glass, and there were no less than thirteen of them. Similar outrages were committed in all the churches and public buildings of Bruges, and if only her private citizens had been rich enough to pull down and rebuild their dwellings there would have been little left by this time of the mediæval city.

It is only fair to add that Bruges has long since learned to appreciate her old buildings. Many of them have been carefully restored, others are in course of restoration, the work has for the most part been accomplished with no little skill and taste, and, for the rest, it may be safely said that no other great mediæval city has preserved so much of its old-world character. How long this will continue to be true is another question. Lancelot Blondeel's scheme, or one no less nefarious, is at length being carried out; much havoc has already been wrought in the northern outskirts of the city; old houses have been pulled down, old timber has been felled; in despite of strenuous opposition, the course of one of the loveliest canals has been diverted, and its former bed filled in for the convenience of the jerry builder.

If the projected sea canal should fulfil the expectation of its promoters there can be no doubt that Bruges will lose much of her charm. She will no longer be a city of sleepy streets and of picturesque canals unfrequented save by swans, choked up with water lilies, and fringed with trees and flowering shrubs and dreamy old houses blinking at the water. She will become a second Ghent, a second Antwerp, and the knowing ones aver that all the profit will find its way into the pockets of Jews and Germans. The modern Fleming, it would seem, has little aptitude for commerce.

There is some consolation in this thought, and there is more in this— the scheme is a vast one, and Bruges moves slowly. It took her twenty years to restore the Hôtel Gruthuise. Twenty-five years ago she decided to restore the western façade of Notre Dame. Between that time and this the architect who was commissioned to undertake the work has submitted no less than twenty-five different plans. When the façade has actually fallen, and it is said that it cannot last much longer, perhaps those who are responsible for the delay will select one of them.

We may take it then that mediæval Bruges will at all events last our day.

The following notes will perhaps be of service to those who wish to see the most beautiful and interesting spots in Bruges, and to examine its art treasures.

Let such an one, coming forth from his inn, which, if he be a wise man, will be either *Le Flandre* or *Le Commerce*—there are others cheaper but none so comfortable—unaccompanied by a guide, who would only irritate and confuse him, and keeping his eyes always open, for there is much to see, make his way as best he can to the *Grande Place*, and there let him feast his eyes on the majestic splendour of the Belfry, and fill his ears with the weird music which every quarter of an hour proceeds from it—

Low and loud and sweetly blended,
Low at times and loud at times,
And changing like a poet's rhymes
Ring the beautiful wild chimes
From the Belfry in the market
Of the ancient town of Bruges.

Next let him turn off into the street called Philipstock, proceeding along which he will presently descry, beyond the houses on the left-hand side, all that remains of the old Church of St. Peter, where Bertulph once celebrated the obsequies of Charles the Good. The first turning on the right leads, through a grove of sycamore and chestnut trees planted on the site of St. Donatian's, to the *Place du Bourg*, one of the loveliest squares in Europe. The great Gothic building opposite is the *Hôtel de Ville*; the two-storeyed church of tawny brick hard-by, with a portal at right angles to it of dark grey stone carved into flamboyant panelling and enriched with statues of bronze, the Sanctuary of the Holy Blood; in the gabled edifice on the left, half Gothic and half Renaissance in style, glorious with colour and gold, and altogether beautiful, we have the last architectural effort of the waning prosperity of Bruges—the *Maison de l'ancien Greffe*, built in 1537. It now serves as a Court of Justice, has been carefully restored, and is well worth a visit. The justice-room, with its old oak and old brass, its stained-glass windows and its glorious chimney-piece, is perfect; so too the inner chamber, which serves as the magistrates' private apartment. The *Hôtel de Ville* has also been well restored; the entrance hall is particularly fine, and the great hall above, with its ancient timber roof, and its excellent modern frescoes, not yet completed, is no less charming. In this building there are several interesting pictures of Bruges in days gone by and of the surrounding country. Of the beauty of the two churches we have already spoken. In the upper church there are some interesting pictures, there are more in the adjoining museum, and here too there are some fragments of ancient stained glass, the original designs of the windows in the upper chapel, some beautiful antique lace and embroidery, and the silver-gilt

LANCELOT BLONDELL'S CHIMNEY-PIECE IN THE PALAIS DU FRANC

reliquary studded with jewels—amongst them a splendid black diamond which once belonged to Marie, Queen of Scots—in which the Holy Blood is annually carried in procession through the streets in the month of May. This reliquary was the gift of the burghers of Bruges in 1614; the original reliquary was destroyed by the Protestants in 1578. The relic is exposed for the veneration of the faithful every Friday in the upper chapel from eight till eleven thirty, and the ceremony of Benediction which then takes place is singularly impressive.

The beautiful groined archway which pierces the *Maison de l'ancien Greffe* leads to a region where there are exquisite views: from the centre of the Great Fishmarket, the backs of the buildings of which we have just been speaking—they are no less fascinating than their façades; and from the *Pont de l'âne Aveugle* the loveliness of the Roya, and the façade of the *Palais du Franc* where, in the great council chamber, is Lancelot Blondeel's famous chimney-piece. The approach to this building is through the *Palais de Justice* in the *Place du Bourg*. Bearing to the right through the Little Fishmarket, most picturesque, we presently reach the *Marché aux Herbes*, the *Quai de Rosaire* and the *Dyver*, where the scenery is no less charming. The great red house on the further bank of the Roya is the house where Malvenda hid the Holy Blood, and the majestic spire in the distance the spire of *Notre Dame*. Almost at the end of the *Dyver* there is a little street called the *rue de Grœninghe*, which branches off the main thoroughfare between two walled gardens. That on the left is the site of the ancient abbey of Eeckhout, a very peaceful place, where in summer-time there are roses in abundance and old-world herbs and flowers, and, on a crumbling wall, snap-dragon. The gabled house hard-by, with a little Gothic window, was formerly the residence of the provosts of Notre Dame; the picturesque group of buildings in the distance, which, amid thick foliage, cluster round its spire, is the old palace of Louis of Gruthuise; the garden beyond the narrow stream, the garden of the nuns of St. André. Let the traveller linger awhile in this tranquil spot and, if he will, for twopence half-penny, refresh himself with a beautiful bunch of roses.

Continuing his walk along the *rue de Grœninghe* the tourist will presently see a wrought-iron grill at the end of an *impasse* which gives on the river. Let him approach it and look through the railings. Here there is a nook which strangers rarely find; many who have lived in the city for years do not know of it, and yet it is perhaps the most beautiful of all the beautiful spots in Bruges. To discover this priceless jewel is the main object of our journey. Here the Roya is often a rushing torrent. On one side of the stream, rising clean out of the water, is the oldest wing of the *Gruthuise*; on the other a walled garden with lofty trees spreading their branches over the river which, to the right, disappears beneath an archway piercing an old house, once part of the palace; in the near background, immediately facing the grill, is the choir of Notre Dame with its grove of flying buttresses, and beyond, towering high above all, the majesty of its steeple—the grandest and the fairest thing in brick or stone which the genius of man has yet created. It was from this lovely spot, or rather a few yards higher up stream, that Mr. Railton took the beautiful sketch of the *Hôtel Gruthuise* which appears on p. 287.

Hard-by, on the bank of this same river, a little higher up stream, stands the Beguinage (*see* map), that most picturesque cloister where the quaint dwellings of the nuns—for each Beguin has her own home, her own purse and her own household—fringe a fair and spacious green planted with lofty elms, a very tranquil spot where the ghost of the thirteenth century still lingers. The convent church dates from the year 1245, but it has been so changed and spoiled by repeated restorations that little of the original building remains, and it can no longer, perhaps, be called beautiful. But, notwithstanding, it has a certain charm which is quite its own. It is so picturesque and so clean and so quiet and so comfortable, and with it all there is such a quaint, old-world atmosphere about the place that many a much more beautiful church is far less attractive. And the worshippers who frequent it!—the very precise and deliberate and ceremonious old ladies who totter across the green to church at intervals throughout the day—from *angelus* to *angelus*, and there let down their long black trains and put on their white choir veils, and presently, with much curtseying to one another and many genuflections before the high altar, together chant their breviary in feeble, quavering tones, whilst the old caretaker, in a secluded corner, calmly tells her beads or knits stockings.

The entrance to the Beguinage is by the *Place de la Vigne*, over a bridge which spans the Roya, whence there are beautiful views of that stream, of the Beguins' little gardens, of their church, of the old lockhouse at the head of the Minne Water, of the lake itself beyond, and, in the far background, of those lovely wooded ramparts, where all night long in summer-time the nightingale intones *his* psalmody.

The canals of Bruges are all of them exceedingly beautiful. The great canal, which enters the city on the eastern side between the *Porte de Gand* and the Infantry Barracks, and divides it into two unequal parts, is interesting from end to end, and as there are roads on each side, and it is spanned by five bridges, there is no difficulty in exploring it. The most picturesque route is from the Bourg by the *rue de l'âne Aveugle* and the terrace which skirts the backwater of the Roya—the *Quai des Marbriers*, as it is called, and the *Quai Vert*. Hard-by the spot where the main stream of the Roya—a vista here of ancient gables with the *Poorters Logie* and its charming tower in the distance—empties itself into the canal is the old tavern which Rubens is said to have frequented. It stands in the *rue des Blanchisseurs*, a narrow lane off the road which skirts the right-hand bank of the canal, and is called the *Vlissinghe*. A most interesting old place this, the tourist should not fail to visit it. The accompanying sketch is of the back of the house.

THE VLISSINGHE TAVERN, FREQUENTED BY RUBENS

The Ghent Canal skirts the whole of the eastern side of the town, from the Minne Water Bridge, that is, to the old *Porte de Damme*; on its banks stand the *Porte de Gand* and the *Porte Ste. Croix*. From the high ramparts beyond the latter gate there is a beautiful panoramic view of the city and of the open country on the other side of the water.

There is also a canal which branches off from the Ghent Canal by the Minne Water Bridge in the opposite direction; it runs alongside of the ramparts as far as the *Porte des Baudets*, where it turns off into the open country. Its banks are for the most part well wooded, beyond the picturesque *Porte des Maréchaux* they are high and steep, and from this spot too there is a beautiful view of the city.

Hard-by the hospital for incurable women, a vast and splendid modern building which stands on the banks of the Minne Water, a fourth canal enters the town. This is perhaps the fairest of all the Bruges waterways. The best points of view are from its bridges, which are all save one beautiful and all save one ancient. There are no less than six of them:— the *Pont de la Clef*, which separates the *rue des Bouchers* from the *rue Fossé aux Loups*—Mr. Railton has given us a sketch of it; the *Pont aux Lions*, hard by the *rue du Marécage* and the Church of St. Jacques; the *Pont des Baudets* in the *rue d'Ostende*; the *Pont Flamand*, which connects the *rue Flamande* with the *rue St. Georges*;—this is the oldest bridge in Bruges, originally constructed by the

Augustinian friars in 1294, it was rebuilt by the town in 1391—the *Pont des Augustins* at the end of the *rue Espagnole*, and the *Pont de la Tour* by the *Place des Orientaux*. The tourist will do well to visit all these bridges and also to follow the road which skirts the canal from the last bridge to its junction with the great canal, about five hundred yards further on. The gardens and houses on the opposite side of the stream are most picturesque. It was here that John van Eyck lived, though, alas! his dwelling has been swept away.

Of the Roya and of the beautiful backwater which connects it with the great canal, at the end of the *rue des Dominicains*, we have already spoken in a previous chapter. There are other streams too which wend their way through the city. It is impossible within the limits of this manual even to indicate their whereabouts, so numerous are they and so intricate is their meandering. The tourist will come upon them, in the course of his rambles, in the most unexpected places, and he will find them on that account none the less beautiful.

Bruges possesses seven parish churches—*Notre Dame*, which claims precedence of all the rest; *St. Sauveur*, which is also the Cathedral—a finer but less picturesque and less interesting building; *St. Jacques*, a noble structure spoiled by Calvinist fury and seventeenth century restoration; *St. Gilles*, which suffered more than all, and has now renewed its youth and splendour; *Ste. Anne*, which dates from the opening years of the sixteen hundreds and which, with its carved oak, its old brass, its pictures, its stained glass and its polished marble, is a very pleasing specimen of the work of the period; *Ste. Walburge*, erected about the same date from the design of the Jesuit Peter Huyssens, a native of Bruges, who died in that city in 1637; and *Ste. Marie Madeleine*, a modern building which, if it were in London, would be called 'handsome.'

All of these churches, save the last, are worth visiting, not only because of their intrinsic beauty, but on account of the beautiful and interesting objects which they contain. Pictures, wood carving, wrought-iron, brass, all these things shall here delight the eye—aye, and gold too and silver and precious stones, tapestry, embroidery, lace, if only the custodians can be persuaded to discover their hidden treasures.

Of the other sanctuaries of Bruges, the traveller should at least visit the Chapel of the Hospital of St. John (1473), which is rich in *objets d'art*, and possesses, amongst other treasures, a set of embroidered Mass vestments which date from 1633, and are all sewn with pearls, no less than seventy-three thousand of them, so it is said; the Chapel and Hospice of *Notre Dame de la Poterie* (1358), beautifully restored,

where there is a small collection of early Flemish pictures, some charming old oak furniture and sculpture, and several pieces of fifteenth-century tapestry; the Carmelite Church in the *rue d'Ostende*, built in 1688 from the designs of Frère Patrice de Saint-Hubert; here the dancing angels over the altar are spindle-shanked and ill-proportioned, the cupids which flutter about them have the faces of demons, and seem bursting with evil passions, the sacred figures carved on the confessionals are caricatures, the whole scheme of ornament is in the worst possible taste, but somehow or other, in spite of it all, this church is a very fascinating and a very devotional one; the proportions are good, it is rich in carved oak and sculptured marble, the colouring is harmonious, and the windows, amber-hued and pale green, with beautiful patterns traced in lead, are simply perfect; and of course there is the Jerusalem Chapel and the chapels of the Precious Blood, of all of which we have already spoken, and, if the tourist would go further afield, the stately thirteenth-century Church of Our Lady at Damme, and the no less beautiful shrine of Our Lady at Lisseweghe, which dates from the same period.

Damme is about three miles out of the city. It is situated on the banks of the Sluys Canal. There is a very good steamboat service, and the pleasantest way to reach it is by water. The Damme Town Hall dates from the end of the fourteenth century, and is a charming old building. Here, too, is a convent and hospital which dates from the thirteenth century, and there are some quaint old houses. When Bruges was at its heyday the population of Damme amounted to sixty thousand souls. The number of its inhabitants is now probably less than one thousand.

Lisseweghe is some five miles from Bruges. The pleasantest way to reach it is by walking or driving. About a mile short of the village, a little off the high road on the left-hand side, are the ruins of *Ter Doest Abbey*, well worth visiting. The great Gothic grange or barn dates from the close of the thirteenth century (about 1280), and is still intact, a stupendous building, 187 feet by 75 feet or thereabouts, and nearly 100 feet high from the ground to the ridge of the roof. Lisseweghe can also be reached by rail.

Of the other famous buildings of Bruges we have already spoken. By the aid of the map and the directions previously given, the reader will have no difficulty in ascertaining their whereabouts.

Bruges is a city of considerable size; its ramparts measure nearly five miles round, and it is hardly an exaggeration to say there is no spot within this magic circle devoid of interest.

The stranger who, having hurried through its churches and picture galleries in the morning, and whiled away an hour or so in its streets in the afternoon, fancies that he knows Bruges is vastly mistaken. For our own part, we have dwelt in this enchanted city for many years, and the sum of its loveliness, we feel very sure, has not yet been revealed to us.

FOOTNOTES:

[1] *See* BOLL. ACTA SS., VI. FEB. *Vita S. Amandi auctore Baudemundo ejus discipulo.*

[2] *See* TAINE, *l'Ancien Régime,* livre 1ᵉʳ, ch. I., § II.

[3] *See* Genealogical Table I.

[4] *Memorials of St. Dunstan.* Rolls Series. Introduction.

[5] *Epistola ad Arnulfum Comitem* (MS. Cotton, Tiberius A. 15, fo. 155b).

[6] *See* Genealogical Table I.

[7] The marriage of King Ethelwolf with Judith was not consummated.

[8] Charles's palace occupied the site of the present Palais de Justice.

[9] Bertulph's house occupied the site of that portion of Government House which gives on the *rue Breidel.*

[10] Charles is always depicted in red.

[11] A name given by the Karls to the feudal lords.

[12] In the *rue Breidel.* The Boterbeke has been vaulted over for centuries, and of course the bridge no longer exists; the gates too have disappeared, but the holes into which the bolts were slipped are still to be seen in the facade of a house on the left-hand side at the further end of the street, which once formed part of the ancient gateway.

[13] Immediately after the murder, Bertulph had sent letters to the Bishop of Tournai containing evidence which he deemed sufficient to prove his innocence. These letters never reached their destination. Bertulph's messenger, a monk of Eeckhout Abbey, had hardly left Bruges when he fell into the hands of the Isegrins. *See* also p. 59.

[14] The ruins of this monastery, most picturesquely situated, are well worth a visit. The huge brick barn with magnificent timber roof, a splendid specimen of thirteenth-century architecture, and some other out-buildings are still intact and still fulfil their original purpose.

[15] *See* p. 72, footnote.

[16] *See* Genealogical Table II.

[17] A nephew of Bertulph's.

[18] A vagabond of any description.

[19] *See* Genealogical Table III.

[20] *See* Genealogical Table III.

[21] *See* Genealogical Table IV.

[22] GESTA TREVIR. *Arch. ap. Martène, Coll. Ampliss.*, iv., p. 363. *See* KERVYN DE LETTENHOVE, *Histoire de la Flandre*, p. 77, vol. ii.

[23] The French party—supporters of the lily.

[24] The Nationalists—supporters of the lion of Flanders.

[25] *See* Genealogical Table IV.

[26] *See* KERVYN DE LETTENHOVE. *Histoire de Flandre*, livre 9ᵉ, tome ii., p. 113.

[27] See *Oud. Vlaemsche liederen*, published by Abbé Carton, p. 154.

[28] *Corp. Chr. Fl.* i., p. 190.

[29] *See* KERVYN, vol. ii., p. 262.

[30] *See* GREEN'S *Short History of the English People*, chap, v., sec. i., p. 218.

[31] Chronicles of Boucecault.

[32] Monk of St. Denis.

[33] *Rel. de St. Denis*, iv. 6.

[34] See *Rel. de St. Denis*, xxviii. 30, Monstrelet I.

[35] KERVYN DE LETTENHOVE. *Histoire de Flandre*, livre 14ᵐᵉ, tom. iii., p. 239.

[36] Ann. Nov., ap. Martène, Ampliss. Coll., v. Col. 621; Lettre MS. de Rodolphe Agricola, 1 Nov. 1482.

[37] KERVYN. Livre 19ᵉ, vol. iv., p. 247.

[38] *See* Genealogical Table V.

[39] See p. 287.

[40] GACHARD. *Lettres inédites de Maximilian*, i., p. 80.

[41] *Chronique de Despars*, vol. iv., p. 178.

[42] The freehold of this property is still held by a descendant of the Adornes family.

[43] See *Revue de l'Art Chrétien*, 1892, p. 396.

[44] See *Revue des Deux Mondes*, June 15, 1900. *De van Eyck à Van Dyck.*

[45] *Revue de l'Art Chrétien*, 1900, 4ᵐᵉ livr. *Les Frères van Eyck*, JAMES WEALE.

[46] *See* LÜBKE. *History of Art*, vol. ii., p. 326.

[47] This lady followed her husband's calling. Mr. Henry Willett of Brighton is the possessor of three beautiful miniatures in the form of a triptych, which are certainly her work. The central panel shows the Madonna and Child, and in the background the old manor house at Oostcamp of Louis of Gruthuise.

[48] This date has every appearance of being authentic, but it may have been added later.

[49] *See* DE LABORDE. *Les Ducs de Bourgogne. Memoriaux de Jean Robert, Abbé de Saint-Aubert.*

[50] *Les Ducs de Bourgogne. Etude sur les lettres, les arts et l'industrie pendant le quinzième siècle*, vol. ii., Preface, p. xliv.